D0894189

Multiculturalism in Turkey

Over the past couple of decades, there have been many efforts to seek a solution to the often violent situation in which Kurdish citizens of Turkey find themselves. These efforts have included a gradual programme of political recognition and multiculturalism. Here, Durukan Kuzu examines the case of Kurdish citizens in Turkey through the lens of the global debate on multiculturalism, exploring the limitations of these policies. He thereby challenges the conventional thinking about national minorities and their autonomy, and offers a scientifically grounded comparative framework for the study of multiculturalism.

Through comparison of the situation of Kurds in Turkey with that of other national minorities – such as the Flemish in Belgium, Québécois in Canada, Corsicans in France, and Muslims in Greece – the reader is invited to question in what forms multiculturalism can work for different national minorities. A bottom-up approach is used to offer a fresh insight into the Kurdish community and to highlight conflicting views about which form the politics of recognition could take.

Durukan Kuzu is a research fellow and senior lecturer at Coventry University. He holds a Ph.D. in Comparative Politics from the London School of Economics and Political Science, and has taught courses on the theory and problems of nationalism in the Government Department at the LSE. He was the co-Chair of the Association for the Study of Ethnicity and Nationalism, UK, and has published in political science journals including *Nations and Nationalism* and *Comparative European Politics*. He contributes to media outlets such as CNN International and advises the Immigration and Refugee Board of Canada on the treatment of Kurds in Turkey.

Multiculturalism in Turkey

The Kurds and the State

Durukan Kuzu

Coventry University

CAMBRIDGE
UNIVERSITY PRESS

CAMBRIDGE
UNIVERSITY PRESS

University Printing House, Cambridge CB2 8BS, United Kingdom

One Liberty Plaza, 20th Floor, New York, NY 10006, USA

477 Williamstown Road, Port Melbourne, VIC 3207, Australia

314–321, 3rd Floor, Plot 3, Splendor Forum, Jasola District Centre, New Delhi - 110025, India

79 Anson Road, #06-04/06, Singapore 079906

Cambridge University Press is part of the University of Cambridge.

It furthers the University's mission by disseminating knowledge in the pursuit of education, learning, and research at the highest international levels of excellence.

www.cambridge.org
Information on this title: www.cambridge.org/9781108417822
DOI: 10.1017/9781108278461

© Durukan Kuzu 2018

First published 2018

Printed in the United Kingdom by Clays, St Ives plc

A catalogue record for this publication is available from the British Library

ISBN 978-1-108-41782-2 Hardback

Contents

Figures

Tables

1 Introduction

The democratization of Turkey has been the country's main news story for many years, and the fate of the Kurds is one of the key themes in that story. The Kurds constitute one of the biggest stateless nations in the Middle East, and those Kurds who live in Turkey have long been forced to assimilate into the Turkish majority.

Since the Republic of Turkey was founded in 1923, the Kurds – who today make up almost 18 per cent of the country's population (about 14 million, out of 77.8 million people)[1] – have been expected to live under the authority of a state which uses only the Turkish language in its dealings with its citizens. A number of Kurdish rebellions during the 1920s and 1930s were repressed by the armed forces; the use of the Kurdish language in public offices and education was banned; and, since then, no movement based on ethnicity has been tolerated. All ethnic differences in the country have been ignored by the 'state that constitutionally consists only of "citizens of Turkey"'.[2] According to Article 66, paragraph 1 of the 1924 Constitution, 'Everyone bound to the Turkish state through the bond of citizenship is a Turk'.[3] The term 'Turk' was comprehensively explained in that document which stated that 'The nation of Turkey with respect of citizenship is called Turk, irrespective of religion or ethnicity'.[4] In Turkey, nationality has been reduced to citizenship and, according to the Turkish Citizenship Law No. 5901, citizenship can be determined by either *jus soli* (right of land) or *jus sanguinis* (right of the blood). The right of land declares that children born in Turkey's territories do not acquire the nationality of either parent at birth but acquire Turkish nationality from birth; meanwhile the right of blood confers citizenship on children whose parents must be a Turkish citizen at the time of birth.[5]

The 1923 Lausanne Treaty, a peace treaty officially concluding World War I in the Middle East, signed between Turkey, heir to the defunct Ottoman Empire, and the Allied Powers (Britain, France, Italy and Japan), is still accepted as the one and only legal document that treats the issue of minorities in Turkey.[6] The concept of minority was not very well known to the Ottomans until the nineteenth century. Although *ekalliyet*, the Ottoman word for minority, was translated from the Western languages and used during the last fifty years of the Empire, it was not a popular word, and non-Muslims were mostly referred to as *Gayrimuslim* in the Ottoman documents.[7] The minority regime as we know it in Turkey today was introduced for the first time with the Treaty of Lausanne in 1923. Although the concept of minority (*azinlik* in modern Turkish) was new at the time, the fact that it has only been applied to the non-Muslims in modern Turkey has its roots in the old Ottoman *millet* system. The Ottomans used the *millet* system to give minority religious communities within their empire limited power and autonomy to act as legal entities with specific communal – 'segmental' – rights and privileges. As such, the Kurds and other Muslim subjects were not considered as entitled to the privileges that other religious minorities had in regulating their own affairs. The same tradition has continued in modern Turkey following the collapse of the empire, and the Lausanne Treaty instituted the minority status in modern Turkey by simply excluding Muslim groups like the Kurds, Caucasians, Laz, and Romani people, who spoke languages other than Turkish.[8] The adoption of the Lausanne Treaty created a situation where the Turkish constitutional scheme dealt with the question of minorities without fully addressing it.[9]

For some years, international law with a focus on the egalitarian[10] interpretation of individual rights and assimilationism[11] also excluded minority/group rights from its framework which the Turkish State often referred to as a source of legitimacy in justifying the way it treated its Kurdish national minority.[12] The Universal Declaration of Human Rights (1948), The United Nations Declaration on the Rights of Persons Belonging to National or Ethnic, Religious, and Linguistic Minorities (1992), the International Covenant on Civil and Political Rights (1966), the International Convention on the Elimination of All Forms of Racial Discrimination (1969), and the European Convention for the Protection of Human Rights and Fundamental Freedoms (1955) did not attribute any normative value to cultural identities but instead valued the equal rights of free individuals to live out their cultural identities without being exposed to discrimination. As Claude argued in 1955, 'The doctrine of human rights has been put forward as a substitute for the concept of minority rights, with the strong implication that minorities whose members enjoy individual equality of treatment cannot legitimately demand facilities for the maintenance of their ethnic particularism'.[13] A long series of conventions and declarations identified the individual as the only legitimate agent of liberal rights, and, in this framework, minority rights were simply subordinated to human rights that granted minority members the freedom of association.[14]

At the international level, the tide has since turned somewhat against this approach, however, because the drivers for individual human rights and the equal citizenship regime mentioned above have proved over time to be insufficient to settle ethnic conflicts and rectify the injustices of assimilation or exclusion.

In Turkey, for example, in the 1980s and 1990s, the separatist Kurdistan Workers' Party (PKK) was involved in an armed conflict with Turkish government forces that led to the deaths of more than 35,000 people on both sides.[15] The 10 per cent electoral threshold in Turkey made it very difficult for the Kurdish minority nationalists to be represented in the Turkish parliament. Most Kurdish political parties have also been closed down with charges of working with and being a political branch of the PKK, which is listed as a terrorist organization by the Turkish State, the European Union and the USA. The Kurdish question has long been seen by the Turkish state as primarily a security problem rather than a matter of equality and civil liberties, and therefore those injustices that emerged as a result of neglecting cultural differences in public were not addressed until very recently.

In reaction to similarly negative developments regarding the minorities across the globe, multiculturalism has started to earn credibility in international law as early as the 1990s. Advocates of this approach argue that members of a national ethnic minority should have differentiated group rights that would emanate from membership of their cultural communities. In a general sense, these rights are understood as being needed to rectify the unjust practices that led to the neglect, exclusion, discrimination, or forced assimilation of minorities in the past.[16] This approach, which proactively attempts to promote ethnic minority cultures, has long been accepted as a valuable strategy for redressing some of the imbalances generated by individual human rights and its universalized emphasis on toleration and neutrality. Multiculturalists respond to the 'neutral' approach to diversity by suggesting that it is simply utopian. They argue that the practical necessity for a state to use at least one official language means that no political community can remain culturally neutral. Multiculturalists further suggest that when the representation of culture at the state level is inevitable, it is important to represent not just the cultural identities of dominant groups but also those of minorities if a fairer society is to be achieved. Multiculturalists argue that a liberal state needs to legalize and make official the public use of the languages used by its national minorities alongside the language used by its majority group. According to the precepts of multiculturalism, groups should have differentiated rights and ought to become arbiters on issues related to their own communities. This view suggests that those national minorities which historically inhabited a given territory and were accustomed to use their own language before their subordination to the state should now be entitled to self-government rights, just like the majority which has had the right to decide which language is to be officially used in relation to the state.[17] These self-government rights – which might include regional autonomy, multi-national federalism, or the right to use their own languages in public life – can be used to increase the cultural freedom of minorities and to redress situations where their will was previously ignored and oppressed in the nation-building process carried out by the dominant community which forms the ethnic core of the state.[18]

In accordance with the 1990 Copenhagen criteria and the 1992 European Charter for Regional or Minority Languages, the protection of linguistic minorities in candidate and member countries became more important, and members of the European Union (EU) were advised to allow the use of minority languages in public education and services. According to Article Fourteen of the Framework Convention for the Protection of National Minorities, states should 'endeavour to ensure adequate opportunities for being taught in the minority language or for receiving instruction in this language'.[19] Moreover, the EU found it necessary to extend these rights to include self-government, which would generate regional administrative units for minority communities by accepting the terms and policy advice of other international organizations such as the Council of Europe, the conventions and reports of which are referred to as decisive in the European Commission's progress reports on candidate countries.[20] Especially its European Charter of Local Self-Government takes a central place in the EU's negotiations with candidate countries.

The charter commits the Parties to applying basic rules guaranteeing the political, administrative and financial independence of local authorities. It provides that the principle of local self-government shall be recognised in domestic legislation and, where practicable, in the constitution...Local authorities, acting within the limits of the law, are to be able to regulate and manage public affairs under their own responsibility in the interests of the local population.[21]

The EU's minority norms have been created with reference to best practice in relation to the cases of the Catalans in Spain, the Flemish in Belgium, the German-speaking minority in South Tyrol in Italy, and the Alanders in Finland. Their cases were used as examples to show that the problems of national minorities could be solved if minorities were granted differentiated group rights that in some situations could be extended to include self-government rights. These success stories encouraged international and supranational organizations to export the policies used in these scenarios to solve national minority problems in other contexts and countries.

Turkey as a candidate country for accession to the EU was put under pressure to fulfil the conditions the EU has set for the protection of minorities. In this realm the current government, which has ruled Turkey for the past fourteen years, has been working towards a radical change in the way that Kurds are accommodated and has initiated a gradual program of political recognition and multiculturalism. The government led by the Justice and Development Party (AKP), which has been in power for fourteen years, has carried out a gradual program aimed at radically changing the ways in which the Kurdish population is accommodated in Turkey. Changes to improve political recognition and multiculturalism for the Kurds have included the Constitutional Amendment Law no. 4471 of 2002 and Law no. 4903 of 2003, which guaranteed a legal basis for the use of ethnic groups' languages or dialects in education and the media. The state television channel TRT6 was dedicated to broadcasting in Kurdish only,[22] and, as a result of these legal changes, the language has now become more evident and publicly used than ever before.[23]

Reasons for Writing

In June 2015, the pro-Kurdish minority political party, the People's Democratic Party (HDP), crossed the electoral threshold in Turkey for the first time in the history of Turkish Republic, and its representatives are now in the parliament. The politics of recognition, and Kurdish demands in particular, are increasingly gaining momentum in Turkey, and so there is an urgent need to analyze these trends and communicate about them in ways informed by a liberal perspective that has long been lacking in the country. The violent conflict between the Kurds and the state, which was persisting in an increasingly violent fashion as of January 2016, begs the question as to why a transition towards the politics of recognition in Turkey has failed to bring about a just peace. The multiculturalist idea of differentiation between Turks and Kurds created great turmoil among people who thought it would lead to further inequalities in Turkey. For example, the Lazes, Arabs, Georgians and Circassians in Turkey, whose groups are not as sizeable as the Kurds and would find it difficult to make claims for autonomy, felt it unfair that the Kurds might be given differentiated cultural and political rights over and above those allotted to smaller groups.[24] The gradual shift from policies of oppression to those which recognized Kurdish identity in Turkey was ironically accompanied by increasing levels of hostility between different ethnic groups. The offices of the pro-Kurdish BDP party (*Baris ve Demokrasi Partisi*) were heavily attacked by civilians in 2011,[25] and a mob looted and set fire to Kurdish premises in the city of Kutahya in May 2016.[26] What once was an armed conflict between the PKK and the Turkish army has almost evolved into a civil war. This violent conflict has escalated to the extent that more than sixty civilians were killed by two bomb attacks in Ankara in February and March 2016, and the Kurdish militia took responsibility for both attacks.[27]

Most scholars are still trying to puzzle out 'why the insurgent PKK which was militarily defeated, which renounced the goal of secession, and whose leader was under the custody of the Turkish state, remobilized its armed forces in a time when opportunities for the peaceful solution of the Kurdish question were unprecedented in Turkey'.[28] Despite apparently positive changes, the poverty problem which is correlated with historical policies of assimilation and discrimination remains to trouble the majority of the Kurds even though their cultural identity has been explicitly recognized in the public sphere. Perhaps most importantly, the Kurds themselves do not have any sense that they are becoming better off just because their ethnic identity is gradually becoming more valued. On the contrary, recent research indicates that, since reforms began, Kurds have been increasingly marginalized.[29] Meanwhile, the further ethnicization of Turkish politics has swept away any hopes for substantive democracy in the country. These developments in Turkey challenge the conventional wisdom which presumes that a positive relationship exists between tolerance and group rights on the one hand and the fundamental principles of liberalism, such as freedom, peace, and equality, on the other.

To understand why reforms have not worked as expected, it is important to analyze the government's plans for 'multiculturalism' and their compatibility or incompatibility with liberalism and democracy in the context of the social realities of contemporary Turkey.

Ethno-cultural diversity is a reality in Turkey, and its management is as important as it has ever been, but questions persist about how the desirable goal of multiculturalism can be achieved and in what form it can be realized. Can multiculturalism, the politics of recognition, and ethnocultural group rights be mobilized in ways that ensure freedom, dignity, equality, and peace for all of the citizens of the modern Turkish state? Such questions are not peculiar to modern Turkey. Claims for autonomy, the tension between individual rights and group rights, and the right of self-government for national minorities have always been controversial in the fields of international law, political theory, nationalism, and conflict studies.[30]

In each of these fields, scholars have raised issues that states need to deal with if they are to accommodate minority claims within a political system in which equality, peace and freedom can be achieved for all. In particular, liberal theories demonstrate the importance of the ways in which national minorities are approached and of the roles that states play in dealing with citizens who come from different backgrounds. They have been extensively discussed from both theoretical and legal perspectives in relation to national minorities elsewhere for decades. Indeed, there is much that can be learned from considering the Kurds of Turkey in relation to the wider history of the treatment of national minorities, and from an examination of different understandings of how diversity should be accommodated.

My main motivation in writing this book was therefore to inform the Kurdish question in Turkey by contributing to a theoretical debate about multiculturalism that has not, so far, been taken up within Kurdish and Turkish studies. The politics of identity and recognition for the Kurds in Turkey has gained momentum since 2002, but the trajectory of this politics has never been fully recognized, studied, or assessed. Critics such as Ozkirimli[31] and Gunter[32], who rightly emphasize the persistence of the state's authoritarian character, have not, to date, questioned the possibility that their own normative suggestions might not be theoretically consistent or sociologically grounded. Minority nationalists as well as liberals, and scholars such as Ozkirimli and Gunter in Turkey, have presumed the virtues of ethno-cultural autonomy and have focused their ire on external factors such as the party politics that have hampered its realization in the country. As a consequence, there is a strong tendency on the part of 'liberals' in Turkey to overlook the global debate on multiculturalism, its normative flaws, inegalitarian outcomes, and essentialist tendencies. Also unexplored are its negative impacts on conflict and, most importantly, how they apply to contemporary developments in relation to the Kurdish question in Turkey. This book, based on my fieldwork and other contemporary social surveys, shows that there are seriously conflicting views within the Kurdish community about the forms that the politics of recognition could take. This book explores these conflicts of interest amongst the Kurds using a bottom-up approach and shows that recognition of an authentic Kurdish identity is especially difficult because of these intractable conflicts within their group. This is the first academic text of its kind to explain how the quest for an authentic Kurdish political identity, as well as attempts to generate it, actually have the potential to limit the autonomy of individual Kurds and exacerbate existing disparities between Turks and Kurds in Turkey.

Careful observation of various cases has shown that the success and consistency of multiculturalism with respect to the accommodation of national minorities has significantly varied from one case to another. While theories of multiculturalism have been successful in helping to resolve issues for minorities in Canada and Belgium, they have failed in other countries. For example, during the process of incorporating the multiculturalist paradigm into the European Union legal framework, the compatibility of multiculturalist policies with these new contexts sometimes emerged as doubtful.[33] In some instances it was unsuccessful in promoting equality or pacifying ethnic conflicts, and in other cases it could not even be put into practice despite government efforts. The Roma people in Hungary who were given self-government rights to administer education in their own language still suffer from inequalities which have not been rectified by the introduction of multicultural discourse.[34] In France, the idea of legalizing Corsu as the language of public education in Corsica could not be achieved, despite the French government's intention to introduce this measure through a referendum in 2003.[35] A total of 114,970 voters cast their ballots on July 6, 2003, in a referendum that would have allowed the island of Corsica to exercise a degree of autonomy. The referendum asked voters whether they would accept a new territorial assembly and an executive body that would manage more of the island's affairs. Based on the results released by the French Ministry of the Interior, a marginal majority voted against autonomy.[36] Similarly, in Turkey, Kurdish identity started to be officially recognized in the 2000s, and Kurds were gradually granted simple cultural rights such as state broadcasting and private language education in Kurdish.[37] Nevertheless, the Turkish government's adoption of weak multiculturalist initiatives in the period of accession to the EU did not evolve into the kind of strong policy envisaged by the EU, which required the provision of state-funded education for the Kurds in their own language.[38] The gradual implementation of the multiculturalist discourse in Turkey has so far, as briefly introduced above, disappointingly failed.

This puzzle is worth exploring, not least because theorists of multiculturalism speak with such certainty about the success that will follow its realization.[39] Their view involves taking the positivity of multiculturalism for granted and disregarding the ways in which multiculturalism – as an idea employed in different forms by political institutions and other actors – causes instability and even perpetuates inequality in some cases. The consistency of the political theories in question and their overarching presumptions about political behaviour need to be tested against evidence informed by political sociology and its understanding of national minorities.

This book makes the case that it is imperative to undertake a closer examination of different cases of multiculturalism in practice, not only to expose its good and problematic aspects, but also to remedy the insufficient theorization and analysis of its assumptions, which are being used to underpin projects involving national minorities across the globe. I aim to reassess what might be termed an idealistic popular theory of multiculturalism in order to identify its actual capacity to deal in real situations with the continuing problems of heterogeneity and national minorities.

This book, which takes a comparative approach, represents the first contribution towards bringing the Turkish/Kurdish case into the global debate about multiculturalism and its flaws. Theoretical discussions around the topic are extremely important in informing new developments in Turkey and in explaining why peace, freedom, and equality might not yet be on the horizon. This book suggests that these universalized concepts will need to be modified to be effective in the Turkish situation. Equally important, however, is this book's focus on an empirical analysis of the Kurds. It seeks to contribute to the theoretical literature on universal minority rights by locating the Kurdish question in relation to the treatment of other national minorities such as the Québécois in Canada, Republican Catholics in Northern Ireland, Corsicans in France, and Muslim Turks in Greece. This book invites the reader to question in what forms multiculturalism can actually work for different national minorities. The central questions this book addresses to an equal extent can be summarized as follows:

- How did the transition to the discourse of multiculturalism in Turkey between 2002 and 2015 impact on the conflict between the Kurds and the Turks, equalities and freedoms?
- What is the impact of multiculturalism discourse on national minorities, especially the Kurds? Does it encourage ethnic nationalism, polarization and conflict while challenging the state hegemony?
- Can we categorize national minorities and identify the extent to which different types of multiculturalist policies can produce the desired outcomes of peace, equality and freedom for each category?
- Where do the Kurds in Turkey stand in comparison to other minorities, how do their peculiarities complicate the implementation of multiculturalist discourse in Turkey and what are the more suitable approaches to the Kurds in Turkey from a liberal perspective other than the current discourse explained in this book?

What Themes, Concepts, and Ideas Does This Book Develop? What Unique Features or Focus Does It Have?

This book's most important contribution is to Turkish and Kurdish studies. There are many such studies which criticize the unequal treatment of minorities in Turkey and highlight the need to improve equality between Kurds and Turks. However, while the focus remains on this possible transformation, new inequalities that are emerging from the current multicultural discourse in Turkey remain unanalyzed. There has, to date, been no study about how and to what extent the contemporary discourse of multiculturalism affects the ethnic conflict between Kurds and Turks. Recognition of minority identities and the viability of accommodating diversity in a liberal democratic system have been at the center of arguments about the conflict in Turkey, but the effects produced by this idealistic approach have not been subjected to scrutiny. This book elaborates on the global debate on multiculturalism, its normative flaws, and its essentialist tendencies, and it examines how they apply to the Kurdish question in Turkey.

It is clear that state policies of forced assimilation have radicalized a remarkable number of the Kurds in Turkey, but the slow transition from assimilationism to multiculturalism has not subdued ethnic conflict either. Increasing numbers of terrorist incidents and ethnic violence in the country since 2004 suggest that the country's 'politics of recognition and multiculturalism' may in fact be heightening the conflict that they are designed to settle. This book explains to what extent and how the contemporary discourse of multiculturalism affects the ethnic conflict and inequalities that exist between the Kurds and the Turks. It furnishes an understanding of what multiculturalism means for national minorities in general, and it also establishes how multiculturalism impacts in particular on the Kurdish question and its possible solutions.

This book will be useful to scholars in a variety of disciplines who want to study whether state nationalism and multiculturalism are compatible on theoretical and practical levels. It explains the importance of being sensitive to different types of nationalism and assesses their implications for various interpretations of multiculturalism. Conventional academic wisdom suggests that multiculturalism is a civic project which challenges the ethnic domination of the majority in a nation-state, yet, as this book shows, multiculturalism for national minorities is in fact an ethnocentric project. When multiculturalism challenges the nominally constructivist notion of nationality, it assumes, to all practical and theoretical intents and purposes, that nationality is an ethnic category. Chapter 3 elaborates on this argument and explains it in detail. By examining the problematics of multiculturalist theory in the context of Turkey and Kurdish rights, this book develops a unique and substantive discussion of that theory's ethnic and civic aspects and its impacts on national minorities.

The book develops a new context-sensitive approach to both the theory of multiculturalism and the minorities that it impacts. While the multiculturalist debate tends to dwell on the distinction between immigrant minorities and national minorities, this book argues that it is not sufficient to differentiate between these two groups, because national minorities are not identical to each other. In fact, when we decide from a liberal perspective on the rights that certain minorities should have, we also need to distinguish between national minorities which have experienced different types of state nationalism during their histories. It is vital to be mindful of the different positions and choices of the ethno-cultural groups that multiculturalism is supposed to accommodate because '[i]t is the differing location of particular ethnic groups within the nation state that shapes and constrains the ethnic options available to them'.[40] Contemporary theories of ethnocentric multiculturalism are especially problematic in cases where there is a history of assimilationist and integrationist civic state nationalism which has produced increased intersectionality as well as complex hyphenated identities. Multiculturalism proves a more difficult project when it is used to try to accommodate these complex minorities rather than those which were marginalized and mobilized as a result of historical state policies of discrimination and exclusion. This book provides an in-depth case study of the Kurdish situation in order to illustrate this idea and draws key insights through its use of a comparative perspective in order to contextualize its claims. It offers significant insights into the theory of multiculturalism and makes key suggestions for its future uses. In particular, it shows how insights from social science and political theory can be used to refine ideas about multiculturalism and improve its usefulness in a variety of cases in which it currently struggles to produce results.

The politics of recognition and therefore of multiculturalism tend towards the elevation of mere fragments into totalizing and 'authentic' entities. Political activists require a solid group identity to advocate for, as well as a group identity on behalf of which they can base their claims to autonomy, and so, in their hands, group identities often become reified even as they are being deployed for strategic ends. It is not uncommon to find data on minorities that has been collected through either a limited analysis of nationalist minority parties and activists or a study of ethnic conflict frequency.[41] The outcome of this kind of research, as Kalyvas notes, 'boils down to the claim that individuals will tend to act in support of organizations claiming to represent their ethnic identity – so much so that individuals and organizations can be conflated into a single actor, the "ethnic group"'.[42] This book serves to challenge this multiculturalist presumption that ethnic and cultural identities will almost inevitably translate into political entities and dispensations.[43] The remarkable number of Kurds in Turkey who have refused to politicize their ethnicities can be seen as proof that not all cultural nationalisms are also political.[44] Cultural 'national identity' does not necessarily translate into the kind of political ideology which holds that the political and the national unit should be congruent.[45] This book criticizes any overemphasis on the ethno-political nature of national identity and aims to explicate under what circumstances an ethno-national minority is more or less likely to politicize its cultural distinctiveness.

This book challenges the scholarly argument that policies of assimilation in civic states rarely work. It also questions the idea that such policies are indeed more likely to strengthen than to erode differences because they provoke a reactive mobilization against such assimilatory pressures. It is usually accepted that the assimilation process poses a challenge to the very existence of the subject's identity, and that therefore the subject who senses a danger of extinction will develop a motivation for social struggle. The scholars who suggest that this relationship exists between assimilation and social struggle fail, however, to account for the lack of mass mobilization in the cases of Kurds and Corsicans. In this book, I develop the idea that the structural effects of assimilationist political systems on minority political cultures are actually much more complex and multifaceted than is suggested in the current academic literature. When assimilation does not necessarily require minority individuals to leave their culture of origin behind, and in situations where the minority and majority cultures are not mutually exclusive, as is usually the case with linguistic minorities who can develop bilingual identities and multiple loyalties, it is hard for a multiculturalist approach to assume that everyone in a minority group will almost always reject assimilation in an attempt to follow their groups leaders who raise claims to self-government rights or self-determination. The Kurdish case in Turkey in particular indicates that this profound complexity exists and must be addressed.

The lack of a coherent political culture is not exclusive to the Kurds in Turkey. Most ethnic communities are internally segregated by linguistic, religious, gender, class-related, geographical, or political divisions. However, some minorities are likely to be able to overcome their internal divisions and combine in support of a collective form of ethno-political representation, while some others are not. When internal disagreements within an ethnic group persist, as is the case for the Kurds in Turkey, it becomes more and more difficult for group members or other parties to answer questions about which fragments of an internally conflicted minority should be recognized and whose demands need to be addressed most urgently.

This book also makes a significant contribution to the field of applied political theory as it relates to multiculturalism because it explores the complex issues involved in finding and implementing ways to accommodate national minorities successfully. Multiculturalism has been prescribed by many as a universal panacea to the problems of all those national minorities which possess a 'societal culture'. Multiculturalism has also been presented as a stepping-stone towards ending ethnic conflict and liberalizing countries in transition. These extraordinary claims about the power of multiculturalist approaches are the main reason why this topic has drawn so much attention from all over the world, including from scholars and governments in Eastern Europe,[46] Africa,[47] Asia,[48] and the Arab world.[49] Although it is widely asserted that 'one size does not fit all' in relation to the transferability of government policy, scholars and policy makers alike have generally accepted the fundamental premise of multiculturalism, which is that national minorities with their own societal cultures should be given self-government rights one way or another. While many scholars have studied the topic from a case-specific perspective and have suggested necessary configurations for institutionalizing this approach, there has, as yet, been no analysis as to why ethnocentric multiculturalism is more successful both normatively and practically in some cases than in others. Scholars have worked to outline the preconditions that will allow multiculturalist arguments to start shaping the political agenda and producing effects. However, the possibility that ethnocentric multiculturalism itself can, in some cases, be destructive of a democratic political life is yet to be studied.[50] This book addresses this crucial problematic and suggests ways in which it can be overcome.

In doing so the book also builds an unprecedented bridge between normative works on multiculturalism in their attempt to respond to the problems of national minorities from a liberal perspective on the one hand and evidenced based empirical/ statistical studies documenting and analyzing the success of decentralization and self-determination in solving ethnic conflicts on the other. These empirical analyses offer useful insights for the normative theories of multiculturalism, which often promote decentralization and self-government rights in different forms but hardly engage with empirical works that test the success of such practices in real-world cases. For example, multiculturalism theorists could extensively benefit from the works of Cunningham,[51] who scrutinizes why self-determination conflicts are more intractable in divided minorities than in others. Similarly multiculturalism theorists could benefit from the works of Brancati,[52] who used a statistical analysis of thirty democracies from 1985 to 2000 to explain why decentralization is more successful in reducing conflict and secessionism in some countries than in others. Bringing such works into the discussion on the capacity of multiculturalism in solving ethnic conflicts this book combines political science and political theory and challenges the conventional thinking about national minorities and their autonomy.

Last, this study will be of significant benefit for policy makers who use legal political theory to inform the solutions they develop for the problems they are experiencing in dealing with minorities. It will be especially important for international and supranational organizations, as well as for non-governmental organizations, which are engaged in extra efforts to find solutions for national minority problems. The United Nations, the European Union, the Organization for Security and Co-operation in Europe (OSCE), and the European Council are just a few of the organizations which are currently engaged in work with minorities. There are several books in existence which explore minority rights from a legal perspective,[53] and, although they try to establish a universal standard for minority rights, all of these works make the argument that each case has its own unique circumstances and that policy makers should be sensitive to them when dealing with the problems faced by each national minority. This book moves beyond this approach and shows that it is possible to categorize national minorities and their problems according to the state policies they have been exposed to in the past. Equipped with the insights made available through this detailed analysis of causes and effects in the implementation of multiculturalist approaches, policy makers and theoreticians will for the first time be able to understand which approach is most likely to provide a solution for the type of national minority with which they are concerned.

Chapter Overview

Chapter 1: Introduction

So far this introduction chapter has summarized the evolution of international law on national minorities and explained the ways in which minorities are treated by states as well as by other international organizations such as the European Union and the United Nations. The discussion sets out two alternative views of liberalization and modernity with regard to the accommodation of national minorities, namely ethnocentric multiculturalism and civic individualist egalitarianism/assimilationism.[54] It identified the multiple and conflicting interpretations of multiculturalism offered by the international organizations which are working to design a liberal form of diversity in modern Europe. The chapter briefly contextualized these interpretations in a discussion about how their conflicting interpretations of modernity were implemented and subsequently failed in Turkey.

Chapter 2: The Theory of National Minorities: From State Nationalism to Multiculturalism

This coming chapter sets out a detailed theoretical background for the discussion that will follow about the best ways to accommodate national minorities. Multiculturalism and egalitarianism/assimilationism – as the two theoretical approaches that liberal modernity has to offer – seem to have informed most states and international and supranational organizations in their efforts to find a liberal democratic solution for the problems of national minorities. There has been an ever-increasing tension between these two different approaches to the treatment of national minorities in Turkey since the foundation of the country in 1923. Difference-blind egalitarianism clings to a monolithic definition of citizenship, while ethnocentric multiculturalism strives for the decentralization of the state along ethnic lines. This chapter explains what the various interpretations of multiculturalism have to say in relation to possible solutions for the problems of national minorities. It also elaborates on the remaining problems with these theoretical approaches and shows how they fail or succeed in specific cases. This chapter therefore explains the substance of multiculturalist theory.

The many and conflicting strategies that international organizations have offered for how best to accommodate diversity have all been implemented in Turkey, albeit in limited ways, and they consequently failed. A brand-new legal framework tailored to the peculiarities of Turkey and its Kurdish minority is clearly needed. This chapter gives a balanced picture of the theoretical discussions that could inform such a legal system. By focusing on these theoretical discussions, the chapter also explores the general weaknesses of the theory of multiculturalism and the relationship of those weaknesses to its practical failure in Turkey.

In doing so, it argues that, while everyone is free to retain diversity in their culture and lifestyle, this diversity does not justify the perpetuation of any ethnic prejudices; nor should it encourage the development or strengthening of rigid boundaries between ethnic groups. In conclusion, the chapter explores the question as to whether it is really possible to recognize ethnicity as a legitimate justification for differentiated rights without either perpetuating and encouraging ethnic polarization or creating the kinds of further inequalities experienced by the Kurds in Turkey.

Chapter 3: Multiculturalism for National Minorities: One Size Does Not Fit All

The third chapter sets out an understanding of national minorities from a sociological perspective. The book as a whole argues that different types of national minorities can be accommodated best through a variety of different methods, and this chapter clarifies how these minorities differ from each other depending on the different structures of their communities and of the states in which they live. It explores why Kurds differ from other national minorities like the Francophone communities in Canada or the people of Flanders, and why Turkey cannot be understood as a similar state to Canada or Belgium, the host states for these other minorities. The chapter identifies examples of success and failure that have emerged when national minorities have been treated in the ways recommended by conventional theories of multiculturalism. It focuses particularly on the kinds of failure that that followed the application of these conventional strategies to the complicated situation experienced by the Kurds in Turkey. These failures have rightly led people to question exactly how liberal and effective ethnocentric multiculturalism actually is. This chapter develops a unique and substantive discussion about whether multiculturalism has the fundamental capacity to address injustices arising from the treatment of 'minorities of assimilation' like the Kurds in Turkey.

Chapter 4: Turkey's Kurdish Dilemma: 'Segmented Forms of Assimilation'

By focusing on the Kurdish case, I contextualize the argument that it is more difficult for ethnocentric approaches to accommodate minorities which were subjected over a long period to state policies of assimilation and integration. The historical context of forced assimilation and integration is explained through a depiction of the history of Turkish nationalism vis-à-vis Kurdish identity, from the foundation of the Republic of Turkey in 1923 up until the 2000s. Chapter 4 explains that Kurds have experienced state policies on a range of different fronts in the past, but vary considerably in their opinions today rather than sharing views on how their collective future might be realized. This variation corresponds to Kurds' diverse political orientations and expectations in the context of modern Turkey, the conditions of which make minority representation more difficult than it is in other cases.

Chapter 5: When Multiculturalism Does Not Fit: Kurds and Turkey in the 2000s

This chapter first shows how policies of assimilation and integration in Turkey impacted on the social, economic, and political positioning of the Kurds in the 2000s. It then applies arguments from the second chapter to the contemporary relationship between the Kurds and the state in Turkey. Multiculturalism is often referenced by a range of political institutions and political actors who appeal to its ideas when they discuss and reflect on the outstanding problems that affect Kurds in Turkey. The views of these institutions and actors are shown here to be highly correlated with the theoretical perspectives offered by multiculturalism and egalitarianism/assimilationism, and indeed these ideas can be seen to have further exacerbated the problematic relationship between the Kurds and Turkey. This chapter shows how further violations of Kurds' freedom and equalities are being justified in terms of these frameworks, and so it provides key empirical evidence for the main argument of this book. Ethnocentric multiculturalism is subjected to scrutiny in order to establish whether or not its approaches can actually bring about equality and freedom in Turkey. The chapter also elaborates on the need for a new approach which would draw on moderate multiculturalist theory as opposed to ethnocentric multiculturalism to provide solutions that are best suited to the realities of the situation at hand.

Chapter 6: Can Multiculturalism Really End Ethnic Conflicts?

It is very common for academics to look at examples of conflict resolution and democratization elsewhere in order to recommend what can and should be done to solve the Kurdish question in Turkey. There is, for example, a tendency to draw on lessons from case studies from places such as Northern Ireland, where the politics of recognition have been relatively successful in subduing ethnic conflict and tensions. Less common are attempts to understand why the ethnocentric multiculturalist solutions which have featured in some of the most successful examples of conflict resolution internationally have not been, and cannot actually be, effectively applied in Turkey. This chapter adds to the empirical evidence provided earlier in the book in respect of the Kurdish case in Turkey and also touches on the case of Corsica, where ethnocentric multiculturalist projects have failed in some respects. In doing so, the chapter answers questions about where and when autonomy, as promoted by ethno-centric multiculturalism, is likely to be a democratic and realistic solution that subdues violent conflicts. It also illustrates where the Kurds stand in relation to this bigger picture.

Chapter 7: Conclusion

The book's conclusion has three functions. First, it summarizes the problems that arise when multiculturalism is presumed to be a natural good which can be applied in undifferentiated ways to resolve the problems faced by Kurds. Second, it reiterates that the historic treatment of national minorities in given situations is highly correlated to the viability of the solutions offered for the issues they face today. Finally, it argues that more considered, moderate, and case-specific applications of multiculturalism will need to be developed to resolve the problems faced in currently intractable cases such as that of the Kurds in Turkey. A new emphasis is needed on responding to territorial needs and empowering local administrations with key competencies in order to help resolve the Turkish-Kurdish conflict that undifferentiated forms of ethnocentric multiculturalism have inadvertently helped to inflame in recent years.

Notes

1 World Fact Book, Turkey, www.cia.gov/library/publications/the-world-factbook/geos/tu.html.
2 Henri J. Barkey and Graham E. Fuller, 'Turkey's Kurdish Question: Critical Turning Points and Missed Opportunities', *The Middle East Journal* (1997): 59–79.
3 Constitutional Court of the Republic of Turkey, 'The Constitution of the Republic of Turkey (1982): Chapter Four, Political Rights and Duties. Article 66', Türkiye Büyük Millet, www.tbmm.gov.tr.
4 Mustafa Baysal, 'National Minorities in the Turkish Law', Tribunal Constitucional, http://tribunalconstitucional.ad.
5 Turkish Citizenship Law, No: 5901, European Union Democracy Observatory on Citizenship, http://eudo-citizenship.eu.
6 Yeşim Bayar, 'In Pursuit of Homogeneity: The Lausanne Conference, Minorities and the Turkish Nation'. *Nationalities Papers* 42, no. 1 (2014): 108–25.
7 Yavuz Ercan, 'Türkiye'de Azınlık Sorununun Kökeni (Osmanlı'dan Cumhuriyet'e Gayrimüslimler)'. *OTAM-Ankara Üniversitesi Osmanlı Tarihi Araştırma ve Uygulama Merkezi Dergisi* 20, (2006): 14.
8 Thomas W. Smith, 'Civic Nationalism and Ethnocultural Justice in Turkey', *Human Rights Quarterly* 27, no. 2 (2005): 436–70.
9 Minority Rights Group, *A Quest for Equality? Minorities in Turkey* (London: Minority Rights Group, 2007), 10.

10 Egalitarians stress the importance of equality, and that equality – assessed at the level of the individual – is expected to prevail with no recognition or quarter offered for cultural differences. In egalitarian terms, members of every cultural group should have the same rights before the law, and everyone should be equally entitled to live and perform their cultural practices in the private sphere, as long as their practices do not infringe upon the rights of other individuals. The adoption of this view involves consent for the assumption that the injustices of the past cannot be rectified by granting differentiated rights like self-determination or exemption from citizenship law to groups that have been marginalized or oppressed. The downplaying of past grievances that this approach entails is justified by the belief that any focus on cultural identities or on genealogical descent, and any bid to foreground those things in modern politics, would violate the equal opportunities available to individuals in various ways and would also fuel the mobilization of further conflict between ethnic groups.

11 Assimilationism is a political ideology that valorizes the practice or policy of assimilating or encouraging the assimilation of people from all ethnic groups and cultures of origin into the dominant language and/or culture in their country of residence.

12 A national minority has been defined as 'a group numerically inferior to the rest of the population of a state, in a non-dominant position, whose members – being nationals of the state – possess ethnic, religious, or linguistic characteristics differing from those of the rest of the population and show, if only implicitly, a sense of solidarity, directed towards preserving their culture, traditions, religion or language'. Jennifer Jackson Preece, *National Minorities and the European Nation-States System* (Oxford: Oxford University Press), 28. This definition is limited, because it does not include migrant minorities, though a consideration of those groups is not central here. This book focuses only on national minorities which inhabited a given territory and were already accustomed to using their own languages before their involuntary subordination to the state project.

13 Inis L. Claude, *National Minorities: An International Problem* (Cambridge, MA: Harvard University Press, 1955), 211.

14 Rosalyn Higgins, 'Conceptual Thinking About the Individual in International Law', *British Journal of International Studies* 4, no. 1 (1978): 1–19.

15 Metin Heper, *The State and Kurds in Turkey: The Question of Assimilation* (Houndmills, UK: Palgrave Macmillan, 1992).

16 Will Kymlicka, *Multicultural Citizenship: A Liberal Theory of Minority Rights* (Oxford: Clarendon Press, 1995).

17 Kymlicka, *Multicultural Citizenship*.

18 A. D. Smith, *Ethnic Origins of Nations* (Oxford: Basil Blackwell, 1986).

19 Council of Europe, 'Framework Convention for the Protection of National Minorities and Explanatory Report, Article 14', Council of Europe, www.coe.int.

20 Durukan Kuzu, 'A Self-Governing Group or Equal Citizens? Kurds, Turkey and the European Union' *Journal on Ethnopolitics and Minority Issues in Europe* 9, no 1(2010): 32–65.

21 Council of Europe, 'Details of Treaty No. 122 – European Charter of Local Self-Government', www.coe.int/en/web/conventions/full-list/-/conventions/treaty/122. Also see Jane Wright, 'The Protection of Minority Rights in Europe: From Conference to Implementation', *The International Journal of Human Rights* 2, no. 1 (1998): 1–31.
22 Baysal, 'National Minorities in the Turkish Law'.
23 Dilek Kurban, 'Confronting Equality: The Need for Constitutional Protection of Minorities on Turkey's Path to the European Union', *Columbia Human Rights Law Review* 35, no. 1 (2003): 151–214. See also Ergun Özbudun, 'Democratization Reforms in Turkey, 1993–2004', *Turkish Studies* 8, no. 2 (2007): 179–96.
24 *Radikal Newspaper*, 'Meclise Zaza, Laz ve Gürcü Dillerinde TV Kurulsun Dilekcesi' ('Petition to the Turkish Parliament to demand TV channels in Zaza, Laz and Georgian languages'), *Radikal Newspaper*, www.radikal.com.tr.
25 *Hurriyet Daily News*, 'Attacks on Pro-Kurdish Party's Election Offices Called "Political"', *Hurriyet Daily News*, www.hurriyetdailynews.com.
26 Siyasi Haber, 'Kütahya'da Kürt İşçilere Linç Girişimi: Kaldıkları Barakalar Ateşe Verildi' ('A Mob Looted and Set Fire to Kurdish Workers' Dwellings in Kutahya'), *Siyasi Haber*, June 1, 2016, accessed June 1, 2016, http://siyasihaber3.org.
27 Raziye Akkoc, 'Ankara Explosion: Turkish President Vows War on Terror as Officials Say One Bomber Was "Female Kurdish Militant"', *The Telegraph*, www.telegraph.co.uk.
28 Güneş Murat Tezcür, 'When Democratization Radicalizes: The Kurdish Nationalist Movement in Turkey', *Journal of Peace Research* 47, no. 6 (2010): 775–89.
29 Cengiz Saracoglu, 'Exclusive Recognition: The New Dimensions of the Question of Ethnicity and Nationalism in Turkey', *Ethnicity and Racial Studies* 32, no. 4 (2009): 640–58.
30 Peter Jones, 'Human Rights, Group Rights, and Peoples' Rights', *Human Rights Quarterly* 21, no. 1 (1999): 80–107. See also Jack Donnelly, 'Human Rights, Individual Rights and Collective Rights', in J. Berting, ed., *Human Rights in a Pluralist World: Individuals and Collectivities* (Westport, CT: Meckler, 1990), 39–62; and Marlies Galenkamp, *Individualism versus Collectivism the Concept of Collective Rights* (Deventer: Gouda Quint, 1998).
31 Umut Ozkirimli, 'Multiculturalism, Recognition and the "Kurdish question" in Turkey: The Outline of a Normative Framework'. *Democratization* 21, no. 6 (2014): 1055–73.
32 Michael Gunter, 'Reopening Turkey's Closed Kurdish Opening?' *Middle East Policy* 20, no. 2 (2013): 88–98.
33 As this study is related to the problems of national ethnic groups, the term multiculturalism will primarily refer to the views of Kymlicka, who clearly described the way in which national minorities should and would be treated in compliance with the general lines of the liberal multiculturalist perspective as summarized in this chapter.

34 Robert Koulish, 'Hungarian Roma Attitudes on Minority Rights: The Symbolic Violence of Ethnic Identification', *Europe-Asia Studies* 57, no. 2 (2005): 311–26.
35 Thomas Benedikter, *Solving Ethnic Conflict Through Self-Government: A Short Guide to Autonomy in Europe and South Asia* (Bozen/Bolzano: Eurac, 2009).
36 Stéphane Guérard, 'Local Referendums in France: A Disappointing Experience', in Theo Schiller, ed., *Local Direct Democracy in Europe* (Wiesbaden: Springer, 2011).
37 Ergun Özbudun and Yazici Serap, *Democratic Reforms in Turkey (1993–2004)* (Istanbul: TESEV Publications, 2004).
38 European Commission against Racism and Intolerance, *Third Report on Turkey* (Strasbourg: ECRI, 2005).
39 Will Kymlicka and Magda Opalski, *Can Liberal Pluralism Be Exported? Western Political Theory and Ethnic Relations in Eastern Europe* (Oxford: Oxford University Press, 2002).
40 Stephen May, Tariq Modood and Judith Squires, *Ethnicity, Nationalism, and Minority Rights* (Cambridge University Press, 2004).
41 James Mahoney, 'Qualitative Methodology and Comparative Politics', *Comparative Political Studies* 40, no. 2 (2007): 122–44.
42 Stathis N. Kalyvas, 'Ethnic Defection in Civil War', *Comparative Political Studies* 41, no. 8 (2008): 1043–68.
43 Will Kymlicka, 'Multicultural Citizenship Within Multination States', *Ethnicities* 11, no. 3 (2011): 281–302.
44 John Hutchinson, 'Nations and Culture', in Montserrat Guibernau and John Hutchinson, eds., *Understanding Nationalism* (Cambridge: Polity Press, 2001), 74–96.
45 Ernest Gellner, *Nations and Nationalism* (Oxford: Blackwell, 1983).
46 Will Kymlicka and Magda Opalski, *Can Liberal Pluralism Be Exported?*
47 Will Kymlicka, Bruce J. Berman and Dickson Eyoh, *Ethnicity & Democracy in Africa* (London: J. Currey, 2004).
48 Will Kymlicka and Baogang He, *Multiculturalism in Asia* (Oxford: Oxford University Press, 2005).
49 Will Kymlicka and Eva Pföstl, *Multiculturalism and Minority Rights in the Arab World* (Oxford: Oxford University Press, 2014).
50 Yasutomo Morigiwa, Fumihiko Ishiyama and Tetsu Sakurai, *Universal Minority Rights? A Transnational Approach: Proceedings of the Fifth Kobe Lectures, Tokyo and Kyoto, December 1998* (Stuttgart: Franz Steiner, 2004).
51 Kathleen Gallagher Cunningham, *Inside the Politics of Self Determination* (New York, NY: Oxford University Press, 2014).
52 Dawn Brancati, 'Decentralization: Fueling the Fire or Dampening the Flames of Ethnic Conflict and Secessionism?' *International Organization* 60, no. 3 (2006): 651–85.
53 OSCE, *National Minority Standards* (Strasbourg: Organization for Security and Cooperation in Europe: 2007); M. Weller, ed., *Universal Minority Rights: A Commentary on the Jurisprudence of International Courts and Treaty Bodies* (Oxford: Oxford University Press, 2007); G. Pentassuglia, *Minorities in International Law* (Strasbourg: Council of Europe Publishing, 2002); A. Phillips

and A. Rosas, eds., *Universal Minority Rights* (London, Turku/Abo: Institute for Human Rights Abo Akademi University and Minority Rights Group, 1995); D. Fottrell and B. Bowring, eds., *Minority and Group Rights in the New Millennium* (Hague: Kluwer Law International, 1999).

54 It is important to clarify that although egalitarianism and assimilationism can interact, they, as already defined earlier in the manuscript, are not necessarily the same thing. It is important to note that whenever the two are mentioned together in this book, the purpose of doing so is to refer to a peculiar context where they merge. It will become clearer in Chapter 3 that not all assimilationist policies are rooted in egalitarianism.

2 The Theory of National Minorities
From State Nationalism to Multiculturalism

Most liberals in non-Western countries like Turkey, as well as national minorities like the Kurds, idealize the value of cultural recognition and multiculturalism in different forms. However, multiculturalism for national minorities is a highly controversial topic in Western political theory, and its imperfections as well as its merits deserve close analysis. This chapter explores the evolution, strengths, and weaknesses of multiculturalism before assessing if and how it might actually be made to work for Turkey and the Kurds.

The discussion here establishes a general understanding of why we need multiculturalism as opposed to hegemonic state nationalism to solve problems in these kinds of complex situations, but it cautions that ethnocentric multiculturalism and its overemphasis on communitarianism might create further inequalities and violations of individual freedom. In Chapter 5 these arguments will be applied to the specific case of the Kurds in contemporary Turkey, but this chapter first presents a preliminary and detailed theoretical discussion about why multiculturalism in its ethnocentric manifestation might have been problematic in Turkey. It concludes by setting out a modified version of multiculturalism which proves useful in addressing the problems faced by national minorities in countries, like Turkey, where neither centralized state nationalism and its difference-blind approaches nor contemporary ethnocentric multiculturalism have solved the Kurdish question.

Structure

Each section in this chapter has a clear purpose. The first chapter has already explained some alternative views in practice with regard to the best ways of accommodating national minorities; however it is not yet clear what are the theoretical justifications for their occurrence and the consequences of their adoption. The following two sections first explain the evolution of minority regimes from ethnic nationalism to civic nationalism and political liberalism; the third section explains why political liberalism and civic nationalism, with its emphasis on difference-blind equal citizenship as an ideological response to ethnic nationalism, has not been successful in solving the problems of national minorities either, so that we need a new multiculturalist interpretation of liberalism. The following fourth and fifth sections will show that multiculturalism is desirable but, when multiculturalist theory turns its attention to national minorities, it tends to have an ethnic conception of nationalism of which classical liberals are strongly critical. This section therefore substantiates one of the central tenets of the book, which is that multiculturalism, so far as its focus on national minorities is concerned, is in fact an ethnocentric project. Following this, the chapter describes the multiculturalists' attempt to justify and accommodate ethnic demands in liberalism with introducing the concept of liberal ethnicity. The last section first questions whether ethnic nationalism and liberalism can ever have a happy marriage, and then answers that this might not be always possible.

Ethnic Nationalism

National identity has often been understood as a matter of inheritance rather than choice. The belief that a nation is a fact of nature was reflected by the German romantic thinker Johann Gottfried Herder, who argued that nationality is 'as much a plant of nature as a family, only with more branches'.[1] According to this view, a German cannot *not* be German, and a Turk cannot *be* German, whatever his grasp of the German tongue or her understanding of German cultural practices. Nationhood, in these terms, is less a matter of political voluntarism than of organic determinism, and human will is subordinated to naturalistic criteria. Whatever his or her migratory movements, each individual is understood to remain 'ineluctably, organically, a member of the community of birth, [being] forever stamped by it'.[2]

   This ethnic conception of national identity has had catastrophic implications for minorities throughout the history of nation-states. It has led to cases of ethnic cleansing, such as that carried out in the Bosnian war in Former Yugoslavia, as well as to genocide in Rwanda, the forced deportation and decimation of the Greek and Armenian populations in Turkey, the isolation of Muslim Turks in Greece, and ongoing discrimination against minorities such as the Uyghurs in China, Tamils in Sri Lanka, and Tatars in Russia. In fact, this list of examples could be multiplied many times over.

Between 1919 and 1939 a distinct set of linguistic and cultural characteristics were widely accepted as proof of nationhood by the League of Nations.[3] 'If the peoples inhabiting a particular area had a unique language and culture then they could legitimately claim a right to national self-determination. If an ethnic nation was unable to form its own independent political unit and instead was forced to exist as a national minority within another ethnic nation's state, then this minority nation was entitled to preserve its own distinct identity as reflected in its language and culture'.[4] However, this principle created many problems and led to many national minorities stirring a wave of conflicts between their kin states. A kin state refers to a state which has some of its co-nationals living in another country (called the host-state or home-state) and so Germany was, for example, a kin state for the large German minority population in Poland. In that particular case, Germans who had been mistreated in Poland gave Germany a reason to treat its Polish minority badly. A more widespread series of revenge acts saw kin states using their ethnic fellows in other countries to justify their irredentist policies. As Hechter notes, 'Irredentist nationalism occurs with the attempt to extend the existing boundaries of a state by incorporating territories of an adjacent state occupied principally by co-nationals (as in the case of the Sudeten Germans)'.[5] While the 'minority guarantees' issued by the League of Nations were intended to be emancipatory, their championing of an ethnic conception of nationhood was co-opted as an ideological basis for the Nazism Hitler would later use to justify both irredentist policies abroad and racism at home.

Political Liberalism and Civic Nationalism as a Response

The problems that arose from the minority guarantees issued by the League of Nations became, for egalitarians, evidence that a focus on group identity would escalate conflict between ethnically separate groups. Such groups have dissimilar capacities to mobilize and claim autonomy and, egalitarians argue, the liberal state loses its neutrality if it only recognizes the right to self-determination of its most able groups. There is certainly some basis for the idea that the multiculturalist politics of recognition violate liberalism's principle of neutrality and can also have negative effects on vulnerable members within the minority group, such as children, women, or political dissidents who are marginalized or mistreated within their own cultural communities.

In seeking to respond to the excesses of nationalisms focused on ethnicities, scholars, lawyers, and activists have identified a number of issues relevant to the protection of the rights of minorities and have chosen to act in ways which prioritize civic nationalism and a focus on individual rights.

The liberal solutions proposed for minority problems have mostly involved attempts to enhance the inclusivity of polities that have previously excluded minorities from the body politic and public life on the basis of their ethnicity, race, or cultural practices. Liberals have distanced themselves from ethnocentric approaches and instead have idealized what they call 'civic nationalism'.

It has become orthodox to argue that, as Zimmer suggests, the civic nation derives its 'legitimacy from its members' voluntary subscription to a set of political principles and institutions'.[6] The civic nation, in these terms, is 'a community of equal, rights-bearing citizens, united in patriotic attachment to a shared set of political practices and values',[7] and voluntary association becomes the cornerstone of national identity. According to this view, 'man is the slave neither of his race, nor his language, nor his religion', and 'man, with his desires and his needs' is left, as an individual, to determine his own sense of national belonging.[8] Kuzio notes that, for advocates of civic nationalism, 'Political reality was based on individual liberty and rational cosmopolitanism and the government was considered to be dependent upon trust from freely consenting citizens'.[9] Liberalism can be understood, then, as only being compatible with this type of civic nationalism as opposed to ethno-politics,[10] and constitutional patriots defend the idea that the very criteria upon which political legitimacy is based should be different from ethno-cultural affiliations, ascriptive characteristics, and descent.[11]

According to the precepts of civic nationalism, a state should acknowledge and respect all individuals as citizens, no matter what their ethnic identity is, as long as they commit to the civic values of the shared political community. Rawls, who is sympathetic to this view, explains in *Political Liberalism* that the civic values upon which the construction of the body politic is to be based in a liberal state should stem from, and evolve around, the concepts of overlapping consensus and public reason. Civic values within this kind of system should reflect and help to foster values that are understood to represent the common good for all of the citizens in a state.[12]

Why Do We Still Need Multiculturalism?

A multiculturalist approach encourages us to question if such a common good can even exist, and whether it is ever possible to reach the kind of overarching consensus in public reason that Rawls assumes can be achieved. There are some strong reasons for questioning the assumption that people of different backgrounds will easily find an overlapping consensus in so-called civic nation-states.

Reinforcing the Dominant Core

Civic nationalism, just like its ethno-cultural counterpart, draws on 'the cultural heritage of dominant ethnic core', especially at the very beginning of nation-building processes,[13] and so it produces, however unintentionally, inegalitarian outcomes for already marginal ethnicities. This is clear when we examine the ways in which states have used language to recreate a common national identity. Even those nations which have claimed to be civic and inclusive have not been able to avoid choosing an official language for use by their subjects in relation to the state.

France chose to use French to create a common national identity and consciousness and thereby oppressed Corsican and Breton peoples who had different mother languages.[14] Meanwhile in Turkey, after the collapse of the Ottoman Empire, administrative power was concentrated in the hands of an elite group who established the terms of the new Turkish nationality on the basis of citizenship and commitment to the liberal political values of the new state. Turkish was declared to be the only official language of the country, and all Muslim citizens, even if they came from Kurdish or Arabic linguistic backgrounds, have since been required to use the Turkish language in public discourse.[15] Even America, renowned for its inclusivity and civic nationalism, forced non-English-speaking Hispanic people to learn English, a move which generated Puerto Rican nationalism as a response. Clearly, the imposition of a dominant culture on national minorities has occurred even in the most feted situations in which civic nationalism has been introduced.[16]

In fact, the civic concept exhibits its own brand of ethnocentrism and superiority, and it is ironic that, in disputing a romantic ethnocentric explanation of nationalism, proponents of the civic model have offered proposals for an alternative that is every bit as rose-tinted, lofty, and idealized as anything from the German romantic tradition. As Yack observes, 'A purely political and principled basis' for national solidarity is the stuff of fairy tales.[17]

Ethnic Descent and Deprivation

The assumption that the project of developing civic states is equally good for all is also undermined by the ongoing correlation between ethnic descent and socio-economic deprivation for minority groups.[18] Membership of a community on moral grounds and legal citizenship are two different concepts that need to be carefully elaborated. Tunisians who became citizens of France but not French,[19] and Pakistani and Bangladeshi people who became British by citizenship but not English, mostly remain in the lowest income groups in their adopted countries.[20]

Meanwhile, children from minorities begin school with economic and linguistic disadvantages which have a great impact on their motivation and chances of success in later life. The outlawing of the use of minority languages at school, which has occurred in Turkey for example,[21] is generally understood to create inequalities for children whose parents use the minority language at home. They need a bilingual education in order to access the medium of instruction properly and in a timely way; and when the state is indifferent to the cultural identity of children, it is likely to produce inequalities that these children will experience for a lifetime.[22]

The Co-optation of Minorities

Classical liberalism[23] is arrogant because, as Kozma points out, 'it presumes the perpetual inclusion of minority nationals in an ongoing civic project that is not their own'.[24] When political liberals couch their theories in the language of social contract theory, they act as 'if there is a universal agreement to build an ideal state, and so the inclusion of minority nations in this project is unproblematic'.[25] In deeply diverse societies in which the conflicting interests of the different groups participating in public discourse leave no room for finding a common good, political liberalism can only serve as an elusive and potentially unobtainable ideal. The persistence of national minorities' claims for autonomy speaks volumes about the impracticality of attempts to develop an overarching consensus in civic nation-states.

Habermas argues that different cultural groups find the justification of a law reasonable if the law's 'burden appears reasonable to them in comparison with the burden of the discrimination which is thereby eliminated'.[26] For example, the compulsory teaching and use of an official state language might be justified on these terms if the erosion and disuse of minority languages was to lead to a concomitant falling away of the discrimination attendant on language difference. An egalitarian can, through this type of logic, justify the granting of official status to the language of the majority and excuse the work of forcing minority members to learn that language, which is now understood to provide members of all ethno-cultural groups with equality of opportunity and the potential to move beyond the limitations of their own cultural groups. In these circumstances, members of underdeveloped minorities will generally feel obliged to opt into education in the official state language because they believe that the lack of it will leave them, and their children, ill-equipped to compete with their peers in the market economy. Their participation in the system that disempowers them is taken as a form of consent for the status quo, and their apparent acquiescence allows others to erase the significance of the sacrifices being made by members of national minorities.

Many liberals feel able to downplay the negative impact of universal laws and endorse some version of the idea that 'all laws have a different impact on different people depending on their preferences and beliefs, for instance speed limits inhibit only those who like to drive fast'.[27] By this logic, a differential effect 'does not constitute unequal treatment provided the law can be justified as advancing some legitimate public objective'.[28] None of this erases the fact that minority members might still want to speak their own language in public discourse more than anything else; it also fails to account for the fact that members of minorities might well care about freedom more than they do about equality. It is not surprising that most of the minority nationalists and insurgents listed as belonging to terrorist organizations actually call themselves freedom fighters.[29] It does not make any sense for a state to justify its decisions on the basis that there is a consensus around legitimate public objectives when some minority members do not even share with the majority a sense of belonging to the same public. Many ethno-cultural groups have been radicalized and further cultural inequalities have been generated by the denial of cultural differences in public discourse and by the entitling of the state to make decisions solely on the basis of equality of opportunity.[30]

Is Multiculturalism the New Liberalism?

In response to the kinds of internal inconsistencies and inegalitarian outcomes produced by allegedly inclusive civic trajectories, the ideology of multiculturalism promotes the idea that cultural groups should be treated differently and given special rights to remedy their disadvantaged positions in their respective communities: 'Inclusion and participation . . . in full citizenship remains the goal', Iris Marion Young argues, 'but "*differentiated* citizenship" now presents itself as a better route to that goal than equal treatment for all groups . . . Equality, defined as the (equal) participation and inclusion of all groups in institutions and positions is sometimes better served by differential treatment'.[31]

Any real equality of opportunity cannot be achieved by providing people with undifferentiated rights and duties because, as Bhikhu C. Parekh argues, 'opportunity should be understood as subject-dependent and a facility, a resource, or a course of action is just a mute and passive possibility and not an opportunity for an individual if she lacks the capacity, the cultural disposition, or the necessary knowledge and resources to take advantage of it'.[32] It means nothing for minorities to have an opportunity if their cultural practices prevent them from making use of it. In civic polities, people who share a particular identity are not systematically prevented from being entitled to the same opportunities as everyone else; however, the context in which these opportunities are offered often indirectly results in discrimination. People benefit who are fully capable of taking up an opportunity, unlike those for whom cultural reservations or pressures give them pause. For example, Sikhs who have the equal right to apply for construction work are not equally treated if a job requires them to wear a helmet instead of a turban, the use of which is a part of their cultural practice. Similarly, women whose beliefs require them to wear the hijab are not equal and free in France, where the education system requires girls to remove this item of clothing. Furthermore, when certain opportunities are offered on supposedly equal terms in civic societies but require the use of the state's official language, linguistic minorities cannot take advantage of them without leaving their own languages behind, at least while participating in the public sphere.

On the face of this argument, the multiculturalist position seems to be informed by distinctions between positive and negative freedoms.[33] Negative freedom refers to the absence of coercion, while positive freedom implies that an active effort has been made to enable an individual's capacity to use their freedom or rights.[34] Scholars who promote the idea that positive freedom offers a more inclusive definition of liberty argue that, when individuals lack the capacity to take advantage of opportunities, they are not free, even in the absence of any coercion. Taking this assumption as a starting point, the ideology of multiculturalism establishes an 'understanding of freedom which will be repositioned from negative to positive, that is, [it will move] from protecting against coercion to providing the context of autonomy'.[35] For example, a 'group's members might be exempted from certain laws, or the group's leadership might be awarded some degree of autonomous jurisdiction over the group's members'.[36]

Multiculturalism and Ethnic Nationalism: Enemies or Friends?

Although there is a common rationale behind multiculturalism, the approach does not offer a unified perspective, and its proponents differ on some very important points, not least on which groups should be entitled to what types of differentiated rights. The question as to who is going to get what rights is an important one that different multiculturalists answer in quite divergent ways.

It is generally agreed that multiculturalism should be concerned with any group of people with a 'stigmatized or marginalized' identity. Indeed, an extensive variety of state measures can be devised to facilitate the values and distinct ways of life of such groups.[37] However, when multiculturalist theory turns its attention to national minorities, it tends to have a rather monist notion of what an ethnic group or culture is: it assumes that self-respect and dignity can only be generated in the context of an ethno-societal culture which, in Will Kymlicka's words, 'provides its members with meaningful ways of life across the full range of human activities including social, educational, religious, recreational, and economic life, encompassing both public and private spheres'.[38] Ethno-national identities are valued on the basis of their capacity to provide their members with this complete set of life opportunities. Carens critiques this idea because, 'Instead of claiming (as is plausible) that the language and national culture of the place where one lives will normally play an important role in shaping the sorts of choices one faces, societal culture is presented as if it were the sole and comprehensive determinant of one's context of choice. Societal culture is what makes freedom possible'.[39]

A multiculturalist approach is also problematic because it privileges national minorities and marginalizes other, non-linguistic and often less-organized minority groups such as LGBT and religious minorities. Members of these minorities, which of course overlap with social and ethno-cultural groupings, should be free to live lives of their choosing without being discriminated against, yet multiculturalism implies that only linguistic ethnic minorities qualify for certain group rights or autonomy because only they have sufficient means to facilitate the full range of human activities within their own *nomos*. This view assumes that all other non-societal cultures are already and inevitably reliant on the existence of a wider societal-linguistic culture. It is clear that multiculturalism has a tendency to defend the rights of autonomy for ethno-cultural groups within diverse societies with little regard for other, often overlapping, disempowered minorities.

The complexity of ethno-cultural groups means that they are not singular in their experiences or needs, and multiculturalists subscribe to the idea that there should be two categories of minority rights for the different types of ethnic minorities that they see as worthy of consideration. They support the idea that self-government rights are needed for national minorities while poly-ethnic rights are required for immigrant minorities. An immigrant minority group is understood to need the state's differential policies to help its members integrate into the societal culture of the host country. This view presumes that immigrants 'have accepted the assumption that their life chances and even more the life chances of their children will be bound up with participation in mainstream institutions operating in the majority language'.[40] To prevent the emergence of unequal outcomes for the minority's members after the state's integration process has been completed, multiculturalists suggest that accommodation policies need to be put in place to recognize the poly-ethnic rights of immigrant minorities.[41] Examples of this kind of accommodation include minority religious holidays being granted, or exams and work shifts being timetabled to accommodate Muslims who fast during Ramadan in Britain, for example.

Multiculturalism for immigrant minorities is understood to involve the implementation of a coherent set of policies that are designed to secure unity in diversity. By contrast, the same theory of multiculturalism assumes that national minorities, which historically inhabited a given territory, should now be entitled to self-government rights. Equality and freedom, according to this view, can only be achieved if those national minorities whose people insist on living in their own societal culture are given equal opportunities to voice their demands. These chances are to be secured by the national minority acquiring self-government rights or even complete independence. Multiculturalism, then, has two distinct facets: it calls for the integration of migrants into the majority society, yet it also advocates the liberation and separation of distinct ethno-national minorities from the same majority.

In short, multiculturalists think that self-government rights are not feasible and cannot increase equality for immigrant minorities because immigrants are perceived to lack a concentrated population and a socio-economic network, features which are deemed to be important elements of a societal culture that can accommodate its own members and their every need. In the absence of this societal culture, any rights to education and government services in an immigrant's own language would be likely to prevent them from learning the language of the dominant socio-economic network, the language which offers them the best option for integrating into the communities and economies within the borders of their host states.

Although this distinction between immigrants and national minorities makes sense to some extent, it does not correspond to the real experience of minority groups, which is much more complex than the theory of multiculturalism suggests. This complexity arises because 'the extent to which national minorities have been able to maintain a separate societal

culture . . . varies considerably',[42] and this variety is reflected in the experience of immigrants too. It can be more important for some national
minorities to have the right to enjoy their culture than it is for them
to have self-government rights which would have little impact 'in countries which are essentially ethnically homogenous – e.g. where the dominant group forms 90 to 95 per cent of the population – and where the
remaining ethnic groups are small, dispersed, and already on the road
to assimilation . . . None of the minorities in these countries are in fact
capable of exercising regional autonomy or of sustaining a high degree of
institutional completeness (e.g. of sustaining their own universities), and
most already show high levels of linguistic assimilation'.[43] The case of the
Roma people in Hungary provides empirical evidence for the argument
that self-government rights do not necessarily increase equality between
the majority and the minority if the national minority is not concentrated
and lacks a societal culture with mature institutions.

The inequality that prevails in Hungary between the national Roma
minority and the non-Roma citizens who form the country's majority
is a clear indication of the fact that self-government rights do not comprise an appropriate solution for minorities which have not developed
a single, representative, and institutionalized economic unit. Segregated
minority education did not become successful in Hungary, as there was
no qualified human resource base to facilitate the maintenance of a good
quality education system in the Romani language. Although the number
of minority students in segregated elementary schooling increased, the
educational profile of disadvantaged minority pupils decreased remarkably in quality, and, correspondingly, the unemployment rates among
Roma people grew.[44] 'According to a 2002 study by the World Bank,
slightly more than 80 per cent of Roma children completed primary
education, but only one-third continued studies into the intermediate
(secondary) level'.[45] The majority's prejudices against the Roma people,
who had a reputation for lacking educational and professional qualifications, remained unchanged, and recognition of their differences in public
discourse did not produce the increase in mutual respect between non-
Roma and Roma citizens in Hungary which had been theorized as an
outcome of these measures.[46]

It is widely accepted that not all national minorities can generate a
full societal culture. However, most minority activists and scholars of
multiculturalism believe that this does not negate the need to give self-
government rights to national minorities which are sizeable and territorially concentrated, such as the Flemish in Belgium, the Catalans in
Spain, and the Québécois in Canada.[47] Even the most fervent critics
of multiculturalism tend to agree with Brian Barry that 'the existence

of different linguistic communities within a single country is compatible with equality of opportunity, on condition that these communities are able to maintain educational and economic institutions capable of providing a range of opportunities of roughly equal value. Belgium (for French and Dutch speakers), Canada (for English and French speakers) all meet these conditions adequately. The politics of wonderland begin to encroach only where such conditions are not fulfilled'.[48]

However, one can argue that, even if the minority in question does not currently have a developed societal culture to the extent that it can offer its members the entire range of conceivable life choices, it can develop this over time. After all, any national community defines itself in relation to, and through the exclusion of, others.[49] This is evident, for example, in the troubled relationship between Muslim Turks and the Greek state in Western Thrace. The dialectical nature of nations might therefore generate trust between nationals who are assured that their own interests, no matter how internally conflicted, would be protected and prioritized against those of other nations.

As Levy argues, 'Nationalism and policies of minority cultural preservation gain the most plausibility when the alternative to some particular national or cultural community is imagined to be either undifferentiated humanity or alienated individualism'.[50] Although the alternative is often some other community to which individuals also have some attachment, multiculturalists insist that ethnic identity cannot be shrugged off in favour of assimilating to another community that provides an alternative cultural context. On the contrary, multiculturalists stress the validity of Kymlicka's view, which is that 'we can't just transplant people from one culture to another, even if we provide the opportunity to learn the other language and culture. Someone's upbringing is not something that can just be erased; it is, and will remain, a constitutive part of who that person is. Cultural membership affects our very sense of personal identity and capacity'.[51]

Liberalism and Ethnicity: A Happy Marriage or a Recipe for Disaster?

Multiculturalism accepts ethnicity as a legitimate subject for public policy, and so it differs from cosmopolitanism and civic nationalism which work on the assumption that ethno-cultural 'membership cannot be the basis for determining membership in the polity .... [because our] political responsibilities to each other must be based on a concept of justice as fairness that transcends all cultures, as opposed to one that is mediated by culture'.[52] Albeit clearly different from cosmopolitanism, the ideology

of ethnocentric multiculturalism is still presented as an attempt to combine the liberal values of cosmopolitanism (consent) and ethnic communitarianism (descent). Its approach can best be explained by the term
'liberal ethnicity'.[53]

Liberal ethnicity differs from traditional ethnicity in some key ways.
While ethnic nationalism can be held responsible for tragic events such
as genocide, decimation, and persistent discrimination, liberal ethnicity is established as inclusive: in fact, 'barriers to entry to the [liberal]
ethnic community would be minimal... [E]thnicity is not a source of
exclusive membership but only a beacon or resource of identity and liberal ethnicity would treat all groups as equal'.[54] Most minority nationalists stress that they are there to stand for their ethno-cultural rights, but
acknowledge that 'they will operate within the larger framework of liberal constitutionalism, and as such any powers devolved to autonomous
minority institutions on the basis of ethnic differences are typically subject to the same common standards of respect for human rights and civil
liberties'.[55]

For example, the HDP – a pro-Kurdish Political party (the People's Democratic Party) – claimed in 2015 to be a party for all people which was committed to protecting the human rights, not only of
Kurds, but also of LGBT people, children, workers, and women. It is
therefore important to stress that the HDP's approach to diversity is not
entirely ethnocentric. The party's manifesto, issued that April, promised
to create a new constitution which would be based on humanity and
would reflect the multi-identity, multicultural, multi-faith, and multi-
lingual structure of Turkey. Nevertheless, the party bases its claims to
autonomy on the rights of the Kurds, and its policies call primarily for
self-government rights and regional assemblies in areas densely populated by their ethnic group. The HDP is not calling for non-territorial
groups to be awarded rights or assemblies. Instead, it assumes that as far
as non-ethnic groups are concerned – those groups organized for women
or LGBT people, for example – individual human rights offer a panacea
for their problems. As promising as it sounds, the defense of ethnocentric multiculturalism in the name of liberalism, or more accurately the
placing of ethnicity and ethnic group rights at the center of liberalism,
has some serious implications, and it causes problems that emerge on a
number of levels.

'Authentic' Ethnicity: Natural or Political?

First of all, it is fundamentally problematic to bring together liberal
universalism/cosmopolitanism and the politicization of ethnicity. This

is because, no matter how open it is to strangers, an ethnically defined polity would be necessarily exclusionary for members of other ethnic groups and would be restrictive even for its own members if the survival of that group identity was threatened. Moreover, any move to protect and promote ethnic values may freeze the culture of a group in ways that limit future opportunities for its members to make flexible and advantageous choices. Those minority members who tacitly or expressly advocate an intra-group change may become vulnerable to the accusation of cultural treachery and may accordingly be punished or shunned. This was evident when the PKK, in the name of freedom and equality, executed almost 100 of its own members in 1989 and 1990 'on suspicion of [them] being real or potential traitors'.[56] Cunningham, Bakke, and Seymour,[57] who assembled a data set on 22 separatist disputes including 242 factions/internal divisions, also showed that targeting of co-ethnic civilians is not uncommon in internally divided separatist groups where the factions compete with each other over political influence.

As Kukathas explains, 'Cultural groups are not undifferentiated wholes but associations of individuals with interests that differ to varying extents'.[58] It is quite a difficult task to solve a conflict between two opposing groups when conflicts of interests within each group pervade the resolution process. This was clear when the majority of the Corsicans who took part in their region's 2003 referendum voted by a narrow margin against the radical Nationalist Liberal Front's proposal which demanded the right to education in the mother language. A majority of people in Corsica did not want education in Corsu to be made obligatory as this would have negatively affected their children's future economic interests; Corsicans believed that their children would fare better if they were educated through the medium of the French language.[59] The kinds of ideological differences which arise in connection with education policies also occur in situations in which minority members who are in conflict with each other over religious differences disagree to the extent that they cannot act in harmony under the banner of their ethnic commonality.

This situation arises in Sri Lanka, for example. There, Tamil nationalism has mostly been defined in terms of language interests but has never been successful because Sri Lankan Tamils are segregated by religion. Linguistic issues cannot take priority while '[t]he Hindus constitute 85% of the Tamil community. A well-organized and well-funded Tamil Christian minority also exists. [... And the] Moors define themselves by the Muslim religion, not by language'.[60] Sri Lankan Tamils cannot arrive at a consensus around key issues and, for this reason, Tamil nationalism is not likely to be able to secure or maintain a deliberative democracy. The idea that people can compromise easily just because they are members of the same ethnic group is based on a fundamental overestimation of the coherency of ethnic culture.

It is understandable that multiculturalists, as well as ethnic minority nationalists, need a solid group identity to advocate for, on behalf of which they can base their claims to autonomy. Yet, in using this identity for strategic ends, they tend to reify and ascribe an idealized stability to the fragment of the group identity they choose to endorse, generally underestimating the extent to which minority groups are fragmented in their character and aspirations. Their lack of attentiveness to the ideological and cultural diversity that exists within minorities means that multiculturalists fail to see the very real problems that accompany the politics of recognition. Instead, they too often tend towards an elitist and overly stable understanding of ethnic groups which denies them any semblance of internal pluralism and relies too heavily on the notion of the 'authentic' fragment. When they employ a limited and inflexible account of an ethnic group's nature, multiculturalists betray their lack of respect for that culture's depth and complexity and overlook those histories which have been thwarted, suppressed, and silenced. Multiculturalism does not only consist of claims to social and cultural identity; it also affirms the importance of certain ethnic likenesses above all others, yet, crucially, multiculturalists cannot explain why the fragment they have chosen to endorse as authentic has been selected to represent the essence of the political community in question.[61]

Ethnocentric Multiculturalism, New Inequalities, and Polarization

When members of a minority have conflicting interests and political demands and there is no unanimous group to be recognized as such, the adoption of multiculturalism becomes severely problematic. This is because, under these circumstances, recognition-based multiculturalism means that the state also 'indirectly partakes in the ongoing Process of redefining the established traditions that constitute a group's nomos'.[62]

Ethnicity is not as authentic as the theory of multiculturalism suggests. The state's participation in the political construction of unanimity or authenticity within an ethnic minority might indeed create further instability and inequality in different forms, and any such moves would especially disadvantage those subgroups which lack the capacity to mobilize effectively on behalf of their members. It is not certain which subgroup(s) should be given the right and authority to shape the future of Tamil or Corsican groups as a whole, for example. As Cunningham rightly points out, states often take advantage of internal divisions within self-determination groups that challenge their authority. In such cases the state gets an opportunity to cooperate selectively with some specific factions of the group who are then offered some concessions that might satisfy them, but not the entire group. Resorting to this strategy, the state reduces the costs of the dispute without fully resolving it.[63] From a liberal perspective, the neutrality of the state is a precondition for equal treatment, and, for the reasons explored here, the public recognition of cultural rights does not always satisfy this requirement.

It is, of course, reasonable that multiculturalists should refuse to accept the undisputed authority of the dominant ethnic majority. However, the state needs to make sure that the multiculturalist legitimization of ethnicity for the purpose of making public policy does not violate the freedom and equality of individuals such as children, women, and political dissidents within minorities. Multiculturalism potentially increases the difficulties that vulnerable people encounter in attempting to evade problematic traditions and practices, particularly when such practices are positioned as cultural freedoms by dominant members of their own ethnic groups. Forced marriages and female circumcision, for example, are accorded privileged status as traditions in some patriarchal ethno-cultural groups but serve to damage and disadvantage women within those minorities.[64] Most liberal states accept the view that an extreme form of ethnocentric multiculturalism that puts cultural rights before human rights can actually be bad for women and for other doubly marginalized individuals in these kinds of cases.

The difficulty with ethnocentric multiculturalism is not simply that it creates further intra-group inequalities. Experience also shows that 'institutionalizing group representation offers opportunities and incentives for political entrepreneurs to whip up intragroup solidarity and intergroup hostility in the pursuit of power. The Northern Ireland power-sharing system is simply the latest illustration of this process of polarization'.[65]

The following chapters, which focus on the Kurds, will illustrate in detail the additional intra-group inequalities and inter-group tensions that the projects of ethnocentric multiculturalism can bring about in practice. Before the discussion moves to these issues, it is important to elaborate on a third reason why multiculturalism, in the form of liberal ethnicity, might actually not be that liberal at all.

When Ethnicity Is One's Prison: Escape to Freedom and
Right to Exit

When autonomy is granted to ethnic groups which need protectionist measures for their own survival, liberalism may not be achieved because the very project of ensuring the survival of ethnic identity violates the fundamental freedoms of individuals who want the right to exit from it. 'Given that many forms of association such as group membership are unchosen', as Kukathas points out, 'the critical issue is whether or not individuals can exit from an association'.[66] The state may, and indeed should, find it necessary to facilitate this exit if, for example, parents' cultural interests limit their children's capacity to enjoy liberty. This issue can arise in relation to education policy in circumstances where the parents' freedom to have instruction delivered to their children solely through their mother language might violate those children's equal opportunities to learn the language of the dominant socio-economic network; lack of access to that language would make it difficult for children to compete with children from the dominant group on the basis of merit. 'The ongoing promotion of a minority language – a language with less power and prestige in a given (national) context than that of the dominant group – is actively detrimental to the mobility of minority language speakers'.[67] This is clear in the example provided by Puerto Rican students in the United States: 'In New York, only 16 *percent* of Puerto Rican students earned academic high school diplomas, qualifying them for admission to college . . . The situation was much the same for Puerto Ricans in Boston and Chicago'.[68] Egalitarians interpret this statistic as a sign of the liberal state's failure to provide students from different backgrounds with the equality of opportunity that would allow them to take advantage of opportunities in higher education, which is the most important gateway to well-paid employment.

Multiculturalists argue to the contrary that such problems can be overcome because an individual's freedom of association – the principle of consent in terms of group membership and freedom of exit – should allow group members a way out if they are not satisfied by the practices of the cultural group to which they belong. People who do not approve of the practices of their cultural groups are, in principle, free to leave. If this freedom is assumed to be available, cultural rights cannot be regarded as a source of any further inequality for those who would be disadvantaged if autonomy was granted to the leadership of their cultural group. This assumption is often invoked in relation to the Kurds in Turkey by pro-Kurdish HDP members who claim that Kurds are free to make their own choices, to opt in or out of education in the minority language, and to develop their lives in the direction that they think offers them the most optimal future. However, neither membership based on consent, nor the right to exit from cultural groups, always constitute realistic and practical alternatives available to everyone.

Some cultural groups, when they are freed from civic rule or simply put beyond state control, systematically prevent their members from taking advantage of exit options. This kind of unequal treatment affects members of the Amish community in the United States when they reach sixteen years of age. Their community prohibits participation in modern life and does not allow its children to continue in education after the eighth grade, and young Amish individuals may not be formally capable of using their right to exit from the cultural group into which they were born. Amish identity requires its holders to refrain from using modern inventions such as electricity, photography, radios, cars, televisions, and so on. Moreover, the Amish community also has the right to say what is acceptable for group members, and, on these grounds, it prohibits activities such as dancing, drinking, or dating. From a liberal point of view, there is nothing wrong with this way of life, as long as people choose to associate with it out of their own free will; 'only after the chance to taste life with cars, electricity, alcohol, and rock and roll at the age of 16 do Amish-raised teens decide whether to be baptized and enter the church'.[69] However, the extent to which children's expressed consent for baptism can be considered as a product of their free will is certainly arguable.

We take it for granted that people are content if they have other alternatives available to them and nonetheless do not leave, but, as Mazie points out, 'why should we read consent into someone staying put? Maybe the person sticks around out of fear, poverty, too little information, too much inertia, and poor health. Maybe s/he just has no better options available'.[70] The most important of all the restrictions on group members' free will is usually that the cost of exit from the community is so high. Women in rural settings and patriarchal groups are usually financially dependent on their spouses and families and are often, therefore, unable to make decisions freely when it comes to leaving their cultural communities, although this is presented to them as an option. This problem certainly became very evident in my conversations with some Kurdish women in rural areas. Similarly, Amish children who do not receive high school education because of their family's beliefs are not eligible for university admission and they are not qualified for many of the jobs that would allow them to earn money and sustain a life in the outside world. The risks that they would encounter on leaving their community are so great that these teenagers usually choose to stay put and take advantage of the well-paid jobs offered by Amish farms and factories.

Limited education restricts the options available to them after the point of departure, and so the Amish community's exemption from the law that enforces a child's right to twelve years of education actually increases the cost of exiting from the community. In such instances, the state needs to reduce this cost to a minimum, and so should require the community to keep sending its children to school beyond eighth grade. This change, in the Amish case, would mean that children would have the chance to gain least the minimum qualifications needed to support a freely chosen life outside their birth community. Without such a change, we cannot assume that people who want, but are unable, to leave their group will have been treated equally with people who are free to choose the lifestyles they wish. In these circumstances, the equal protection of citizens' freedoms by the state may require intervention in the cultural practices of a group which limits the freedom of its members to choose between staying or leaving.

As far as linguistic ethnic minorities are concerned, the archetypal example of the problems caused by undifferentiated equality involves the judge in Amarillo, Texas, who issued an order in 1995 that forbade a mother from speaking Spanish to her child and made compliance a condition of custody. He argued that the mother's use of Spanish in speaking to her daughter at home was equivalent to a form of 'child abuse': 'If she starts [school] with the other children and cannot even speak the language that the teachers and others speak, and she's an American citizen, you're abusing that child . . . Now get this straight: you start speaking English to that child, because if she doesn't do good in school then I can remove her because it's not in her best interests to be ignorant'.[71]

A strong emphasis on equal treatment does not deny the freedom of people to associate with different ways of life, to decide how their children will be educated, or to choose the rules according to which they wish to be judged. It simply ensures that all individuals are given the same fundamental rights, such as freedom of religion or association; they are then free to choose what they wish to do with those rights at a later point, provided that these choices do not infringe on the equality of other individuals to use their freedom of exit. However, if a choice by an individual or a group itself systematically causes a burden on other vulnerable individuals – such as children who thereby become incapable of making choices freely in the future, for example – and if it increases the cost of exit, as in the Amish group, one cannot claim that granting autonomy would provide equal treatment for group members.

In these terms, the autonomy of an individual can be limited only when it infringes upon the autonomy of another individual. The 'harm principle' frees individuals from having to bear the burdens of others and therefore achieves more than theories of multiculturalism which 'attempt to address one form of inequality, namely cultural inequality, but in doing so . . . undermine the prospects of addressing other forms, such as [economic and educational inequalities]'.[72]

Conclusion

Multiculturalism can clearly be very problematic in some cases, and it is difficult to imagine that multiculturalist models can be effectively implemented in contexts where states have an understandable concern that they could lead to further inequalities, instability, and violations of personal freedoms. As Kymlicka points out, 'It is important therefore to distinguish what is feasible in the short term from what is desirable in the long term... [In such cases,] we can imagine a theory of the progressive implementation of liberal multiculturalism with different minority rights provisions kicking in as the underlying conditions are established'.[73] It is apparent that there are various ways of responding to cultural diversity even within the multiculturalist paradigm itself, and the question therefore is 'not whether one wants be a multiculturalist at all but the kind of multiculturalist one wants to be'.[74]

In cases where neither difference-blind egalitarianism/assimilationism nor ethnocentric multiculturalism is able to promote the values of equality and freedom, a third way, characterized by 'moderate multiculturalism', seems to offer the optimal solution. Moderate multiculturalism, as Parekh rightly asserts, 'begins by accepting the reality and desirability of cultural diversity',[75] yet it also puts emphasis on equality, individual rights, and freedom of exit. Ethnocentric multiculturalism, in its attempt to recognize authentic identities, has the potential to generate isolationism and polarization between ethnic groups, while difference-blind egalitarianism is likely to cause excessive interventionism as it works to achieve equality between people with disparate capacities. Moderate multiculturalism stands against both isolationism and interventionism,[76] and in doing so it makes sure that any liberal solution for the problems of national minorities will not be predominantly shaped by concerns with either cultural freedom or individual equality.

Notes

1 Oliver Zimmer, 'Boundary Mechanisms and Symbolic Resources: Towards a Process-Oriented Approach to National Identity', *Nations and Nationalism* 9, no. 2 (2003): 173–93.

2 A. D. Smith, *Nationalism and Modernism* (London: Routledge, 1998), 180.

3 Before the League of Nations was established in 1919, 'the most detailed consideration of national minority protection was conducted by certain private organizations. Two noteworthy examples are the Office des Nationalités and the Central Organization for a Durable Peace. The Office des Nationalités held two conferences in 1915 and 1916, which culminated in a Draft Declaration of the Rights of Nationalities. This document laid down general principles of racial, religious, and linguistic freedom and recognized the

rights of homogeneous nationalities to independent statehood wherever possible and, failing that, to local, religious, and educational autonomy in states where they formed a significant national minority. The Association for a Durable Peace took these ideas one step further. In 1917, it released a Draft International Treaty on the rights of National Minorities. This proposed treaty gave national minorities civil and political equality as well as control over educational and religious institutions and proportional representation in government'. Preece, *National Minorities and the European Nation-States System*, 71.

4 Jennifer Jackson Preece, *National Minorities and the European Nation-States System* (Oxford: Oxford University Press), 73.
5 Michael Hechter, *Containing Nationalism* (Oxford: Oxford University Press, 2000), 17.
6 Zimmer, 'Boundary Mechanisms and Symbolic Resources', 175.
7 Bernard Yack, 'The Myth of the Civic Nation: A Critical Review', *Journal Politics and Sociology* 10, no. 2 (1996): 193–211.
8 Ernest Renan, 'Qu'est-Ce Qu'une Nation? (What Is a Nation?)', in O. Dahbour, M. Ishay and R. Michelin, eds., *The Nationalism Reader* (Atlantic Highlands, NJ: Humanities Press International, 1995).
9 T. Kuzio, 'The Myth of the Civic State. Hans Kohn Revisited: Civic and Ethnic States in Theory and Practice'. Paper presented at the Annual Convention of the Association for the Study of Nationalities, Columbia University, New York, April 13, 2000.
10 Michael Ignatieff, *Blood and Belonging: Journeys into the New Nationalism* (New York, NY: Farrar, Straus and Giroux, 1993). Also see William Pfaff, *The Wrath of Nations. Civilizations and the Fury of Nationalism* (New York, NY: Simon & Schuster, 1993).
11 Jan-Werner Müller, *Constitutional Patriotism* (Princeton, NJ: Princeton University Press, 2009). Also see Jürgen Habermas and Ciaran Cronin, 'The European Nation-State: On the Past and Future of Sovereignty and Citizenship', *Public Culture* 10, no. 2 (1998): 397–416.
12 John Rawls, *Political Liberalism* (New York, NY: Columbia University Press, 2005).
13 A. D. Smith, *Ethnic Origins of Nations* (Oxford: Basil Blackwell, 1986).
14 James E. Jacob and David C. Gordon, 'Language Policy in France', in W. R. Beer and J. E. Jacob, eds., *Language Policy and National Unity* (Totowa, NJ: Rowman & Allanheld, 1985).
15 David Kushner, *The Rise of Turkish Nationalism, 1876–1908* (London: Frank Cass, 1977). Also see Nergis Canefe, 'Turkish Nationalism and Ethno-Symbolic Analysis: The Rules of Exception', *Nations and Nationalism* 8, no. 2 (2002): 133–55.
16 Lillian Guerra, *Popular Expression and National Identity in Puerto Rico: The Struggle for Self, Community, and Nation* (Gainesville, FL: University Press of Florida, 1998).
17 Yack, 'The Myth of the Civic Nation', 196.
18 Amy Gutmann and Charles Taylor, *Multiculturalism and 'the Politics of Recognition': An Essay* (Princeton, NJ: Princeton University Press, 1992). Also see Iris Marion Young, *Justice and the Politics of Difference* (Princeton, NJ: Princeton University Press, 1990).

19 Jean-Pascal Bassino and Jean-Pierre Dormois, 'Were French Republicans Serious about Equality? Convergence in Real Wages, Literacy, and the Biological Standard of Living in France 1845–1913'. Paper presented at the third Economics and Human Biology Conference, Strasbourg, June 22–24, 2006.

20 New Policy Institute, *London Poverty Report: Ethnicity, Low Income and Work* (London: New Policy Institute, 2009).

21 Durukan Kuzu, 'The Politics of Identity, Recognition and Multiculturalism. The Kurds in Turkey', *Nations and Nationalism* 22, no. 1 (2016): 123–42.

22 David Corson, *Language Diversity and Education* (New York, NY: Routledge, 2000).

23 This only refers to the views of liberal scholars such as Rawls, Habermas and Ignatieff, whose approach to the topic was explained above under the sub-section 'Political Liberalism and Civic Nationalism as a Response'.

24 Troy Kozma, 'Liberalism and Civic Assimilation: A New Look at Minority Nations'. Paper presented at the annual meeting of the Midwest Political Science Association, Palmer House Hilton, Chicago, IL, April 20, 2006. Also see Avishai Margalit and Joseph Raz, 'National Self-Determination', *The Journal of Philosophy* 87, no. 9 (1990): 439–61.

25 Kozma, 'Liberalism and Civic Assimilation', 2.

26 Jürgen Habermas, 'Equal Treatment of Cultures and the Limits of Postmodern Liberalism', *Journal of Political Philosophy* 13, no. 1 (2005): 1–28.

27 B. Barry, 'Equal Treatment and Same Treatment'. Paper presented at The New York University Department of Politics Seminar Series, 2009, www.politics.as.nyu.edu, 1–20.

28 Barry, 'Equal Treatment and Same Treatment', 15.

29 Durukan Kuzu, 'A Self-Governing Group or Equal Citizens – Kurds, Turkey and the European Union', *Journal on Ethno-politics and Minority Issues* 9 (2010): 61. Also See James Hughes. 'The Chechnya Conflict: Freedom Fighters or Terrorists?' *Demokratizatsiya* 15, no. 3 (2007): 293.

30 Roeder shows that in ethnically divided societies power-dividing between the majority and minority groups not only provides more credible commitments to the rights of all minorities but also lowers the stakes of ethnic conflict in government by providing check and balance mechanisms. See Philip G. Roeder, 'Power Dividing as an Alternative Ethnic Power Sharing', in Philip G. Roeder and Ronald Rothchild eds., *Sustainable Peace: Power and Democracy after Civil Wars* (Ithaca, NY: Cornell University Press, 2005), 51–83.

31 Iris Marion Young, 'Polity and Group Difference: A Critique of the Ideal of Universal Citizenship', in Ronald Beiner, ed., *Theorizing Citizenship* (Albany, NY: New York University Press, 1995), 176, 195.

32 Bhikhu C. Parekh, *Rethinking Multiculturalism: Cultural Diversity and Political Theory* (Cambridge, MA: Harvard University Press, 2002), 241.

33 Isaiah Berlin, 'Two Concepts of Liberty', in Isaiah Berlin, ed., *Four Essays on Liberty* (New York, NY: Oxford University Press, 1970).

34 Gerald C. MacCallum, 'Negative and Positive Freedom', *The Philosophical Review* (1967): 312–34.

35 Alina Silian, *Liberal Nationalism and Deliberative Democracy*, unpublished master's thesis submitted to Central European University Nationalism Studies Program, Budapest, Hungary, 2002, 36.

36 Ayelet Shachar, 'On Citizenship and Multicultural Vulnerability', *Political Theory* 28, no. 1 (2000): 64–89.

37 T. Modood, *Multiculturalism* (Cambridge: Polity Press, 2007).

38 Will Kymlicka, *Multicultural Citizenship: A Liberal Theory of Minority Rights* (Oxford: Clarendon Press, 1995), 76.

39 Joseph H. Carens, *Culture, Citizenship, and Community: A Contextual Exploration of Justice as Evenhandedness* (Toronto, ON: Oxford University Press, 2000), 69.

40 Will Kymlicka, *Politics in the Vernacular: Nationalism, Multiculturalism, and Citizenship* (Oxford: Oxford University Press, 2001), 30.

41 Will Kymlicka, *Finding Our Way: Rethinking Ethnocultural Relations in Canada* (Oxford: Oxford University Press, 1998).

42 Kymlicka, *Multicultural Citizenship*, 79.

43 Will Kymlicka, 'National Minorities in Postcommunist Europe: The Role of International Norms and European Integration', in Zoltan Barany and Robert G. Moser, eds., *Ethnic Politics after Communism* (Ithaca, NY: Cornell University Press, 2005), 191–218.

44 Robert Koulish, 'Hungarian Roma Attitudes on Minority Rights: The Symbolic Violence of Ethnic Identification', *Europe–Asia Studies* 57, no. 2 (2005): 311–26.

45 Minority Rights Group International, 'Hungary–Roma', Minority Rights Group International, http://minorityrights.org.

46 Yael Tamir, *Liberal Nationalism* (Princeton, NJ: Princeton University Press, 1995).

47 Will Kymlicka, 'Assessing the Politics of Diversity in Transition Countries', in F. Daftary and F. Grin, eds., *Nation-Building, Ethnicity and Language Politics in Transition Countries* (Budapest: Open Society Institute-ECMI/LGI Series, 2003).

48 Brian Barry, *Culture and Equality* (Cambridge: Polity Press, 2001), 105.

49 Tamir, *Liberal Nationalism*.

50 Jacob T. Levy, *The Multiculturalism of Fear* (Oxford: Oxford University Press, 2000), 71.

51 Will Kymlicka, *Liberalism, Community, and Culture* (Oxford: Oxford University Press, 1991), 175.

52 Siobhán Harty, 'The Nation as a Communal Good: A Nationalist Response to the Liberal Conception of Community', *Canadian Journal of Political Science* 32, no. 4 (1999): 665–89.

53 Eric Kaufmann, 'Liberal Ethnicity: Beyond Liberal Nationalism and Minority Rights', *Ethnic and Racial Studies* 23, no. 6 (2000): 1086–119.

54 Kaufmann, 'Liberal Ethnicity'.

55 Will Kymlicka, 'Liberal Multiculturalism and Human Rights', CEU E-Learning Site, https://ceulearning.ceu.edu.

56 Aliza Marcus, *Blood and Belief: The PKK and the Kurdish Fight for Independence* (New York, NY: New York University Press, 2007).

57 Kathleen Gallagher Cunningham, Kristin M. Bakke and Lee J. M. Seymour, 'Shirts Today, Skins Tomorrow: Dual Contests and the Effects of Fragmentation in Self-Determination Disputes'. *Journal of Conflict Resolution* 56, no.1 (2012): 67–93.

58 Chandran Kukathas, 'Are There Any Cultural Rights?' *Political Theory* 20, no. 1 (1992): 105–39.
59 W. Alejandro Sanchez, 'Corsica: France's Petite Security Problem', *Studies in Conflict & Terrorism* 31, no. 7 (2008): 655–64.
60 R. Jayaratnam, 'Ruminations of a Sri Lankan Tamil', *Sri Lanka Guardian*, February 17, 2010.
61 Craig Calhoun, 'Nationalism and Ethnicity', *Annual Review of Sociology* 19, no. 1 (1993): 211–39.
62 Ayelet Shachar, 'On Citizenship and Multicultural Vulnerability', *Political Theory* 28, no. 1 (2002): 64–89.
63 Kathleen Gallagher Cunningham, *Inside the Politics of Self-Determination* (New York, NY: Oxford University Press, 2014), 6.
64 Susan Okin, *Is Multiculturalism Bad for Women?* (Princeton, NJ: Princeton University Press, 1999).
65 Barry, *Culture and Equality*, 211.
66 Chandran Kukathas, 'The Life of Brian, or Now for Something Completely Difference-Blind', in P. Kelly, ed., *Multiculturalism Reconsidered* (Cambridge: Polity Press, 2002).
67 Stephen May, 'The Politics of Homogeneity: A Critical Exploration of the Anti-Bilingual Education Movement', in James Cohen, Kara T. McAlister, Kellie Rolstad and Jeff MacSwan, eds., *Proceedings of the 4th International Symposium on Bilingualism* (Somerville, MA: Cascadilla Press, 2005), 1560.
68 Barry, *Culture & Equality*.
69 Steven V. Mazie, 'Consenting Adults? Amish Rumspringa and the Quandary of Exit in Liberalism', *Perspectives on Politics* 3, no. 4 (2005): 745–59.
70 Steven V. Mazie, 'Consenting Adults? Amish Rumspringa and the Quandary of Exit in Liberalism', 746.
71 May, 'The Politics of Homogeneity', 1561.
72 Avigail Eisenberg and Jeff Spinner-Halev, *Minorities within Minorities: Equality, Rights and Diversity* (Cambridge: Cambridge University Press, 2005), 8.
73 Will Kymlicka, *Politics in the Vernacular: Nationalism, Multiculturalism, and Citizenship* (Oxford: Oxford University Press, 2001), 304–5.
74 David Miller, *On Nationality* (Oxford: Oxford University Press, 1995), 13.
75 Parekh, *Rethinking Multiculturalism*, 340.
76 Chandran Kukathas, 'Anarcho-Multiculturalism: The Pure Theory of Liberalism', in G. B. Levey, ed., *Political Theory and Australian Multiculturalism* (New York, NY: Berghahn Books, 2008).

3 Multiculturalism for National Minorities
One Size Does Not Fit All

The previous chapter explained the difficulties that the theory of ethnocentric multiculturalism creates for national minorities, and it also explored critiques of its assumptions. Yet, although ethnocentric multiculturalism looks theoretically flawed, in practice it has been thriving in certain countries where the national minorities which have made use of it have become more prosperous than they were before it was implemented. Québécois people in Canada and the Flemish population in Belgium are two groups that have benefited from its use, for example. Inspired by its successful implementation in Canada and Belgium, many national minorities, such as the Kurds, have continued to idealize multiculturalism, and it has also appealed to countries that, like Turkey, are engaged in a transition towards liberalism.

Chapter 2 has already shown that multiculturalism can be very problematic in some cases, and it seems that relatively moderate multiculturalist policies might be more suitable in certain situations. This raises the hitherto unanswered question as to which types of national minorities can best be accommodated by which theoretical approaches. This chapter analyzes the differences that exist between certain types of national minorities, and it explains why ethnocentric multiculturalism has been more problematic for some national minorities such as Kurds than it has been for others.

Multiculturalism for National Minorities

We live in a world of nation-states. However, some ethnic groups or nations, such as Kurds, do not have a state they can call their own. In fact, in a world where there are fewer than 200 states, there are approximately 5,000 ethnic minority groups and 600 language groups in existence;[1] of these language groups, 174 are involved in struggles for self-determination.[2] The factors that underlie the emergence of nation-states and fuel their passionate, and often violent, expression impact on ethnic minorities in various ways. The dominant form of state nationalism in any given country, and the particular understanding of nationhood associated with it, will inform the prospects for that country's ethnic minorities. It will, for example, shape a state's decisions as to how minorities will be treated, and it will also establish whether they should be assimilated, differentiated, or excluded. Some minorities will experience problems including discrimination; others will find that their members are dispossessed of equal citizenship rights; still others will be forced by the state to assimilate.

The ideology of multiculturalism, which disregards these variations, is based on the overarching argument that all minority nations should have the right to govern themselves. It suggests that minorities should be given self-government rights and territorial autonomy within the state where they reside, as long as they were the majority group in their ancestral homelands and are not on the road of assimilation.[3] The assumption here is that non-assimilating minorities will always resort to nationalism and claim self-government rights and that these inevitabilities must be accommodated. Kymlicka and Opalski suggest that indigenous people and 'national minorities have typically responded to majority nation-building by seeking greater autonomy which they use to engage in their own competing nation-building, so as to protect and diffuse their societal culture throughout their traditional territory'.[4] Smith suggests similarly that 'whenever and however a national identity is forged, once established, it becomes immensely difficult, if not impossible, (short of total genocide) to eradicate'.[5]

The theory of multiculturalism actually has a strong basis because, most of the time, a national minority's members are simply unwilling to relegate their ethnic particularity to the realm of private discourse.[6] According to the Minorities at Risk Project, 'none of the 117 ethnic groups that raised economic grievances [in 1999] failed to raise issues of political rights, and only 1 of the 98 ethnic groups that raised cultural grievances failed to raise political grievances'.[7] This evidence can be used to justify a somewhat simplistic model in which a case for political autonomy and multiculturalism is conflated with an ethnic minority's desire for cultural autonomy of various kinds.[8]

Cultural groups vary in the extent to which they can offer a holistic range of services to their members. In fact, the question as to 'whether a cultural group can be thought of as a societal culture whose practices and institutions cover a full range of human activities, is certainly a matter of degree, rather than the either/or distinction'[9] that some would make it. Any attempt to understand societal culture as a dichotomous variable which either exists or does not exist is flawed because culture forms a continuum. At a certain point on that continuum it may be possible to identify traces of habitual unity, shared vernacular, high population, and concentrated settlement, but this does not mean that these things will be accompanied by institutionalization, common expectations from the polity, similar experiences, and shared memories.

It is a mistake to treat national identity independently from the individuals who are supposed to share it because their beliefs, decisions, and interests are actually open to change with indefinite possibilities. Unlike individuals, who are able to make decisions for themselves, national minorities are collections of people whose interests may lie in different directions and be informed by different causes. For this reason, the picture of the relationship between a national minority and the state set out by Kymlicka, Opalski, and Smith is too simplistic: it simply fails to capture the complexity of the relationships that exist between a minority's members, some of whom may choose to resist while others voluntarily assimilate. Cunningham, for example, explains this grand complexity in her work *Inside the Politics of Self-Determination*.[10] Contrary to separatists' claims, some group members may well be willing to integrate with the dominant community while continuing to enjoy their culture in the private sphere.[11] This is the kind of choice being made by Corsicans in France,[12] the Kurds in Turkey,[13] and by many Scottish people in the United Kingdom.[14]

Of course, there are various circumstances in which ethnic cultures are translated into ethno-nationalist political entities and supported by the masses in a consistent manner, but theorists of multiculturalism do not attend to these circumstances.[15] This chapter suggests that, even if such an investigation were carried out, it would not be possible to locate within any culture any one factor that determines the ways in which its members make certain political decisions. It is much more reasonable to assume that people make different uses of their culture depending on the options available to them and that those options will tend to have been limited by the modern state, which is still the ultimate arbiter in world politics and exerts determining force, to some extent, over the lives of its citizens. It is, therefore, important to examine the nuances of state policies and the options that states make available to national minorities before making overarching assumptions about the reactions of national minorities to the state's nation-building project.

One Size Does Not Fit All

Ethnocentric projects of self-government and multiculturalism encounter more difficulty in some cases than others, and any problems become apparent when the nationalist parties concerned fail to mobilize their ethnic constituencies. In the Corsican referendum of 2003, for example, 57,180 people voted against limited autonomy while 54,990 voted in favour of a new government structure.[16] The Corsicans' reluctance to push for greater autonomy was reiterated in the 2010 regional elections in which *Corsica Libera* sought independence and chose not to condemn the terrorist *Fronte di Liberazione Naziunale Corsu* (the National Liberation Front of Corsica, or NLFC). The party won only 9.85 per cent of the votes cast, and even the *U Partitu di a Nazione Corsa* (Party of the Corsican Nation, or PNC), which rejects terrorist activities and wants only limited autonomy, could gain only 25.88 per cent in the same election.[17]

Ethnocentric theories of multiculturalism are unable to account for, or respond, to the heterogeneity of minorities such as the Corsicans. When millions of Corsu-speaking citizens in France voluntarily adopt French identity and avoid any identification with Corsican nationalism, their refusal to see assimilation as a challenge to their existence is simply not discussed by adherents of multiculturalism. Still less discussed are those minority members who strongly believe that it is not in their interests to have armed groups entering into conflict to secure a cultural autonomy that not all group members want. It is important to remember that individuals will not always act in support of organizations that claim to represent their ethnic identities.

Similar patterns can be noted in Turkey where, in 2007, 41 per cent of southeastern Kurds supported the *Adalet ve Kalkinma Partisi* (Justice and Development Party, or AKP) instead of the pro-Kurdish *Demokratik Toplum Partisi* (Democratic Society Party, or DTP), which at that time was explicitly defending its connections with the PKK.[18] The 2011 general election demonstrated the continuation of this trend. The Kurdish nationalist party, *Baris ve Demokrasi Partisi* (Peace and Democracy Party, or BDP), claimed the right to autonomy and state-funded education of all grades in the Kurdish language in fifteen eastern and southeastern Anatolian cities, each of which has a significant Kurdish population. In the 2011 general election, however, the independent candidates who were supported by the BDP secured majorities in only five of these cities.[19] In the course of my research, I engaged in extensive discussions with Kurds in the cities of Diyarbakır and Mardin and found that the numerical data that emerged from the election results in these two cities may inflate the level of support that exists for the BDP's goals. It became clear in interviews that even people who voted for the BDP cannot agree upon a definition that would explain clearly what is meant by the regional autonomy its leaders are so eager to claim. It emerged that the demands that conciliatory Kurds wish to make are not reflected in the policies pursued by the hawkish BDP representatives they voted for.

At the current juncture, theories of multiculturalism offer no suggestions as to what should be done when a radical subgroup within a minority is engaged in ethnic conflict but the minority as a whole lacks political unanimity for various reasons. It is clear that group interests do not emerge organically as part of a natural order but take their particular form because of certain circumstances including financial benefits, historical relations with other groups, and power politics.[20] Preece points out that '[e]thnic identification and association is not only driven by fate (descent) but also by choice (consent). We cannot choose our ethnicity but we can choose to suppress or express it in our social relations – and it is precisely that element of choice which makes ethnicity a legitimate subject for public policy'[21] in some cases. In Quebec and Flanders, for example, an absolute majority of minority members have consistently chosen both to express their ethnicity openly and to make it politically relevant. Kresl suggests that in Quebec the Liberal Party and the *Parti Québécois* have dramatically divergent views on some policy issues, but they are very much on the same wavelength where cultural policy is concerned.[22]

Yet there are other situations in which the majority of people in a national minority group have chosen not to affiliate with ethno-politics. Both Corsicans and Kurds made these kinds of choices consistently in the first decade of this century. If it is true that some national minorities choose not to prioritize their ethnic identities, and others choose not to prioritize them all of the time, then we need to ask if it is possible to identify when and which national minorities are less likely to develop this kind of particularistic pan-ethnic orientation. More importantly, we might want to establish whether multiculturalism and self-government rights should be offered to minorities as a solution to any problems they face in situations where the absolute majority of a minority's members have rejected their nationalist parties and are choosing to support integrationist policies instead.

In this regard, a recent special issue of the *Journal of Conflict Resolution* on 'Disaggregating the Study of Civil War'[23] examines how the relationships between non-state actors affect the onset, duration, and outcome of conflict. McLaughlin and Pearlman's article[24] in this issue argues that most studies in the field take the existence of internal divisions and fragmentation amongst non-state actors as given and hence makes no effort to explain their emergence in the first place. They also question why internal fragmentation is persistent, politically relevant, and so conducive to prolonged conflicts in some cases but not so much in others.

This chapter introduces a typology of national minorities which will depend on their past experiences with various different types of state nationalism. It will emerge that in-group visions of national identity and political expectations are more diverse within groups when their members have been simultaneously exposed to the forced assimilation and 'open door' policies of civic state nationalism. It is less likely that coherence and harmony will be found in this kind of minority because individuals will have experienced different kinds of lives and social status and different kinds of economic consequences arising from their relationships with the state and fellow minority members. Finally, this chapter explains why multiculturalism lacks the capacity to respond effectively to the continuing problems faced by the hugely complex minorities that populate this category.

State Nationalism and National Minorities

National minorities distinguish between civic and ethnic state nationalisms because of the different effects produced by their respective policies of forced integrationist assimilation on the one hand, and social and political exclusion or differentiation on the other. Although nationalism is a dynamic phenomenon, some national minorities have been consistently and exclusively exposed to ethnically exclusionary and/or differentiating policies while others have been subjected to assimilation. This variation has a significant impact on the extent to which multiculturalism can work for different national minorities today, as can be seen from a comparison between the experiences of the Kurds in Turkey who have been forcibly assimilated and those of other national minorities such as the Québécois whose needs have been recognized and differentiated in Canada for centuries. It is possible to identify three different categories for the kinds of state nationalism that national minorities have experienced.

A Typology of National Minorities and Multiculturalism: Where Do the Kurds in Turkey Stand?

1   Recognized Minorities: The Flemish and Québécois Experience

This first category consists of national minorities which have been given options either to integrate into the majority or to remain living in their own regions under special arrangements that have allowed them language rights and federalization. The Québécois in Canada and the Flemish in Belgium are examples of this category, and they are generally accepted as providing the best modern examples of successful multiculturalism at work. This is not least because systems of federalism and language rights have already been in place for centuries in both Canada and Belgium and have facilitated a strong demarcation between the different cultural blocs they were designed to accommodate. Ethnocentric multiculturalism in these countries is not as new as is usually thought.

Kymlicka and Opalski assert that '[the] British in Canada stripped the Quebecers of their French language rights and institutions, and redrew political boundaries so that the Quebecers did not form a majority in any province',[25] but this reductionist account of Canadian history, while true to some extent (especially in relation to the period between 1840 and 1867), omits the very important fact that 'although the Canadian Model continued to evolve well into the 1980s, many of its key features had been in place since the mid-nineteenth century'.[26] French culture was never thought to be a part of English Canadian culture; on the contrary, historical rivalry and enmity between the French and English has existed since the Battle of Hastings in 1066 and has echoed throughout history.

The boundary between the two communities has persisted in Canada. Although the United Province of Canada, a British colony, was founded by merging the two colonies of Upper Canada (modern Ontario) and Lower Canada (modern Quebec), Francophone citizens have dominated the latter and the former has been largely populated by Anglophone citizens.[27] According to the rights given to them in the Constitution Act of 1867, these two groups were able to elect the same number of representatives to the legislative assembly, but its official language was English, and Francophone people were given no option but to use that language if they wanted to participate in the assembly. Federalism was, however, soon introduced, and 'Quebec has been granted a mix of concurrent and exclusive jurisdiction over a wide range of policy areas that give it the tools to ensure the survival of a Francophone society'.[28] This federal solution created linguistic dualism, and French was soon added as an official language in addition to English. Sections twenty-one to twenty-four of the Constitution Act have allowed the use of both English and French in the Quebec National Assembly and require legal provisions to be decreed and practiced in both languages. Through the enactment of the Charter of the French Language in 1977, the *Parti Québécois* even endeavoured to legislate to make the French language the only official language of the region. The Supreme Court of Canada, which is the ultimate arbiter on provincial matters, was also designed to guarantee regional representation, and three of its nine seats have been secured for judges from Quebec since 1982.[29] Quiet Revolution in Quebec in the 1960s first brought about the nationalization of economic assets. By 1978 the provincial government seized control over its immigration policies and controlled immigration to increase the use of the French language. The use of French language is so central to Quebec that, according to a government document, 'to live in Quebec is to live in French'.[30] A more comprehensive Canadian multiculturalism prioritizes a civic conception of nationality and recognizes the intersectionality of plural identity references, but the Québécois approach that is known as interculturalism rather emphasizes the singular ethnic/linguistic component of identity (French in this case) as the primary source of legitimate membership of the polity in Quebec. As such, Kymlicka's ethnocentric multiculturalism theory has much more in common with the Québécois interculturalism than it has ever had with the Canadian multiculturalism in practice.

Canada's Indian Act of 1876, which banned the use of aboriginal languages in education, has never applied to Francophone groups, which have always had the right, albeit limited, to use their language in a whole range of activities including education and administration. Cultural homogeneity has never been assumed in Canada, and there has always been a split between English and French groups. Voluntary assimilation into the Anglophone community has always been an option for Francophones in Canada, but in practice it has mostly remained an underrated symbolic option for most French speakers. There are, of course, exceptions to this pattern. For Francophone people who live in Alberta, the only official language has been English.[31] This remains the case even in the northwest, although the state has recognized that the French language has an important role to play in the education of Franco-Albertans. Franco-Albertans have rights to separate schools, as well as other poly-ethnic rights, but the reality is that they have largely assimilated in terms of their language use.

The situation in Alberta supports the argument that, when integration and assimilation is a realistic option, there is no reason to presume that ethnic distinctions will keep determining political behaviour. The example they provide suggests that the integrationist ideal of civic nationalism in Canada has facilitated a limited heterogeneity within the country's Francophone community. The same structure has also allowed the emergence of a small English-speaking community, as well as pan-Canadian nationalism within Quebec. Schertzer and Woods observe that 'some French Quebecers simply are not Quebec nationalists and some

French Quebecers are even pan-Canadian nationalists in the same way that many English Canadians are'.[32]

It is important to note that those Francophone Québécois who detach themselves from ethno-nationalism comprise only a small minority and do not pose an existential threat to the operational capacity of the Québécois nationalists who form the majority within their community. In Canada, there has not been enough social and political space for ethnically separated Francophone and Anglophone communities to mix. Therefore, ethnocentric multiculturalism in Canada is not as challenged by cultural intersectionality as it is in other places where the policies of integration and assimilation have created plural identities, varied social status, and conflicting interests amongst national minority members.

The Flemish case offers similar lessons to the Québécois experience. Before Belgium detached from the Kingdom of the Netherlands in 1830, a Dutch dialect called Flemish was the dominant language in Flanders and had already been institutionalized. Under the hegemony of France, it was downgraded and confined to the private interactions of people who lived in that region, but Flemish citizens retained their rights to use their own language not only in private but also at public meetings or when publishing magazines. Notwithstanding the existence of French as the official language, Flemish people were allowed to maintain their distinct economic and cultural unity and, therefore, a national political identity. They were never exposed to the kind of violent assimilation that would have seen them forced to integrate into the dominant linguistic community. Instead, Flemish people were able to secure the kind of limited recognition that gave them the opportunity to consolidate their cultural unity to a point where societal institutions in that language were gradually constructed.

Flanders was also an economically developed region, and, in spite of the oppressive policies of state nationalism, it remained so. The Flemish group therefore enjoyed a developed industrial economy in which its members could enjoy the right to work in their own language. In 1866, Antwerp, dominated by the *Antwerp Meeting Partij*, was the first province to declare Flemish as the official language. 'The year 1878 saw the use of Flemish in administrative documents, but it was only after 1893 that pressure started to build up significantly with the demand of officially making Flemish a national language, which was achieved in 1898 thanks to the Flemish activists in Parliament'.[33] Throughout the nineteenth century, language legislation in Belgium included a personality principle according to which people in Flanders had the permission to speak Flemish in every part of the public sphere. In the 1930s, Dutch gradually became the sole language of administration and education in

Flanders. In these circumstances, fragmentation of the Flemish group did not occur, and all of its members wanted to use their rights to freedom of association and self-government. Moreover, because their ethnic identity in public has long been recognized, Flemish people have never needed to resort to violent conflict to earn their cultural rights. Their example supports the view that the absence of forced assimilative policies creates a context in which multiculturalism seems more likely to be viable.

Even the most enthusiastic egalitarian thinks that if a linguistic group maintains 'an entire economy and polity within a state' (as has happened in Belgium and Canada) then it could be given autonomy and the right to govern its own education system.[34] The Flemish example illustrates that the viability of ethnocentric multiculturalism actually involves more than a simple adaptation of the demarcation between ethnic groups which have economic parity. The application of contemporary multiculturalist theory is clearly not a simple matter of continuing the policies of positive recognition that have always been there.

2   Multiculturalism for Oppressed Minorities: Muslim Turks in Greece

The persistence of cultural, political, and social boundaries between ethnic groups is also stronger and more stable when integrationist assimilation has not been an option for the members of national minorities. Oppressed minorities have survived the barriers established by exclusionary citizenship regimes but have nevertheless been socially and politically excluded from the majority on a consistent basis.

It is worth noting that assimilation does not always mean inclusion, integration, and/or equality. Many ethnic exclusionists are assimilationist even as they continue to exclude minority groups. Uyghur Turks in China,[35] Muslim Turks in Greece,[36] non-Muslims in Turkey,[37] Indian Tamils in Sri Lanka,[38] and Hungarians in Slovakia represent examples of this category.[39] Although they experienced policies of assimilation in the sense that they were not allowed to use their own languages in most public spheres, they were never accepted as members of society in the fullest sense of the term. Discrimination against these groups remained evident in job applications, university admission processes, and class divisions. In such cases, minority groups were differentiated and marginalized in ways that positioned them in opposition to the majority along ethnic lines. Although internal divisions remain, members of these minorities have also typically united as political groups along ethnic lines. When assimilation was not an option, when it was not aimed at integration, or when differentiation between ethnic groups has strongly persisted and facilitated discrimination in social life, national minorities have not had many options other than to opt into their own ethno-national communities.

Policies of segregation, discrimination, and differentiation along ethnic lines seem to be the most relevant sources of motivation for people to develop a shared sense of belonging and to claim ethno-national autonomy: 'Ethnic group formation is a process of social closure [and] high degrees of closure imply that the boundary cannot be easily crossed'.[40] This also explains why differentiation and segregation increase support for ethno-nationalism.

From a normative perspective, multiculturalism is much more likely to be operational in situations like that experienced by Muslim Turks in Greece. Although it is well known for its assimilationist policies, Greece differs from nations like France or the United States where integration has been the norm. The foremost reason for this is that Greece's assimilationist policies have never sought to integrate Muslim Turks into the majority but were instead designed to intimidate or exterminate them. Greece's Muslim Turks were deprived of citizenship rights between 1955 and 1998,[41] discriminated against by the law, ignored, and left to their own destiny.[42] As a result of their experience of exclusion, which was justified by the ideas of ethnic state nationalism, Muslim Turks also became demographically concentrated in Western Thrace. The exclusionist policies of the Greek state isolated Muslim minority members and left them with no other option than to develop an inferior socio-economic network within which they could work and earn money away from the Greek majority. Mostly they were confined in rural areas of the country where the main form of work was agriculture. Their participation in the body politic and the mainstream of Turkey's economic life has always remained limited.[43]

The Muslim Turkish minority in Greece is economically disadvantaged, and this has led to several problems in terms of the institutional capacity of the Muslim community to provide its members with efficient welfare services and opportunities. Nevertheless, the possibility remains that a progressive form of multiculturalism could be useful and feasible in their case for several reasons. Firstly, it is more feasible to provide public services and education in the language of minority members if they are demographically concentrated in certain regions; secondly, those Muslim minorities, including non-Turks, which have been identified and historically excluded by the persistent association of Greek identity with Orthodox Christian characteristics are inclined to mobilize voluntarily around Turkish ethnicity.[44] The Muslim community in Greece is not ethnically homogenous because '[t]here are an estimated 120,000

Muslim Turks in Greece'.[45] Approximately 35,000 of them are Pomaks whose mother tongue is actually a Bulgarian dialect, and there are nearly 5,000 Muslim Gypsies who are of Romany origin, but although the Muslim community in Greece is fragmented, most of its members still find it more appealing to classify themselves as Turkish rather than Greek.[46] All ethnic groups are internally fragmented. However, minorities which have been systematically excluded from the majority in society are more likely to overcome their internal divisions and resort to ethno-political forms of representation. In such cases, multiculturalism's essentialist and self-reinforcing policies will not create injustice for even the most distinct people, as long as they are willing to attach themselves voluntarily to essentialist orientations of identity.

It is easy to justify the policies of multiculturalism in such cases even if they do not instantly lead to a remarkably better financial situation for the members of a minority. It can be argued, for example, that because 'Western Thrace is the least developed and poorest region in Greece',[47] the Turkish language does not offer any prospects for having a good career for anyone who does not want to become a farmer in rural Greece. Despite the fact that speaking the Turkish language does little to maximize the material interests of an ethno-cultural politics in Greece, the Muslim community of Western Thrace is increasingly adhering to that kind of politics. This is mostly because the alternative to the solution of ethno-national autonomy for them is to be pushed into a Greek society in which they are subject to social discrimination and isolation.

3   *Multiculturalism for Minorities of Assimilation and Integration: Corsicans and Kurds*

The third category of national minorities consists of groups which were forced to assimilate into the ethnic core of a state's dominant ethnic majority. The Kurds in Turkey, the Corsicans in France, the First Nations in Canada, and Native Americans belong to this category and experienced, among other things, the prohibition of minority languages in education (which lasted for Canada's Aboriginal people until the 1980s), punishment for the use of such languages in public as well as in the private sphere (experienced by the Kurds in Turkey until the 2000s), resettlement of minorities from their historical homelands, and difference-blind state policies, such as those experienced by Corsicans in France until the 1990s.

There are several reasons why multiculturalism has been especially problematic in cases where there is a long history of assimilation and integration. First of all, such minorities became relatively mobile after the forcible displacement of their populations. Today, for example, almost 40 per cent of the Kurds in Turkey are dispersed across the country rather than living in their historical homeland. American Indians and Corsicans in France followed a similar pattern.[48] The rate of assimilation in those uprooted minority groups has usually been 'considerably higher than the rate of assimilation among the secluded populations of villages close to the soil'.[49] In such cases, the multiculturalist policies proposed in the homelands of minorities have very limited executive reach. When members of these minorities are scattered, it is difficult to make any territorial arrangements that respond to their needs. Moreover, even in their homelands, there is usually an ethnically mixed population and it is difficult for ethnically focused self-government mechanisms to represent this diversity appropriately.

Another reason why multiculturalism has proved problematic is that this trajectory of integration and assimilation creates hyphenated identities. Ethnically defined political rights are hardly appealing to those people who refuse to describe themselves in singular terms. Some scholars, such as Young, have suggested that when, as in most of these cases, state nationalism has consistently denied and ignored minorities over time, the 'norm of the homogenous public is oppressive ... [as] it requires that persons transform their sense of identity in order to assimilate. Self-annihilation is an unreasonable and unjust requirement of citizenship'.[50] Forced assimilation in these circumstances can become a source of radicalization, and this radicalization has typically translated into politics, if not violence.[51]

Young's argument assumes that, for example, people can only become American if they stop being Spanish, Italian, or Arabic. However, this assumption is flawed, especially because assimilation does not always lead to self-annihilation.[52] Additive assimilation refers to a process which involves assimilation into a culture by a person who also chooses to preserve links to their birth culture, so this does not necessarily mean self-annihilation. Absorptive assimilation, on the other hand, implies the kind of assimilation which requires a person to give up their birth culture in order to acquire a new one. While the first category is especially relevant to linguistic minorities, because members can develop bilingual identities, the latter is important to those groups which form part of a mutually exclusive binary. Members of religious minorities cannot be both Muslim and Christian, or Protestant and Catholic at the same time, for instance.

When assimilation is additive, as is usually the case for linguistic minorities, it is hard for a multiculturalist approach to locate individuals on one or other side of the line between resistance and assimilation. In such cases people may undertake forms of resistance in order to preserve their native culture, yet voluntarily assimilate into another at the same time. To portray the reaction of most national minorities to assimilation as resistance, then, is to ignore the reality of cases in which boundaries are permeable and assimilation is additive. Some members of a minority may choose to embrace assimilation, as the Bretons have in France; some will resist it in any form and will go on to generate the kind of conflict produced by radical Chechens in Russia; still others will develop hyphenated national identities such as those formed by British Scots, Latino Americans, or the Catalans in Spain.

There is a third reason why multiculturalism is especially problematic in cases where assimilation has been the predominant state policy. This trajectory has made it difficult for minorities to develop a realistic, cohesive socio-political culture that is sufficiently developed in terms of its institutional capacity to accommodate its members, even when it is allowed to do so. Today's Aboriginal people in Canada have always been divided into Inuit, Métis, and First Nations groups, and in their cases the state has refused to use ethnicity to draw a boundary between the majority and the minority. Their religious particularities, subcultures, and class divisions have remained more relevant than they might have been in circumstances that would have allowed the development of their unified ethnicities. The First Nations' initial lack of unity had nothing to do with government policy. However, the reason they could not eventually develop a shared sense of common ethnic identity can be explained in part by the fact that they were never given the opportunity to foster one. Canada has not genuinely empowered the First Nations to institutionalize their culture. Their members experienced state policies that punished the use of their languages in public and banned ethnic associations; they were also usually deprived of a sense of shared belonging or collective political orientation.

The prohibition of Aboriginal languages in education until the early 1980s represented a particularly important barrier to their cultural institutionalization. In the light of this, it would be wrong to argue that government policies have had no role in these groups' lack of unity. The same argument also applies to the Kurds in Turkey. The utilitarian value of the minority language remains low in this kind of scenario and leads minority people to opt into the language of the community that offers them the greatest possible opportunities. It is not uncommon for minority members who would be put at a disadvantage by the essentialization of ethnic culture to opt into the majority language. In doing so, they complicate those policies of multiculturalism which are aimed at creating an autonomous region where boundaries are drawn along the lines of ethnicity.

The Corsican case in France supports this suggestion. Multicultural-ists tended to assume in the past that the Constitutional Court of France was actively blocking the implementation of regional autonomy and self-government rights in Corsica and that Corsicans would be opposed to a political system with a centralized French administration which legit-imized French as the sole language of instruction in public education. However, the results of the 2003 referendum, in which the majority of Corsicans said no to autonomy, disappointed anyone who assumed that 'France would soon join the bandwagon of states that experienced a shift from suppressing the sub-state nationalisms to accommodating them through regional autonomy and official language rights'.[53] Simi-lar patterns have emerged in Turkey where private institutions that were allowed to teach Kurdish suspended their courses due to a lack of interest from Kurdish people; and 'despite the constitutional reform in Cana-dian society, Aboriginal languages and knowledge (that were assimi-lated once) are not yet flourishing in education systems. The Cana-dian education system has not empowered the enormous creativity in Aboriginal languages, and First Nations schools have not used them widely'.[54]

The integrationist ideal of civic nationalism, in the name of which assimilation policies were used in the first place, appears to be an impor-tant factor in ensuring the persistence of remaining differences within a national minority group.[55] Civic nationalism offers people from different backgrounds an opportunity to identify themselves as equal members of a community in which they can make choices like everyone else. Essen-tially, civic nationalism accepts people with different backgrounds into its own traditions and practices, unlike ethnic nationalism which resists the incorporation of people from different ethno-cultural backgrounds into the dominant core. This incorporation is not an option in a state which has adopted ethnicity as a criterion for membership, no matter how much minority members are willing to integrate into the main-stream community. Indian Tamils in Sri Lanka have obviously suffered from the kind of ethnic nationalism practiced by the Sinhalese major-ity, which did not recognize the citizenship of Indian Tamils in 1949 and discriminated against them in university admissions.[56] Similarly, Uyghur Turks in China cannot enjoy a healthy cultural life in the context of a Chinese mainstream community that even discriminated against any Uyghur Turks who became fluent in Mandarin.[57] In these kinds of cases, people from national minority groups have no option other than to live in their own cultural groups.

In other circumstances, people in a minority can choose to adopt the culture of a civic state and to make use of the equal opportunities it has to offer:[58] as Waldron observes, 'It does not matter if one's own cultural structure is destroyed so long as one has access to some sufficiently rich and healthy alternative cultural materials'.[59] In these kinds of situations, ethnocentric multiculturalism starts to lose viability for minorities that are operating within a civic assimilationist integration paradigm. As long as the doors are opened in civic projects, there will always be some sub-groups that want to enter into the mainstream community and adopt its culture. The fact that a forced assimilation policy is being used in a civic state-building project does not mean that nobody will voluntarily participate in it. Voluntary participation in civic projects happens for various reasons. It may, for example, happen if the subgroup shares some basic characteristics with the dominant culture, as happened in Northern Ireland where Protestant Irish people have spoken for union with Britain. It also happens because the group may want to make use of advantages offered in the mainstream community, as was the case for some Puerto Ricans who chose to live in the United States where they would benefit from improved job opportunities.[60]

Pan-ethnicity occurs only when there exists the kind of clear-cut competition between ethnic groups which might arise over an issue like the ethnicization of bureaucracy or the uneven distribution of materials to certain minority groups.[61] When people from a certain ethnic group are discriminated against, they are more likely to identify themselves in terms of their ethnic descent.[62] Outcomes are more likely to be different in putatively civic communities where people have equal opportunities to take up official roles and are given identical educational opportunities. People who voluntarily integrate into the mainstream community and are able to gain important positions within it have proved to be less likely to prioritize their descent when it comes to defining the kind of polity in which they want to live. Moreover, the combination of equal opportunities and voluntary assimilation under civic nationalism can in time diminish the extent of ethnic mobilization. Subgroups have opportunities to develop different visions of their broader community depending on their experiences, class positions, religious beliefs, and levels of similarity to the dominant culture.[63]

Lastly, multiculturalism is problematic for minorities in this category because, in those cases where societal culture is more fluid than has been assumed, 'multiculturalist policies are not simply a passive adaptation to an ineluctable fact of cultural diversity. Rather, multiculturalism actually creates the reality which is then, in a circular process of self-reinforcement, appealed to as a justification for further extension of multiculturalist policies'.[64] In this process of self-reinforcement, the development of minorities' societal culture and the prizing of their nationhood requires multiculturalism to persist with its essentialization of ethnic culture. However, this can produce some inegalitarian outcomes for those group members who have different interests, values, or perceptions.[65] The protection of one cultural minority may automatically perpetuate inequality between subgroups of that minority. It especially disadvantages whichever subgroup has the least capacity to mobilize. For example, extensive research has revealed that the PKK, in developing its claim to represent the Kurds, has actually heavily suppressed all of the dissident movements within its own organization.[66]

In this context, civic nationalism provides dissidents with an option to exit from their cultural groups, and there are always some people who might seek to use this option. It is usually the case that minority groups choose to teach their children the language of the mainstream community if the utilitarian value of their own language has remained very low due to the assimilationist policies of the past. In this kind of situation, any attempt to establish an autonomous administrative region in which the leadership would stick up for cultural essentialism impedes the opportunities of members who might want to use this exit option for themselves. The critiques of multiculturalism explored here are relevant in this particular context precisely because of these problems. The existence of societal culture is a matter of degree, and so solutions which treat it as an absolute feature of minorities risk failure. The shared practices and expectations of a minority are part of a societal culture, and they are not easily found in cases where a national minority group has been continuously exposed to forced assimilation and integration.

Conclusion

It is apparent that the applicability of multiculturalist approaches in real political situations varies from one instance to another for various reasons. This book does not intend to defend one policy over another; the aim is not to find out whether difference-blind egalitarianism/assimilationism or ethnocentric multiculturalism offers a truer answer (if there is one at all) which might then might be generalized to deal with the whole range of problems that arise in relation to national minorities. Instead, as the chapters that follow make clear, difficulties are bound to arise for multiculturalism in cases where it is hard to find a monolithic national minority group, a majority of the members of which

want the kind of politically autonomous solution which has proved successful in Canada or Belgium.[67]

Especially in contexts where forced assimilation and integration have
been the norm, nationalistic groups become radical; however, the same
system also accommodates those people who voluntarily assimilate. In
such cases, most national minority members require the rectification of
economic and social inequalities more than they desire the political rights
which their radical fellows believe are derived primarily from ethnicity.
Preliminary evidence suggests that when ethno-cultural boundaries are
easy to cross and are rendered socio-politically irrelevant by progressive
civic state-building projects, separation and hierarchy are minimized. In
such contexts, 'classificatory ambiguity and complexity will be high and
allow for more individual choice (compared to those fixed by ethnic distinctions)'.[68] There are evidently some minority members who are primarily concerned with their material well-being, and they are convinced
that only assimilation into the majority can guarantee this. Some other
minority members take pride in, or benefit from, their cultural distinctiveness and resist assimilation for various reasons, and in these cases
questions need to be asked about whether the economic opportunities
that attract voluntarily assimilating groups or the cultural freedoms that
appeal to ethno-nationalists should be taken more seriously. Which set of
freedoms should be given priority when two groups are in conflict about
the future of their community? What should the state do if members of
minorities are not in agreement about the form that political recognition
of their culture should take? What happens to the demands of ethno-
nationalist minority factions in countries where integration is the norm
for most minority members – what demands are legitimate, and who
should be listened to?

The next chapter focuses on the Kurdish case in Turkey in order to
contextualize and address this difficulty. Turkey is somewhat distinct in
that it practices assertive assimilation while at the same time being relatively open to those Muslim minorities that are willing to take part in
the civic nation. This context of forced assimilation can radicalize some
segments in the group, and some people will disagree vehemently with
centralist state nationalism; yet, at the same time the system incorpo-
rates those who have voluntarily assimilated into the majority and provides a base for heterogeneous practices that cross ethnic boundaries.
The following chapters explain this in detail by focusing on the lack of
mass mobilization in a Kurdish population which is fragmented in terms
of political loyalties because its people were subjected to the policies of
forced assimilation and integration for so long. The next chapter explains

the historical background to this contemporary problem of heterodoxy within the Kurdish population in Turkey.

Notes

1 Ted Robert Gurr, *Minorities at Risk – A Global View of Ethnopolitical Conflicts* (Washington, DC: United States Institute of Peace, 1995).

2 David Quinn and Ted Robert Gurr, 'Self-Determination Movements and Their Outcomes', in J. Hewitt, J. Wilkenfeld and T. Gurr, eds., *Peace and Conflict* (Boulder, CO: Paradigm Publishing, 2008).

3 Will Kymlicka, *Multicultural Citizenship: A Liberal Theory of Minority Rights* (Oxford: Clarendon Press, 1995).

4 Will Kymlicka and Magda Opalski, *Can Liberal Pluralism Be Exported?: Western Political Theory and Ethnic Relations in Eastern Europe* (Oxford: Oxford University Press, 2002), 23.

5 A. D. Smith, National Identity: *Ethno-Nationalism in Comparative Perspective* (Reno, NV: University of Nevada Press, 1993), 131.

6 Jacob T. Levy, *The Multiculturalism of Fear* (Oxford: Oxford University Press, 2000).

7 Philip G. Roeder, 'Clash of Civilizations and Escalation of Domestic Ethnopolitical Conflicts', *Comparative Political Studies* 36, no. 5 (2003): 509–40.

8 See John Rex's chapter on 'Multiculturalism in Europe and North America' in his book *Ethnic Minorities in the Modern Nation State* (New York, NY: Springer, 1996), 114–31.

9 Iris Marion Young, 'A Multicultural Continuum: A Critique of Will Kymlicka's Ethnic-Nation Dichotomy', *Constellations* 4, no. 1 (1997): 48–53.

10 Kathleen Gallagher Cunningham, *Inside the Politics of Self-Determination* (New York, NY: Oxford University Press, 2014).

11 Will Kymlicka, 'Multiculturalism and Minority Rights: West and East', *Journal on Ethnopolitic and Minority Issues in Europe* 4, no. 2 (2002): 1–26.

12 W. Alejandro Sanchez, 'Corsica: France's Petite Security Problem', *Studies in Conflict & Terrorism* 31, no. 7 (2008): 655–64.

13 Gunes Murat Tezcür, 'Kurdish Nationalism and Identity in Turkey: A Conceptual Reinterpretation', *European Journal of Turkish Studies*, no. 10 (2009): 1–18.

14 Michael Keating, *Plurinational Democracy: Stateless Nations in a Post-Sovereignty Era* (Oxford: Oxford University Press, 2001).

15 Jeffrey G. Reitz, 'Assessing Multiculturalism as a Behavioural Theory', in R. Breton and K. Dion, eds., *Multiculturalism and Social Cohesion: Potentials and Challenges of Diversity* (New York, NY: Springer, 2009).

16 Stéphane Guérard, 'Local Referendums in France: A Disappointing Experience', in Theo Schiller, ed., *Local Direct Democracy in Europe* (New York, NY: Springer, 2011).

17 Glhermine, 'French Regionals 2010: Second Round', World Elections, https://welections.wordpress.com.

18 Yigal Schleifer, 'Religious Kurds Become Key Vote in Turkey', *Christian Science Monitor*, www.csmonitor.com.

19 *Hurriyet Daily*, '2011 Yili Genel Secim Sonuclari – the 2011 General Election Results', *Hurriyet Daily*, www.hurriyetdailynews.com.

20 Will Kymlicka, 'The Rights of Minority Cultures: Reply to Kukathas', *Political Theory* 20, no. 1 (1992): 140–46.

21 Jennifer Jackson Preece, *Minority Rights* (Cambridge: Polity Press 2005), 161.

22 Peter Karl Kresl, 'Quebec's Culture Policy: Will Increased Autonomy Matter?' *American Review of Canadian Studies* 26, no. 4 (1996): 499–521.

23 Wendy Pearlman and Kathleen Gallagher Cunningham, 'Nonstate Actors, Fragmentation, and Conflict Processes'. *Journal of Conflict Resolution* 56, no. 1 (2012): 3–15.

24 Theo McLaughlin and Wendy Pearlman, 'Out-group Conflict, In-group Unity? Exploring the Effect of Repression on Intra-movement Cooperation'. *Journal of Conflict Resolution* 56, no. 1 (2012): 41–66.

25 Kymlicka and Opalski, *Can Liberal Pluralism Be Exported?*, 25.

26 Sujit Choudhry, 'Does the World Need More Canada? The Politics of the Canadian Model in Constitutional Politics and Political Theory', *International Journal of Constitutional Law* 5, no. 4 (2007): 606–38.

27 Kenneth McRoberts, *Misconceiving Canada: The Struggle for National Unity* (Oxford: Oxford University Press, 1997).

28 Choudhry, 'Does the World Need More Canada?' 613.

29 Peter W. Hogg, *Canada Act 1982 Annotated* (Toronto, ON: Carswell, 1982). Also see Will Kymlicka, *Finding Our Way: Rethinking Ethnocultural Relations in Canada* (Oxford: Oxford University Press, 1998).

30 David Howes and the Centaur Jurisprudence Project, A Clarification of Terms: Canadian Multiculturalism and Quebec Interculturalism' Centre for Human Rights and Legal Pluralism, McGill University (2012): 1–14, http://canadianicon.org/wp-content/uploads/2014/03/TMODPart1-Clarification.pdf.

31 Christine Dallaire and Claude Denis, '"If You Don't Speak French, You're Out": Don Cherry, the Alberta Francophone Games, and the Discursive Construction of Canada's Francophones', *Canadian Journal of Sociology* (2000): 415–40.

32 Robert Schertzer and Eric Taylor Woods, 'Beyond Multinational Canada', *Commonwealth & Comparative Politics* 49, no. 2 (2011): 196–222.

33 Caroline Varin, 'Education in a Federal System: A Case-Study of Belgium', *CUREJ: College Undergraduate Research Electronic Journal*, June 28, 2006, University of Pennsylvania, http://repository.upenn.edu, 206.

34 Brian Barry, *Culture and Equality* (Cambridge: Polity Press, 2001).

35 Nicolas Becquelin, 'Criminalizing Ethnicity: Political Repression in Xinjiang'. Paper presented at the China Rights Forum, 2004.

36 A. Alexandris, 'Religion and Ethnicity: The Identity Issues of Minorities in Greece and Turkey', in R. Hirshchon, ed., *Crossing the Aegean: An Appraisal of the 1923 Compulsory Population Exchange between Greece and Turkey* (New York, NY: Berghahn Books, 2003).

37 Metin Heper, *The State and Kurds in Turkey: The Question of Assimilation* (Houndmills, UK: Palgrave Macmillan, 2007).
38 R. Edrisnha, 'Multination Federalism and Minority Rights in Sri Lanka', in W. Kymlicka and B. He, eds., *Multiculturalism in Asia* (New York, NY: Oxford University Press, 2005).
39 Ivan Gyurcsik and James Satterwhite, 'The Hungarians in Slovakia', *Nationalities Papers* 24, no. 3 (1996): 509–24.
40 Andreas Wimmer, 'The Making and Unmaking of Ethnic Boundaries: A Multilevel Process Theory', *American Journal of Sociology* 113, no. 4 (2008): 970–1022.
41 Human Rights Watch, *The Turks of Western Thrace* (New York, NY: Human Rights Watch, 1999).
42 Christina Borou, 'The Muslim Minority of Western Thrace in Greece: An Internal Positive or an Internal Negative "Other"?' *Journal of Muslim Minority Affairs* 29, no. 1 (2009): 5–26.
43 Bahar Rumelili, 'The European Union and Cultural Change in Greek-Turkish Relations', *The European Union and Border Conflicts* 17 (2005): 1–31.
44 Dia Anagnostou and Anna Triandafyllidou, 'Regions, Minorities and European Integration: A Case Study on Muslims in Western Thrace, Greece', *Romanian Journal of Political Sciences* 6, no. 1 (2007): 100–25.
45 Tozun Bahceli, 'The Muslim-Turkish Community in Greece: Problems and Prospects', *Journal Institute of Muslim Minority Affairs* 8, no. 1 (1987): 109–20.
46 Evangelia Adamou, 'Bilingual Speech and Language Ecology in Greek Thrace: Romani and Pomak in Contact with Turkish', *Language in Society* 39, no. 2 (2010): 147–71.
47 Bahceli, 'The Muslim-Turkish Community in Greece', 114.
48 Paul M. Ong, Douglas Houston, Jennifer Wang, and Jordan Rickles, *Socioeconomic Status of American Indians in Los Angeles County* (Los Angeles, CA: University of California/United American Indian Involvement, 2002). Also See J. B. Carillet and M. Roddis, *Corsica* (London: Lonely Planet Publications, 2007).
49 Karl Wolfgang Deutsch, *Nationalism and Social Communication: An Inquiry into the Foundations of Nationality* (Cambridge, MA: MIT Press, 1953), 152.
50 Iris Marion Young, *Justice and the Politics of Difference* (Princeton, NJ: Princeton University Press, 1990), 179.
51 Donald L. Horowitz, *Ethnic Groups in Conflict* (Berkeley, CA: University of California Press, 1985).
52 Aristide Zolberg, 'Modes of Incorporation: Towards a Comparative Framework', in V. Bader, ed., *Citizenship and Exclusion* (New York, NY: St. Martin's Press, 1997).
53 Will Kymlicka, *Multicultural Odysseys: Navigating the New International Politics of Diversity* (Oxford: Oxford University Press, 2007), 70.
54 Marie Battiste, 'Enabling the Autumn Seed: Toward a Decolonized Approach to Aboriginal Knowledge, Language, and Education', *Schooling in Transition: Readings in Canadian History of Education* (2012): 275–86.

55 There are of course other conditions such as internal diversity, the history of conflict, and kin states across borders that can help us to understand the impotence of some groups being non-monolithic. The focus on state–minority relations here does not exclude the possibility of multiple causation and relevance of plural determinants to explain the lack of ethnic mobilization and mass support for minority nationalism. However, this focus indeed builds upon recent research which, by testing the alternative explanations for ethnic mobilization such as the history of conflict and internal diversity across European cases, concludes that 'whatever the conditions are, it is more likely that only those minorities who have already been systematically differentiated by the state along ethnic lines will resort to ethno-nationalism in masses'. See Durukan Kuzu, 'Comparative Analysis of Political Systems and Ethnic Mobilization: Assimilation versus Exclusion', *Comparative European Politics* 15, no. 4 (2017): 557–76.

56 R. Edrisnha, 'Multination Federalism and Minority Rights in Sri Lanka', in Kymlicka and Baogang, *Multiculturalism in Asia*.

57 Becquelin, 'Criminalizing Ethnicity'.

58 K. Anthony Appiah, 'Identity, Authenticity, Survival: Multicultural Societies and Social Reproduction', in A. Gutmann, ed., *Multiculturalism: Examining the Politics of Recognition* (Princeton, NJ: Princeton University Press, 1994).

59 Jeremy Waldron, 'Minority Cultures and the Cosmopolitan Alternative', *University of Michigan Journal of Law Reform* 25, no. 3 (1991): 751–93. Also see Alan Patten, 'The Autonomy Argument for Liberal Nationalism', *Nations and Nationalism* 5, no. 1 (1999): 1–17.

60 Ronald J. Larsen, *The Puerto Ricans in America* (Minneapolis, MN: Lerner Publishing Group, 1991).

61 Y. L. Espiritu, *Asian American Pan-Ethnicity* (Philadelphia, PA: Temple University Press, 1992).

62 Min Zhou, 'Segmented Assimilation: Issues, Controversies, and Recent Research on the New Second Generation', *International Migration Review* 31, no. 4 (1997): 975–1008.

63 Richard Alba and Victor Nee, 'Rethinking Assimilation Theory for a New Era of Immigration', *International Migration Review* (1997): 826–74.

64 Barry, *Culture and Equality*, 315.

65 Chandran Kukathas, 'Are There Any Cultural Rights?' *Political Theory* 20, no. 1 (1992): 105–39.

66 Aliza Marcus, *Blood and Belief: The PKK and the Kurdish Fight for Independence* (New York, NY: New York University Press, 2007).

67 Michael Keating, *Plurinational Democracy: Stateless Nations in a Post-Sovereignty Era* (Oxford: Oxford University Press, 2001).

68 Wimmer, 'The Making and Unmaking of Ethnic Boundaries', 970–1022.

4 Turkey's Kurdish Dilemma
'Segmented Forms of Assimilation'

The historical relationship that existed between the Kurds and the state in Turkey in the period up to the end of the twentieth century demonstrated that civic state-building and policies of assimilation create complexities which make ethnocentric multiculturalism unworkable. Chapter 3 outlined a typology of national minorities and identified a category/context in which multiculturalism is found especially difficult to implement for normative and practical reasons. This chapter, by focusing on the Kurds in Turkey, epitomizes this context in greater historical detail. The Kurdish community in Turkey is deeply divided in terms of its people's cultural practices and political orientations, and any version of multiculturalism based on an understanding of minorities as a monolithic category seems likely to be non-operational in the Kurds' situation. Still, a huge volume of literature about the ethnic conflict between radical Kurds and the armed forces in Turkey shows that its problems cannot be accounted for by stringent interpretations of difference-blind egalitarianism or assimilationism either, because of the complex historical trajectory of the relationship between Kurds and the state and its ongoing consequences.[1] The discussion that follows examines in detail this complexity, as well as its implications for multiculturalism.

Integrationist State Nationalism and Assimilation

It is not possible to single out one dominant feature that characterizes the kind of nationalism that has been prominent in Turkey throughout its history. The literature on Turkish nationalism tends to embrace an understanding of the Turkish nation that combines both civic and ethnic elements before concluding that 'Turkish nationalism exhibits a highly hybrid character'.[2] Insofar as this chapter refers to civic nationalism in Turkey, it does so only to define the nationalism to which Kurds have been exposed. It does not seek to define the entirety of Turkish nationalism in ways that might exclude the issues generated by its relations with other groups. The term 'civic state nationalism in Turkey' is invoked here specifically to refer to an illiberal form of civic nationalism that reflects the state's integrationist ideal but which has, nevertheless, failed to lead to the voluntary incorporation of all Kurds into the Turkish state. As this discussion will make clear, any Kurds who were unwilling to assimilate have been forced to do so.

Whether a particular nationalism is conceived of as either ethnic or civic has much to do with whether its conception of the nation is informed by primordial or constructivist assumptions about what constitutes nationhood. Although the constructivist approach was accepted by the 1924 constitution which inaugurated the Turkish nation, it can safely be stated that cultural components such as language, religion, and ethno-symbolic resources have affected the ways in which it has been instituted.[3] Kurds have, for example, been included in ways that non-Muslim groups have not.

Any definition of Turkish nationalism which is drawn up without reference to its roles in the state's relationships with particular groups at certain periods of time would be ahistorical and would also erase important kinds of complexity. Due to various historical contingencies, it is quite possible to see Turkish nationalism as exclusionary because of the ways in which the state has treated the non-Muslim population; yet, by contrast, non–Turkish-speaking Muslim groups, including the Kurds, have always been addressed in ways that accord with the civic French conception of nationhood which situates assimilation into the mainstream community as the only possible option.

This chapter examines the assimilation of Kurds in Turkey and asks whether it can be portrayed in any clear-cut way as either voluntary or forceful. Answers to this question in the chapter furnish a historical background understanding which is necessary in order to comprehend better the reasons why multiculturalism and representing the Kurds in Turkey is a complicated matter. It will become clear that the 'state in Turkey should [not] be seen as a monolithic and static entity',[4] nor should any of its ethnic groups be classified in this simplistic way. Any attempt to explain the entirety of Turkish nationalism with reference to a limited number of actors and sources would result in gross oversimplification. This is because nationalism is always an ideological phenomenon which changes depending on its context and on the people who interact with it. A careful analysis therefore depends on tracing these dynamic processes and relationships in order to account for the 'multiple reference populations and correspondingly segmented forms of assimilation'.[5]

Assimilation is a social phenomenon that can only be perceived and experienced subjectively,[6] and for this reason anyone who is inclined to describe the relationship between the Kurds and the Turkish state as a

forceful assimilation of the former by the latter has to come to terms
with the heterogeneity of Kurdish communities[7], as well as with the fact
that some of their members have voluntarily assimilated into the mainstream community.[8] As Tezcür points out, '[t]he relationship between
Turkish and Kurdish nationalisms cannot be adequately captured as the
resistance of the latter to the domineering attempts of the former'.[9] This
chapter explains that Kurds, who have been subjected to a variety of
different state policies on a range of fronts in the past, vary in their opinions today, and this variation not only reflects their past experiences but
also corresponds to their diverse political orientations and expectations
in modern Turkey.

Turkish Nationalism

During the assembly debates about the content of the 1924 constitution,
the French conception of a nation as 'universalist, rationalist, assimilationist and state-centered'[10] was accepted as the foundation of the citizenship regime that would operate in the new nation.[11] Article Eighty-
Eight of the constitution declared that '[t]he people of Turkey regardless
of their religion and race is called Turk by citizenship'. Later, Article
Fifty-Four of the 1961 constitution reaffirmed that '[e]veryone who is
tied to the Turkish State through citizenship ties is Turkish', and this
view was endorsed again in Article Sixty-Six of the 1982 constitution.[12]
In fact, it has been argued that Turkey offers an example of constructive
nationalism because the nation was embodied through the agency of the
state and not vice versa:[13] 'Turkey emerged as a state-nation rather than
as a nation state',[14] and therefore there is no clear direction of influence
between ethnicity and Turkish citizenship.[15]

Atatürk made it clear in his speeches that '[t]he inhabitants of modern Turkey, whom we call the Turks, and who of course are the Turks
in the sense that they compose the modern Turkish nation, are really a
people formed over many centuries out of a mixture of races such as pre-
Hittites, Hittites, Phrygians, Celts, Jews, Macedonians, Romans, Armenians, Kurds and Mongols ... [At some point,] Turks from Asia added
themselves to the stock...'[16]

This idea has, however, has been seriously challenged. At the theoretical level, the constitution refers to Turkishness in terms of a citizenship which automatically yields itself to the understanding that there
is 'another – more authentic – Turkishness' which cannot be acquired
by citizenship alone.[17] For instance, 'the law enacted in 1926 specified Turkishness, instead of Turkish citizenship, as a requirement for
becoming a state employee'.[18] Moreover, in the newspaper *Cumhuriyet*

on July 2, 1938, it was announced that a precondition for admission to the Military Veterinary School as well as to the Air Forces was the candidate 'being a citizen of the Turkish Republic and being of Turkish race'.[19]

Non-Muslims, Exclusion, and Discrimination

Application of these undeniably exclusionary regulations was, however, mainly restricted to non-Muslim citizens who were believed by the state to be unable to assimilate into the Turkish community, or rather were thought to be emerging as a kind of fifth column within the country.[20] Candidates from non-Muslim constituencies had still not been accepted into the military schools and many other security-related institutions in Turkey by 2007. The 'recognition of the non-Muslim as citizens was only in legal, not in sociological, terms', Heper argues, because in reality they were being either excluded from the body politic or deported from the country.[21]

The statistical yearbooks of 1929 and 1934 reveal that 'Christians made up 20 per cent of Turkey's population in 1912; fifteen years later, in 1927, they had dropped to as few as 2.64 per cent'.[22] Historical examples richly illustrate the religious essence of nationalism in Turkey. The Lausanne Peace Treaty, according to which only non-Muslims were accepted as a minority, clearly indicated that, despite the civic rhetoric employed in the constitution, the boundaries of Turkishness were primarily drawn with regard to Islam rather than language use.[23]

The population exchange between Turkey and Greece offers more evidence that the nation was being conceptualized in religious terms. While non–Turkish-speaking Muslim groups were accepted into Turkey, Turkish-speaking non-Muslims whose families had resided in Anatolia for centuries were deported to Greece.[24] Moreover, writings about early immigration to Turkey reveal that non–Turkish-speaking 'Bosnians, Greek, Serbian, Macedonian, Albanian and Bulgarian Muslims, who faced extermination or repression in the newly independent Balkan states, fled to Anatolia'.[25] While Muslim subjects of the Ottoman Empire were easily accepted in Turkey and were naturalized on the condition that they would learn Turkish, non-Muslim residents of Anatolia were treated quite differently. At the beginning of the republican regime, the 'Armenian population of the Ottoman Anatolia was already decimated',[26] and a majority of the Greek Orthodox community was also displaced; those who remained in the country were intimidated and terrorized through policies of discrimination, such as the Property Tax Law (Varlik Vergisi Kanunu).

On 12 November 1942, an additional tax, levied exclusively on non-Muslims, was introduced on the basis of law 4305. This law concerned 4 to 5 thousand of an estimated 28,000 Armenians, Greeks, Jews and even *Dönme* (Jews or Christians converted to Islam)...Those who could not pay up were exiled or condemned to forced labour in 'Turkey's Siberia', namely in the quarries of Aşkale near Erzurum, where 21 forced laborers died.[27]

An inclusive civic rhetoric has been used in Turkey's constitutions, but an exclusionary nationalism has obviously been prevalent and has had damaging effects for the country's non-Muslim minorities. Yeğen says 'it may be safely stated that the pre-eminent other of extreme nationalism, especially in the sixties and seventies, was not the Kurds but rather *non-muslimhood'*.[28] Certainly, Mustafa Kemal, before and during the first years of republic, was involved in a tactical alliance with clerics in a bid to gain the support of all Muslim subjects and mobilize them around a nationalist goal.[29]

During his speech to the Turkish parliament in 1920, Atatürk told his listeners that 'You, the members of this dignified assembly, are not only Turks, or Circassians, or Kurds or Lazes, you are the Islamic element made up all of these'.[30] In his letter to the Caliph, Mustafa Kemal used laudatory language, and praised 'Our Great Khan'. People were mobilized in mosques rather than in military quarters, so that the *Cuma Khutba* (the sermon delivered at the noon prayer on Fridays and on certain other occasions) became a key point of access to the state's business. Notably, the Assembly of the Turkish Republic was opened for the first time in 1920 on a Friday with the accompaniment of prayers. Finally, in the state's founding constitution it was stated that 'Islam is the religion of the state', and this claim was not revoked until 1928.[31]

Kurds, Inclusion, and Assimilation

The boundary drawn by Islam in Turkey created a circle of Muslim people whose linguistic differences remained a barrier to the nation-building project. The number of ethnic groups in Turkey during the early republican era was forty-nine,[32] whereas this number was actually claimed by some scholars to be around a hundred.[33] It was clearly impossible for a newly founded state to operate with such a high number of languages in play, and the founders of the republic believed it was impractical to try to create national consciousness and solidarity without establishing a uniform language.[34] The significance of having one official language in Turkey was continuously accentuated: the 'Citizen, Speak Turkish!' campaign was launched in 1928,[35] and in the same year the Arabic alphabet was replaced with Latin script, not only to ensure a clear break from the Ottoman and Islamic past, but also to make it easier and quicker for people to become literate, and to bring the Turkish nation into line with a 'modern' European outlook.

Obstacles to the nation-building project went beyond linguistic diversity to include the overwhelming religiosity inherited from the Ottoman Empire. Just after the republican regime was established, the foundation of the republic was depicted by the republican cadre as an attempt to move away from the beliefs and practices of the Ottoman Empire which were, accordingly, characterized in terms of failure, backwardness, and a rejection of the Caliph and the asymmetric powers of the sheikhs who maintained a feudal order under his divine authority.[36] 'In Atatürk's opinion, it was the scholastic interpretation of Islam and the irrational approach to religion that were to be blamed for the fall of the Ottoman Empire'.[37] The republicans' mission in this context was to secularize and centralize the administration, and most of all to liberalize the country in ways that would render it similar to its European models; this work was also supposed to replace divine authority and dynastic loyalty with national sovereignty and citizenship.

As early as 1921, Atatürk implicitly revealed his intention to transform the ideological base of the political order from dynastic loyalty to national sovereignty when he said that authority, without any condition and reservation, belongs to the nation. Only after the republican regime was established, however, could he gradually realize this idea by introducing a series of laws which would ultimately eradicate the institutional power of Islam and its political function. Toprak argues that '[t]he abolition of the Caliphate in 1924 was the first step in the de-institutionalization of religious involvement in the politics. This was followed by the abolition, on the same date, of the Office of the Seyhu-l Islam and the Ministry of Religious affairs and Pious Foundations (*Seriye ve evkaf vekaleti*). These three offices had provided an institutional base for the *din-u devlet* (Sharia or theocratic state) concept'.[38]

Mohammedan fanatics were outraged by Mustafa Kemal's policy of secularization,[39] and the Sunni Kurds, who had been very loyal to the Caliph, were also outraged by this idea; indeed, it was especially traumatic for them because Mustafa Kemal had won their hearts and minds partly by appealing to their religious sentiments during the war of liberation which had occurred just a few years previously. Now, with the abolition of this institutional bond between the various ethnic Muslim groups in Turkey, the primary tool employed in the nation-building process became nothing but the idea of sharing a territorial boundary within which the language of the state would be Turkish only. Sheikh Said, in his effort to mobilize an uprising, tried to incite other Kurdish and particularly Zaza Sheikhs by asking them to recognize this work in action: 'Earlier we had a common Caliphate, and this gave to our religious people a deep feeling of being a part of the community that the Turks also belonged to. Since the abolition of the Caliphate, the only thing we are left with is Turkish repression'.[40] On the same day that the republic abolished the Caliphate (March 3, 1924), it also banned all Kurdish schools, associations, and publications.[41] This was the first move to promulgate an assimilation policy that would facilitate the construction of the modern Turkish nation by placing a strong emphasis on its territorial integrity.

Two important points require clarification here in relation to the definitions for assimilation and civic nationalism that will be used from this point on to illustrate the historical relationship between the state and the Kurds in Turkey. Firstly, erroneous interpretations of a civic-ethnic dichotomy extend so far as to amount to an assumption that civic nationalism should be acultural and – in any case of nationalism involving an ethno-cultural dimension – ethnic. It is vital to note that any dichotomy between civic and ethnic nationalisms actually has little to do with the presence or absence of cultural or ethnic aspects in their ultimate outcomes.[42] It is inevitable that any social entity has to have a cultural ingredient and therefore the invisible boundaries of a nation are limited by socio-historical contingencies.

From an ontological perspective, each instance of so-called civic nationalism, no matter how much it claims to be based on territorial and political values, also includes a cultural component.[43] Ethnic boundaries affect policy and politics just as much as they affect ethnic boundaries. When the role of language in creating a common national identity is considered, even the nations that claim to be the most civic and inclusive cannot avoid choosing an official language which is to be used by its subjects in relation to the state. Turkey used Turkish to create a common national identity and consciousness among Kurds, Lazes, Arabs, Romanis, Albanians, and Circassians, whose mother tongues were thereby excluded from the public sphere. Every nation has a cultural boundary, and so what makes the dichotomy relevant is not the suggestion that ethnic nationalism is based on exclusion while civic nationalism is not (they both are exclusionary to some extent);[44] instead, their difference consists in the fact that only civic nationalism permits people of other cultures to become accepted members of a nation, on the condition that they are ready to adopt its political values, culture, and the language of the dominant ethnic core.[45]

In cases where ethnic nationalism prevails, people from other cultures, language groups, or religions are not expected to become members of the nation because ethnic nationalism assumes that the boundaries of nation are primordial. If nationality can be granted by nature alone then it cannot be attained at a point beyond birth.[46] This means that ethnic nationalism never involves projects for incorporation, and so nations that choose this option differ from Turkey where state policies have always been informed by the goal of eventually incorporating and assimilating Kurds and other Muslim ethnicities into the mainstream community. In the Turkish situation, Kurds, like all other citizens of non-Turkish ethnicity, have been expected to relegate their ethnic identities and cultural differences to their private lives.

Criticisms of ethnic nationalism too often endorse the erroneous assumption that civic nationalism is liberal in character while eastern ethnic nationalism is axiomatically illiberal.[47] This false dichotomy has led some scholars to associate assimilationist policies in Turkey with ethnic nationalism, and it is not uncommon for scholars to assume that it was Kurdish identity per se that the state in Turkey endeavoured to 'eliminate'.[48] Scholars who speak pejoratively about assimilation wrongly associate it with ethnic nationalism, which in fact absolutely repudiates the idea that identity can be constructed through means such as voluntary assimilation, amalgamation, or acculturation.

A serious problem arises from the argument that links assimilation to ethnic nationalism in the sense that it encourages confusion between concepts of assimilation and cultural annihilation. This confusion arises when assimilation is understood to be a process of absorption at the end of which the assimilated person's identity of origin ceases to maintain its distinct character. In fact, assimilation can only lead to cultural annihilation for assimilated people if the two cultures involved are mutually exclusive, and this is not necessarily the case in all situations. People cannot be half-Christian and half-Muslim at the same time, but a person might well identify herself as being half-Turkish and half-Kurdish or choose to identify her national identity as wholly Turkish while preserving her ethnic Kurdish identity in some form or another. The learning and use of the Turkish language does not necessitate a person forgetting his knowledge of Kurdish, for example.

There are various modes of incorporation available,[49] and while the sort of assimilation that implies cultural annihilation can be called absorptive assimilation, the second type of assimilation, through which a 'previous cultural membership is retained while acquiring a new one',[50] should be understood as additive assimilation. Those who think that assimilation is annihilation usually assume that one has to cease to be

Kurdish in order to become Turkish. Thus assimilation has been conceptualized by some scholars as the epitome of Kemalist Turkish nationalism, as if it were a form of ethnic nationalism that systematically pursues the cultural annihilation of non–Turkish-speaking Muslim minorities in its efforts to secure homogenization.[51]

The process of acculturation (in the sense of additive assimilation) has not always systematically translated into the absorptive assimilation of Kurds in Turkey, but its occurrence is an irrefutable fact that undermines the legitimacy of Turkish nationalism in relation to the Kurds. Absorptive and forceful state policies were used against those Kurds who rejected the relegation of their identities to the private sphere and who resisted the idea of additive assimilation for various reasons. I will go on to argue that, in these cases of resistance, the civic ideals of additive assimilation have been derogated by policies of repression which reached a stage at which they effectively enacted absorptive assimilation. The following sections explore these complex relations by focusing on two dimensions of Turkish nationalism: first, the persistent idealization of civic nationalism and the idea of incorporation, and then the historical practice of forceful assimilation.

Some Kurds and Voluntary Incorporation

The voluntary incorporation of the Kurdish community into the mainstream in Turkey has often been challenged or ignored by those who understand Kurdish nationalism to be a natural and relatively constant phenomenon which has always existed. David Miller rightly cautions against such assumptions and suggests that '[w]hat we must avoid is thinking of the ethnic identities that we wish to support as "genuine" or "authentic" in contrast to other identities which are "manufactured" or "imposed"'.[52]

The Kurdish community has been as diverse as any other community, and some Kurdish groups, unlike their nationalist counterparts, have supported the centralized administration in Turkey and chosen to incorporate themselves into the mainstream for a variety of reasons which included religious affiliations and their desire to maximize their economic potential. Some of these people went on to reach important positions in Turkey's administration and society, and their trajectories illustrate that incorporation is only possible in a context in which civic, inclusive nationalism prevails.

Kurdish nationalists and some scholars identify the ratification of the treaty from the Lausanne Peace Conference – in which non–Turkish-speaking Muslims were left out of the minority definition – as a disappointing moment which led Kurds to start an armed struggle against the republic. They state that, after the Lausanne Treaty, all possibilities of, and talks about, granting autonomy to Kurds disappeared, and, beyond this point, 'bitterly disappointed, the Kurds turned again to armed struggle in 1925 led by Sheikh Said and . . . organized by Azadi'.[53] However, the record of confidential sessions in the Grand National Assembly of Turkey in March 1923 reveals that almost all Kurdish deputies spoke strongly in favour of the inseparability of the Turkish and Kurdish peoples, and the radicals' depiction of the approach taken by Kurdish members of parliament (MPs) to the Lausanne peace conference is quite different from the reality.

In fact, Kurdish MPs articulated their support for the unity of Kurds and Turks in the following ways. Diyop Agha explained that 'We [Kurds and Turks] are no different from each other . . . We have no conflict among ourselves. We have neither a Turkish nor a Kurdish problem. We are all brothers'. Necati Bey from Erzurum whose mother was a Kurd argued that, '[i]f you can lay bare the true sentiments of the Kurds and the Turks, you would see that they have the same vision for the future of this country. The Turks and the Kurds became so mingled together that our nation that [the allies] are trying to tear apart, constitutes one single entity'. Kurd Necib Bey from Mardin noted that, '[i]n the invitation to the [Lausanne Peace] Conference, there is the term "Non-Turks". I am a Kurd . . . I beg our delegates to tell everybody that the Turk and Kurd together constitute one single nation. I ask our delegates to reject such a reference to the Kurds in the strongest terms possible'.[54]

It is usually accepted that 'the rebellion failed because the Azadi leaders were unable to coordinate the Kurdish officers' rebellion with the anticipated uprisings of tribal leaders',[55] but those who accept this account avoid asking why this was the case. Commentators on Kurdish national movements are rather reluctant to accept that tribal and religious matters were the overriding determinants of these movements, which did not resonate with those Kurds who lacked national consciousness or unity of any sort. On April 19, 1920, the British Prime Minister Lloyd George observed that, 'When it comes to Kurdistan, it is difficult to decide which policy to adopt . . . Once it was thought that separating Kurdistan from Turkey and granting autonomy to it would have been the best policy. Yet it has never been clear what exactly the Kurds themselves preferred. On the basis of a study of this issue that I had asked to be made in Istanbul, Baghdad and elsewhere, I now have the impression that a Kurd does not represent any entity other than his own tribe'.[56]

Given the absence of unity on the part of Kurds, Mustafa Kemal and his associates did not think that they would be challenged by a remarkable threat in the long run. After all, as the 1923 Lausanne Treaty makes clear, the state's policies favoured only those Kurds who defended unity and incorporation. In fact, certain segments of Kurdish society have complied with state policies and have not developed resistance to this ideal. First of all, at the outset of Kurdish resistance, the ordinary people of the Kurdish peasantry did not attach themselves to the rebellions led by Sheikhs and tribal leaders because the Sheikh's revolts 'promised them no relief from exploitative landlords, while Ankara had already announced its desire to curtail feudalism'.[57] The main motivation behind these Kurdish rebellions, like similar ones in Hungary and Poland, was the desire of previously powerful elites to 'be left alone to exercise their feudal tyranny over as many of their countrymen as they can contrive to control'.[58] The religious division between the Alevi and Sunni Kurds also helps to explain patterns of incorporation and resistance among members of Kurdish society. This division is generally accepted as one of the elements that explain the failure of Sheikh Said to mobilize an ethnic revolt by Kurds in 1925. Historical accounts of his efforts seem to endorse this view:

The core of Sheikh Said rebellion's military leadership was drawn from Sunni former Hamidiye commanders, such as Xalid Beg Gibran, to whom Sheikh Said was related by marriage ... Mindful of the depredations of the Hamidiye, the Alevi tribes refused to join the rebellion, considering themselves better off in a secular Turkey, nominally Sunni, than in a self-declared Sunni Kurdistan in which the Naksabandi (Sunni) *tarikat* would assume a major role. The Alevi rejection of his overture greatly limited the potential area of the rebellion.[59]

The Dersim uprising, which is explored later in this chapter, failed for similar reasons, chiefly because 'it appeared to most Sunni Kurds at the time to be merely an Alevi uprising – and thus not in their own interests'.[60] This historical distinction between the more secular Alevis and the religious Sunni segments of the Kurdish population remained relevant in explaining their changing political orientations in the longer term: 'There were, in 1920 and 1937–38, rebellions of Kurdish Alevis against the Kemalist movement and the Republic, but at no time until today did Kurdish Alevis *in significant numbers* join forces with Sunni Kurds against the Kemalist regime. By and large, Kurdish as well as Turkish Alevis were supportive of the secular and populist ideals of Kemalism; many Kurdish Alevis voluntarily assimilated to Turkish culture and came to identify themselves as Turks rather than as Kurds'.[61]

Indeed, not only have a remarkable proportion of Alevis been incorporated into the mainstream Turkish community through the appeal of the secular ideals of the republic, but some Sunni Kurds have also been integrated into the mainstream by those right-wing political parties which have an Islamic focus to some extent or other.[62] A great number of Sunni Kurds have generally voted for parties of this kind in general elections. As can be deduced from party programs, Islam has always been pragmatically employed in Turkey to win the support of the Sunni Kurds, and those right-wing political parties which have adopted this approach have tended to be successful, to varying degrees, in incorporating Sunni Kurds into the body politic.

When the first multi-party politics began in Turkey in 1946, the Democrat Party (DP), which was the only party to compete with the republicans, came to represent traditional Sunni Islamic values in exactly the social and institutional arenas that the republican revolution had sought to secularize. During the era of the DP, which was the first political party to win an election against Atatürk's Republican Party, the relevance of Islam increased in Turkey's eastern regions. An indication of this change can be seen in the fact that, 'after 1950, within a year, 250,000 Quran and thousands of religious books, many of which aimed to lessen Kurdish nationalism, were sold in the region'.[63] While the DP was concerned with undermining Kurdish nationalism, its policies simultaneously sought to bring about incorporation and inclusion and it achieved some successes in these regards. Like many other Kurdish figures from the eastern regions, Abdulmelik Firat, who was Sheikh Said's grandson, became a member of parliament between 1950 and 1960.[64]

The DP's successor, the *Adalet Partisi*, or Justice Party (AP), was also supported by the Kurds, and it rejuvenated the DP's emphasis on the urgent need to rectify regional disparities between eastern and western parts of the country.[65] This approach was evident in AP's government program of 1965 which stated that '[t]o realize a balanced development in a social justice framework, we have to narrow the development gap among the regions. There are great gaps in terms of life and living standards in most parts of the country, especially in East and Southeast regions'.[66] In the 1961 elections, the Justice Party and the New Turkey Party (NTP) shared the votes of the electors in the east. Dr Yusuf Azizoglu from the NTP, who became the minister of health in 1962, was a Kurd. The prime minister, later the president, Özal, who thought it was very likely that ethnic differences could be overcome by recourse to Islam and equal citizenship, was also of Kurdish origin, and he frequently said so in public.[67] After the 1980 coup, even the military, which used to be known as the guardian of the secular regime in Turkey, 'viewed religion as a political tool to boost national unity and weaken the influence of

Marxist and separatist ideas'.[68] Islam was a key factor too in shaping the collaborative attitude and political behaviours of those Kurds who voted for the Islamist-Welfare Party, which won seats for thirty-four members of parliament of Kurdish origin in the 1995 general election.[69]

In 2007's parliamentary elections, 'the Islamist AKP (Justice and Development Party) managed to collect 56 percent of the southeast's votes. Even in *Diyarbakır*, considered a pro-Kurdish DTP stronghold, the AKP took 41 percent of votes'.[70] 'It has been estimated that by the end of the twentieth century... at least one-fourth of the deputies elected to Parliament since 1923 have been of Kurdish origin',[71] and, as of 2007, the AKP had been represented by seventy-five ethnically Kurdish MPs. Although their ethnic origin is never publicly referred to, many Kurds in Turkey have reached high positions in the Turkish state and have enriched many walks of life in the same way that Scottish, Welsh, and Irish people have done in Britain.[72] Yet, Kurds who have been elected to parliament have only been able to operate within the boundaries of an official ideology which dictates that the sole official language is Turkish and that the politics of ethnicity have no place within political debate. Kurdish MPs illustrate that, while citizens of any ethnicity can enjoy influential positions in Turkey, they can only do so as long as they do not make their ethnicity an issue. This helps to explain why Kurds who have cooperated with the state have been condemned and attacked by radical Kurdish nationalists.

Texts such as *The Way of the Kurdish Revolution*, distributed in 1975, contained extremely brutal attacks on the Kurdish bourgeoisie whose members were accused of collaborating with the Turkish state.[73] Some of the former deputies from the DEP, a pro-Kurdish party, were also very intolerant of Kurds in other political parties. Many prominent deputies of Kurdish origin who served parties such as *Hikmet Cetin*, *Kamran Inan*, and *Fehmi Isiklar* were portrayed as traitors who had betrayed the Kurdish cause. The PKK, too, in accordance with its Decree on Village Raids, has attacked and burned 'non-revolutionary villages that do not support national struggle for liberation'.[74]

The next chapter shows how the complexity of motivations behind some Kurds' engagement with voluntary assimilation in the past is still relevant in contemporary Turkey, making it difficult for an ethnocentric discourse of multiculturalism to succeed. Before then, however, it is equally important to give a picture of the other side of the Kurdish population in Turkey, who persistently resisted assimilation and who, by doing so, made it inevitable for the Turkish State to find a way of accommodating ethnic differences in the country.

Some Other Kurds and Forced Assimilation

Although the majority of Kurds who chose to integrate into the mainstream community were given the same 'equal opportunities' as everyone else, no solution other than forceful assimilation was anticipated for those Kurds who were not willing to relegate their ethnic identity to the private sphere and had rejected becoming Turkish in any form. This, in a nutshell, was the issue that caused problems for a significant portion of the Kurdish population.[75]

The abolition of the Caliphate in 1924 and the declaration of the decree banning the use of any language other than Turkish in public offices and schools were followed by a series of laws on secularization. This secularization process, the centralization of the entire administration, and compulsory education in the Turkish language have been key factors in the politicization of the Kurds,[76] and resistance to these developments shaped a wave of mutinies in the 1920s and 1930s: 'Of the 18 rebellions that broke out between 1924 and 1938, 17 were in Eastern Anatolia and 16 of them involved the Kurds'.[77] The first of these insurgencies was Sheikh Said's rebellion, which Atatürk understood to be the outcome of religious fundamentalism or feudal resistance rather than Kurdish nationalism. Atatürk's view is supported by many scholars because the rebellion was led by only one Zaza-speaking Sunni tribe. It was not supported by other Kurdish tribes, let alone by the Alevi Zazas, who felt more secure under the authority of the semi-secular republic than under the rule of Hanafi Sunni Kurds.

There are two very different Kurdish dialects – Kurmanci and Kirmanci (Zaza) – in Turkey. Even today, Kurmanci has nothing to do with the language of the Zaza (Kirmanci) people who demarcate themselves from Kurmanci Kurds in the strongest terms possible: 'As recently as the 1990s, when a former Kurdish separatist leader, Seyfi Cengiz, tried to convince villagers in his region that they were Kurds, the latter responded to him with the following words: we are Kirmanci (Zaza). You are saying we are Kurdish. We are not Kurdish'.[78] It is baseless to assume that Zazas might have revolted in the name of the Kurmanci people at a time when they could not even communicate properly. Whatever the main reason behind the rebellion was, the government's reaction to this movement had further assimilative implications for both the Zaza and Kurmanci people who lived in the region.

While this rebellion was going on, Atatürk declared martial law and introduced 'the 4 March 1925 Law on Maintenance of Order and Peace' – *Takrir-i Sukun* – which would create Independence Tribunals (*Istiklal Mahkemeleri*) that had complete authority to arrest and execute anyone who committed treason and endangered the public order.[79] Independence Tribunals authorized by martial law sentenced Sheikh Said and fifty-two of his partisans to capital punishment. Police forces were established there and authorized with extraordinary powers to maintain the peace. Policies of repression did not just affect those who were engaged in mutiny; they also intimidated ordinary people in the region. One of the most important initiatives to prevent a further rebellion was formulated through the plan for the reformation of the East – *Sark Islahat Plani*. On September 8, 1925, this plan was issued under resolution number 2356. According to Article Fourteen of the Plan for Reformation of the East, '[p]eople who speak a language other than Turkish in state and municipality, institutions, and other organs and administration, in schools, at the marketplace in the district and regional centers of Malatya, Elâziz, Diyarıbekir, Bitlis, Van, Muş, Urfa, Ergani, Hozat, Erciş, Adilcevaz, Ahlat, Palu, Çarsancak, Çemişgezek, Ovacık, Hısnımansur, Behisni, Arga, Hekimhan, Birecik, Çermik, [would] be brought before the courts'.[80]

Meanwhile, the government had also initiated a plan to mix the populations of different ethnicities, and it introduced a resettlement law aimed at producing this effect. In fact, Resettlement Law no. 8885, passed on May 31, 1926, had more specific outcomes because it allowed the government to reconfigure its resettlement policies to strengthen the Turkish character of the population at the national level: 'On 15 October, 1925, Directorate General for resettlement decided that the Maras province whose inhabitants were of various elements, needed Turkish immigrants ... [The] 2nd resettlement law also focused on domestic population issues. Accordingly, it authorized the ministry of interior to relocate the nomadic tribes and others around suitable centres'.[81]

It is possible to argue that Turkey deployed this forced resettlement policy as a means to bully mutinous elements in the country, but it eventually contributed to assimilating Kurds into the Turkish population. In a further bid to achieve complete assimilation and integration of the Kurds through resettlement, the government passed, in 1927, Law no.1097 (Law on the Transfer of Certain People from the Eastern Regions to the Western Provinces) which led to almost 1,400 individuals from Agri province and the Eastern regions being resettled to the Western provinces.[82] Separatism was also discouraged by a policy which banned any associations and political organizations that were established on the basis of ethnicity. Associations as such were banned by Law no. 765, which was published in the official *Journal of the Turkish Republic* on March 3, 1926. Articles 141 and 142 contain the key provisions:

Article 141–4: Any attempt, on the basis of race, to suppress or eliminate the rights recognized by the Constitution, the creation or attempted creation of organizations aiming to weaken or diminish national sentiment and the leadership or administration of such organizations are criminal offences punishable from eight to fifteen years' incarceration.

Article 141–5: Membership to such organizations is punishable from five to twelve years' incarceration....

141–8: For the purposes of this legislation, an organization shall consist of any gathering of two or more persons to pursue a common goal...

142–6: If any of the above mentioned criminal offences is committed by way of publication, the sentence will be increased by one half.[83]

While these oppressive policies were being put into practice, other insurgencies took place around the Agri mountain. These uprisings that were led by Captain Ihsan Nuri and were supported by the Kurdish nationalist organization, the Hoybun, were to be repressed by the government in 1930. Article One of Law no. 1850, published on July 29, 1931, specified that 'Killings, and other acts committed, either individually the state or of its provinces, by civil or military personnel, as well as by local authorities, guards or the militia, or any civilian having aided them or having acted in accord with them, from the 20 June 1930 to the 10 December 1930, in the pursuit and extermination of uprisings which took place at Ercis, Zilan, Agri Dag and surrounding area, also including the region of the first inspectorate and the district of Pulumur, in the province of Erzincan, will not be considered as crimes'.[84]

The Dersim region had been problematic for almost a century. Inhabitants of the region consisted, by and large, of Alevi Zazas. Sheikhs and tribal leaders in the region did not accept any authority other than their own control, and Dersim had, by the mid-1930s, become the last part of Turkey that could not be controlled. Tribal chiefs and Sheikhs insisted on maintaining their right to exercise unlimited authority over the masses, whom they often abused economically.[85] The US ambassador to Turkey stated in his Dersim report that 'Although the Turkish government tried to solve the problem by means of economic reforms, tribal chieftains resisted these reforms, refused to pay taxes, and disrupted the constructions of bridges, roads and schools in the region'.[86] To subdue insurgencies and revoke the feudal order, the government issued the 1934 Law on Resettlement (İskân Kanunu), Law No. 2510, on June 13, 1934, and in that year 25,381 people from 5,074 households in eastern and southeastern cities were resettled to the western parts of Turkey.[87]

As a second step, the government had commanded the army to 'round up and deport the people in the rebellious districts ... to render those who have used arms or are still using them once and for all harmless on the spot, to completely destroy their villages and to remove their families'.[88] After the Dersim rebellion was subdued in 1938, 7,954 persons were reported killed or caught alive, although Kurds claim that the number of people who died in Dersim was much higher. After the rebellion was subdued and the mutineers were executed, reforms were pushed forward in Dersim; Dersim's name was changed to Tunceli in 1935, schools were built, and children were educated so intensively along the lines of republican ideology that most of the subsequent generations in the region not only assimilated into the mainstream very successfully but also ended up being proud of holding Turkish nationality.[89] As of April 2011, the leader of the mainstream Republican People's Party (CHP) Kemal Kilicdaroglu is just one of the Alevi Zazas from Tunceli (Dersim) who has strongly opposed the politicization of ethnicity in Turkey in the modern era. In the end, the number of Kurds deported to western Turkey in the 1930s totalled 25,381,[90] and the repression of the rebellions that took place between 1924 and 1938 resulted in the displacement of Kurds who would later mix with people of other ethnicities in the places where they were resettled.

In the 1930s and 1940s, these assimilationist-integrationist policies went so far as to deny the very existence of a distinct Kurdish ethnicity. It was declared that Kurds were actually (mountain) Turks and that they had forgotten their Turkishness over time. It was only ever in these claims that Turkishness was discussed in terms of ethnic origin rather than citizenship. This deviation from the constitutional spirit that defines Turkishness primarily as a category of citizenship was, however, only prevalent during the 1930s and 1940s, and it evaporated after that era's fascism and Nazism had been quashed. 'German influence was particularly effective *vis-à-vis* at least some officers',[91] and it also affected very limited number of civil servants like the Minister of Justice, Mahmut Esat Bozkurt, who stated that '[t]he Turks are the only lords of this country, its only owners. Those who are not of pure Turkish stock have in this country only one right that of being servants, of being slaves'.[92] It should be stressed that, even in the 1930s and 1940s, Kurds had not been excluded from the ethnically defined Turkish community but were represented as being of Turkish descent. 'On the historiographical level this has been expressed by the Turkish Historical Thesis and the Sun Language Theory, according to which the Turkish language is the source for all existing languages in the world'.[93] According to this theory, the word 'Kurd' was a name given to the one of the twenty-four grandsons of Oguz Khan, the mythological founder of the Turks, and so the Kurds could indeed be accounted for as Turks.

A decade after the Dersim rebellion, and just before the election in 1950, the first easings in relations began.[94] The CHP – *Cumhuriyet Halk Partisi* or Republican People's Party – had allowed previously displaced Sheikhs and Aghas to return to their hometowns in 1947 in the hope that these chieftains would, in return, use their tribal potency to generate local support in the coming election.[95] In fact, 22,516 people belonging to 4,128 households returned to their homes in 1947,[96] but it was too late for CHP to win the backing of the Kurdish chieftains, who were ready to give unequivocal support to any party that opposed the regime that had treated them harshly. In the 1950 election, the Democrat Party came to power with the support of the conservative majority and of Kurdish chieftains who thereby became MPs in the new parliament.

The resettlement of Kurds under state coercion laws was followed by a wave of voluntary migration undertaken by Kurds who wanted to benefit from the development in the 1950s of a national market economy in Turkey's urban industrialized regions.[97] From that time onwards, until the outbreak of the violent conflict between PKK and the armed forces of the state in 1984, there was unlikely to be any serious uprising on the part of the Kurds. What small-scale political activities there were could be repressed without any difficulty. It was illegal to establish a political party that was based on ethnicity, and, for this reason, the political activities of those nationalist Kurds who adopted a Marxist-Leninist ideology were channelled through the Workers' Party of Turkey (TIP or *Turkiye Isci Partisi*) which was mainly concerned with trying to bring socialism to Turkey. In 1971, this party was closed down on the grounds that its Eastern Region Demonstrations – *Dogu Mitingleri* – turned out to be a base for the politicization of Kurdish ethnicity. Later on, in 1974, Kurdish members of the former workers' party of Turkey established an underground organization called the Socialist Party of Turkish Kurdistan. Members of this organization tried to disseminate leftist ideas about Kurdish identity, 'yet they continued to believe in Kurdish-Turkish coexistence within a socialist system'.[98] This Kurdish organization was not well accepted by those Kurdish groups which were instead committed to traditional tribal and Islamic values.

During those times, the PKK – *Partiya Karkerên Kurdistan*, or Kurdistan Workers' Party – emerged from a group led by Abdullah Öcalan, who was a former member of the Ankara Higher Education Association and had been arrested for distributing ideological bulletins. 'In 1977 the *Apocular* (partisans of Abdullah Öcalan) identified the enemies of the Kurdish people as the fascists; agents of the state and those (no matter whether Turks or Kurds) who supported them, the Turkish left which subordinated the Kurdish question to the leftist revolution and finally the exploitative Kurdish Landlord class'.[99]

What separated the PKK from all other Kurdish organizations was its ultimate aim to create an independent Kurdistan. The *Apocular* fought not only with the tribal Kurdish chieftains and villagers who did not support them but also with those Kurds who preferred to stay loyal to the state; it also clashed with any Kurdish leftist group that deviated from the use of PKK's violent techniques or questioned its ultimate goal of creating a separate Kurdistan. The foundations of the PKK had been constructed in terms of Marxist ideology, but it adopted a fascist and intolerant approach which left no room for opposition of any sort within its own community. Not surprisingly, the PKK's first attack was on a Kurdish tribal leader, Bucak, who was also an MP from the conservative Justice Party. While the Kurdish movement was operating on a clandestine basis, the political atmosphere all over the country was chaotic. The vicious conflict between rightist and leftist factions went so far as to be described as anarchy and involved '231 political murders in 1977, 832 in 1978, 898 during the nine months between December 1978 and September 1979, and 2,812 during the following twelve months'.[100]

Atatürk's legacy 'was under assault not only from the war between leftist and rightist groups, but also from Kurdish nationalists, Marxists and Islamic revivalists'.[101] In the military coup of 1980, the army declared a state of emergency and suspended the civil government for two years. According to official statistics, police forces arrested 175,000 political activists and civilians in this period.[102] Most of the detainees were Marxists and leftists and – given that Turkey had been a strong ally of the US in the cold war – it can be safely asserted that the targets of police forces during and after the 1980 coup were generally communists rather than the Kurds per se. Not just Kurdish leftists, but also many Marxists of Turkish origin had to flee the country. The Turkish nation chose communists and separatists, not Kurds, as the nation's 'other'. Most of the Marxist detainees, whether Kurdish or Turkish, were tortured until 1984.

It is a well-known argument that the PKK would have never been able to generate the first wave of support for its cause if leftist Kurds in *Diyarbakır* Prison had not been repressed, tortured, and marginalized by police forces,[103] but those religious Kurds who had nothing to do with Marxist leftist ideology had not been appreciably marginalized by the state in the first place. It is also recognized that the massive support enjoyed by the PKK, even eleven years after its establishment, could not have been generated solely among Kurds. Öcalan even admonished his deputies on this count, complaining that: 'when we look at the experience in other countries, we see that they started with 300 guerrillas. Within two years their numbers rose to 10,000. We also started with 300, but we are still only 1,500. Why?'[104] The PKK was still not a massive movement at this time, yet its existence was posing a great threat both to Atatürk's legacy of national unity and to the patriotic ideal within the country.

New policy measures to prevent acceleration in the growth of separatist movements were not going to differ from earlier policies, which had already impeded the emergence of a distinct Kurdish societal culture in Turkey. In October 1983, the government introduced Law 2932, which forbade 'express[ly], diffusing or publishing in any language other than the official language of the states recognized by the Turkish state. Until 1992, Kurds were not allowed to be engaged in cultural activities and perform songs and plays in Kurdish, or identify certain customs as Kurdish'.[105] Those who wanted to give their children Kurdish names were not allowed to do so because Law 1587 stated that such names contradicted national culture, traditions, and morality and offended public opinion and so could not be legally registered on birth certificates. By 1986, 2,842 of 3,254 villages in mostly Kurdish-populated regions had been given Turkish names as part of attempts to secure further integration and obliterate the Kurdish identity. The government applied the deportation policy again, and by 1995 it had evacuated 2,253 villages for security reasons.[106] More villages were vacated by villagers who fled the terror being fostered by the PKK and the banditry of the village guards who abused their power in the region.[107,108] Some of the villages had been left by inhabitants who found themselves caught in crossfire between the PKK and security forces.

The war on the PKK was to be carried out under the state of emergency (OHAL, or *Olaganustu Hal Durumu*) which was declared in July 1987 and was to be renewed every four months by parliamentary decree.[109] Civilian governors were authorized by this law to exercise certain powers which would not be subject to the supervision of the constitutional court. Civil governors who held this power undertook measures which included limitations on the press and the elimination from the area of people whose actions were thought to be inimical to the public order. Under the state of emergency, both the police forces and civil governors violated a great number of human rights, such as the right to speak one's mother tongue.

Governments that used to see the problem as merely a security issue have gradually evolved their position and are now more concerned with the consolidation of democracy in Turkey. One of the factors in this gradual change is Turkey's candidacy for membership of the European Union: the protection of minorities is a condition for accession, and, partly as a result of the opportunity this creates, Kurdish nationalists have increasingly come to articulate their demands through the rhetoric of democratization rather than that of independence claims. The shift away from talk of independence initially encouraged the government, as well as many liberals, to hope and even assume that the conflict would wane if liberal democracy was consolidated. However, different approaches to that assumption have arisen because Kurds themselves are internally divided as to what they want, and there is uncertainty around which subgroups' demands are legitimate and who should be considered as the ultimate holders of rights. This discussion has not been derived from an informed philosophical view on the part of the government but has emerged a result of attempts to tackle the practical problems of diversity management which have arisen within the country and among the Kurds in particular.

Conclusion

The 'state versus the Kurds' paradigm fails to reflect either the complex relations that exist between the diverse groups within Kurdish society, or the ways in which those relations impact on the agency of the state. A significant number of Kurdish groups have cooperated with the state, whereas radical nationalists have been fighting against its armed forces. As this chapter has shown, the Turkish nation has never established its other as the Kurds per se; it is more accurate to say that it has defined itself against communists and separatists, as well as non-Muslims. As we have seen, the conflict is not solely between the state and separatist Kurds but is one between nationalist Kurds, who reject Turkish identity in any form, and moderate Kurds, who have sought to maintain multiple identities within the current framework. This fragmentation among Kurds cannot be overcome by resort to the ethnic roots that Kurdish people share, not just because the state tried to oppress any nationalist mobilization around particularistic ethnicities, but also because those Kurds who feel able to take up any position in the mainstream have chosen not to adopt an ethnocentric approach.

The assimilation of different segments of the Kurdish community into the Turkish system has been facilitated through equal opportunities, religious sentiments, semi-secularism, and anti-feudal regulations at different points in the past. Yet those people who could not be incorporated into the system by any of these means experienced types of oppression and forced assimilation which encouraged them to become more radical than their contemporaries.[110] Legitimate public objectives for the majority have turned out to be irreconcilable with Kurdish nationalists' prioritization of cultural autonomy. In Turkey, Turks and Kurds have not only fought together in the war of independence but have also shared a religion and a territory for such a long time that Kurdish nationalists' intent to put one ethnicity or likeness above all others is now being rebuffed by a group of intermingled Turks and some Kurds.

Mixed marriages and the resettlement of the Kurds in the western parts of the country mean that a great number of people have come to hold multiple identities. Gultekin's work 'Debates on interethnic marriages: assimilation or integration?' in 2012[111] identified at least 23,138 intermarriages between the Turks and the Kurds in Turkey up until 2000. This number, however, admittedly has its limitations as it uses the Kurdish language as the only proxy for the Kurdish ethnicity and therefore excludes a significant sample population of Kurds who do not speak Kurdish anymore. A more recent work in 2016 by Zeyneloglu, Civelek and Sirkeci focuses on internal migration and intermarriage patterns between the Kurds and the Turks who have moved between the regions of Turkey in the last four decades of the 20th century. Their findings reveal that of all the 8,070 Kurdish women they have identified between the ages of 19 and 45, who live outside their birth place and who are married to a Turkish man, 6,762 don't speak the Kurdish language at all. This suggests that Turkish may in fact 'become the main medium of expression during the early adulthood of a Kurd in Turkey (especially upon entrance to higher education and/or after intermarriage)'.[112] Given that nationalism affirms the importance of certain likenesses above all others, the nationalist mobilization has also turned out to be problematic for some Kurds, who are more concerned with their future prospects or linguistic or religious particularities than with their overall Kurdishness. Zaza and Alevi Kurds' demarcation of themselves from the majority of Sunni and Kurmanci Kurds throughout history remains evident, for example.[113] For the Sunni Kurds the most important thing is that their religious beliefs are valued, and this priority has aligned them with political parties whose members are of diverse ethnicities rather than with groups focused on ethnicity.[114] These forms of fragmentation remain present because the Kurds have not been exclusively labelled in terms of their ethnicity and have never been excluded from the cultural and political mainstreams on the basis of their ethnicity in a way that would lead them to give priority to it in the way that was adopted by Muslims in Greece, the Québécois in Canada, and the Flemish in Belgium.

Obviously, the situation that is being 'transitioned' from affects the limits of transition or change itself.

The next chapter demonstrates that the political actors and state policies that defend the difference-blind, egalitarian position are violating the freedoms of radical nationalists. It will also show that the nationalist minority parties, freedom fighters, and supposedly liberal multiculturalists who defend the principle of autonomy are refusing to acknowledge that their demands are potentially in conflict with the equality and freedoms of those individuals who have assimilated voluntarily.

Notes

1 Bahadir K. Akcam and Victor Asal, 'The Dynamics of Ethnic Terrorism'. Paper presented at the 23rd International Conference of the System Dynamics Society, Boston, MA, 2005. Also see Kemal Kirişci and Gareth M. Winrow, *The Kurdish Question and Turkey: An Example of a Trans-State Ethnic Conflict* (London: Frank Cass, 1997); and Henri J. Barkey and Graham E. Fuller, 'Turkey's Kurdish Question: Critical Turning Points and Missed Opportunities', *The Middle East Journal* (1997): 59–79.

2 Nergis Canefe, 'Turkish Nationalism and Ethno-Symbolic Analysis: The Rules of Exception', *Nations and Nationalism* 8, no. 2 (2002): 133–55. Also see Ayşe Kadioğlu, 'The Paradox of Turkish Nationalism and the Construction of Official Identity', *Middle Eastern Studies* 32, no. 2 (1996): 177–93.

3 Yesim Bayar, 'The Trajectory of Nation-Building through Language policies: The Case of Turkey during the Early Republic (1920–38)', *Nations and Nationalism* 17, no. 1 (2011): 108–28.

4 Gunes Murat Tezcür, 'Kurdish Nationalism and Identity in Turkey: A Conceptual Reinterpretation', *European Journal of Turkish Studies*, no. 10 (2009): 1–18. Also see Murat Somer, 'Defensive and Liberal Nationalisms: The Kurdish Question and Modernization and Democratization', in E. F. Keyman, ed., *Remaking Turkey: Globalization* (Oxford: Lexington Books, 2007).

5 Rogers Brubaker, 'The Return of Assimilation? Changing Perspectives on Immigration and its Sequels in France, Germany, and the United States', *Ethnic and Racial Studies* 24, no. 4 (2001): 531–48.

6 See Raymond H. C. Teske and Bardin H. Nelson, 'Acculturation and Assimilation: A Clarification', *American Ethnologist* 1, no. 2 (1974): 351–67.

7 This does not mean that we cannot study or measure the state policies of forced assimilation from a top-down perspective, but in order to understand how those policies operate on individual and societal levels, what their implications are, and what they mean for the people who are exposed to them, one needs to use a bottom-up approach and account for the diverse ways in which assimilation impacts on different segments. It is important to acknowledge the distinction between 'the policies of assimilation' as

imposed by the state and 'the process of assimilation' as experienced by individuals. It is one of this book's arguments that no hard and fast categorizations can be made with regard to the nature of the relationship between the two.

8   Metin Heper, *The State and Kurds in Turkey: The Question of Assimilation* (Houndmills, UK: Palgrave Macmillan, 2007).

9   Tezcür, 'Kurdish Nationalism and Identity in Turkey', 8.

10 William Rogers Brubaker, 'Immigration, Citizenship, and the Nation-State in France and Germany: A Comparative Historical Analysis', *International Sociology* 5, no. 4 (1990): 379–407.

11 S. Killi, *Turkish Constitutional Developments and Assembly Debates on the Constitutions of 1924 and 1961* (Istanbul: Mentes Matbaasi, 1971).

12 Mesut Yeğen, '"Prospective-Turks" or "Pseudo-Citizens": Kurds in Turkey', *The Middle East Journal* 63, no. 4 (2009): 597–615.

13 A. V. Sherman, 'Turkey – A Case in Constructive Nationalism', *Commentary* 30, no. 2 (1960): 93–101.

14 Heper, *The State and Kurds in Turkey*, 95.

15 David Shankland, *Islam and Society in Turkey* (Hemingford Grey, UK: Eothen Press, 1999).

16 David Hotham, *The Turks* (London: Taylor & Francis, 1972), 72.

17 Mesut Yeğen, 'Citizenship and Ethnicity in Turkey', *Middle Eastern Studies* 40, no. 6 (2004): 51–66.

18 Mesut Yeğen, 'Turkish Nationalism and the Kurdish Question', *Ethnic and Racial Studies* 30, no. 1 (2007): 119–51.

19 A. Yildiz, *Ne Mutlu Turkum Diyebilene: Turk Ulusal Kimliginin Etno-Sekuler Sinirlari (1919–1938) (How Happy Is the One Who Can Say 'I Am Turkish': The Ethno-Secular Borders of Turkish National Identity (1919–1938))* (Istanbul: Iletisim, 2001).

20 Marc Baer, 'The Double Bind of Race and Religion: The Conversion of the Dönme to Turkish Secular Nationalism', *Comparative Studies in Society and History* 46, no. 4 (2004): 682–708.

21 Heper, *The State and Kurds in Turkey*, 91.

22 Soner Cagaptay, 'Passage to Turkishness: Immigration and Religion in Modern Turkey', in H. Gunalp, ed., *Citizenship and Ethnic Conflict: Challenging the Nation State* (London: Routledge, 2006), 62.

23 Omer Taspinar, *Kurdish Nationalism and Political Islam in Turkey: Kemalist Identity in Transition* (London: Routledge, 2005).

24 Renée Hirschon, *Crossing the Aegean: An Appraisal of the 1923 Compulsory Population Exchange between Greece and Turkey* (New York, NY: Berghahn Books, 2003).

25 Cagaptay, 'Passage to Turkishness', 62.

26 Canefe, 'Turkish Nationalism and Ethno-Symbolic Analysis', 145.

27 Tessa Hofmann, *Armenians in Turkey Today: A Critical Assessment of the Situation of the Armenian Minority in the Turkish Republic* (Brussels: The EU Office of Armenian Associations of Europe, 2002), 16.

28 Mesut Yeğen, 'Turkish Nationalism and the Kurdish Question', *Ethnic and Racial Studies* 30, no. 1 (2007): 119–51.

29 Binnaz Toprak, *Islam and Political Development in Turkey* (Leiden: Brill, 1981).
30 Ankara Arastirma Merkezi, *Atatürk'ün Söylev Ve Demeçleri (Atatürk's Speeches and Declarations)* Vol. III (Ankara: Türk Tarih Kurumu Basımevi, 1997), 74–5.
31 Paul Stirling, 'Religious Change in Republican Turkey', *The Middle East Journal* 2, no. 4 (1958): 395–408.
32 Peter A. Andrews and Rüdiger Benninghaus, *Ethnic Groups in the Republic of Turkey* (L. Wiesbaden: Reichert, 1989).
33 Hâle Soysü, *Kavimler Kapısı (The Gate of Ethnicities)* (Istanbul: Kaynak Yayınları, 1992).
34 Mustafa Saatci, 'Nation-States and Ethnic Boundaries: Modern Turkish Identity and Turkish-Kurdish Conflict', *Nations and Nationalism* 8, no. 4 (2002): 549–64.
35 Senem Aslan, '"Citizen, Speak Turkish!": A Nation in the Making', *Nationalism and Ethnic Politics* 13, no. 2 (2007): 245–72.
36 Henri J. Barkey, 'The Struggles of a "Strong" State', *Journal of International Affairs* 54, no. 1 (2000): 87–105.
37 M. T. Demir, *Nurcu Movement in Turkish Political System and 'Fetullahcilar' as a By-Product: Advanced Issues in Turkish Politics* (Izmir: Dokuz Eylul University Press, 2005), 11.
38 Toprak, *Islam and Political Development in Turkey*, 46.
39 J. Palmer and C. Smith, *Modern Turkey* (London: George Routledge and Sons, 1942), 12.
40 Hamit Bozarslan, 'Kurdish Nationalism in Turkey: From Tacit Contract to Rebellion (1919–1925)', in A. Vali, ed., *Essays on the Origins of Kurdish Nationalism* (Costa Mesa, CA: Mazda, 2003), 180.
41 Christopher James Houston, *Islam, Kurds and the Turkish Nation State* (Oxford: Berg, 2001).
42 R. Brubaker, *Nationalism Reframed: Nationhood and the National Question in the New Europe* (New York, NY: Cambridge University Press, 1996).
43 Avishai Margalit and Joseph Raz, 'National Self-Determination', *The Journal of Philosophy* 87, no. 9 (1990): 439–61. Also see Will Kymlicka, *Liberalism, Community, and Culture* (Oxford: Oxford University Press, 1991).
44 Rogers Brubaker, *Ethnicity without Groups* (Cambridge, MA: Harvard University Press, 2004).
45 Jennifer Jackson Preece, *Minority Rights* (Cambridge: Polity Press, 2005).
46 Walker Connor, 'Nation-Building or Nation-Destroying?' *World Politics* 24, no. 3 (1972): 319–55. Also see Edward Shils, 'Primordial, Personal, Sacred and Civil Ties: Some Particular Observations on the Relationships of Sociological Research and Theory', *British Journal of Sociology* 8, no. 1 (1957): 130–45.
47 H. Kohn, 'Western and Eastern Nationalisms', In J. Hutchinson and A. Smith, eds., *Nationalism* (Oxford: Oxford University Press, 1994).
48 N. Entessar, *Kurdish Ethno-Nationalism* (London: Lynne Rienner Publishers, 1992).

49 Aristide Zolberg, 'Modes of Incorporation: Towards a Comparative Framework', in V. Bader, ed., *Citizenship and Exclusion* (New York, NY: St. Martin's Press, 1997).

50 Rainer Bauböck, 'The Crossing and Blurring of Boundaries in International Migration. Challenges for Social and Political Theory', *Public Policy and Social Welfare* 23 (1998): 17–52.

51 Chris Kutschera, *Le Mouvement National Kurde (The National Movement of Kurdish People)* (Paris: Flammarion, 1979). Also see Kendal Nezan, 'Kurdistan in Turkey', in G. Chaliand, ed., *People without a Country: The Kurds and Kurdistan* (London: Zed Press, 1980).

52 David Miller, *On Nationality* (Oxford: Oxford University Press, 1995), 135.

53 Paul White, 'Ethnic Differentiation among the Kurds: Kurmancî, Kizilbash and Zaza', *Journal of Arabic, Islamic, and Middle Eastern Studies* 2, no. 2 (1995): 67–90.

54 Heper, *The State and Kurds in Turkey*, 117.

55 Entessar, *Kurdish Ethno-Nationalism*, 83.

56 Abdurrahman Arslan, *Samsun'dan Lozan'a Mustafa Kemal Ve Kürtler (1919–1923)*, Vol. 4 (Istanbul: Doz Basım ve Yayıncılık Limited Şti., 1991), 47. Also see Heper, *The State and Kurds in Turkey*, 113.

57 David Romano, *The Kurdish Nationalist Movement: Opportunity, Mobilization and Identity* (Cambridge: Cambridge University Press, 2006), 106.

58 John Bulloch and Harvey Morris, *No Friends but the Mountains: The Tragic History of the Kurds* (London: Penguin Books, 1992), 97.

59 Robert Olson, *The Sheikh Said Rebellion and the Emergence of Kurdish Nationalism: 1880–1925* (Austin, TX: University of Texas Press, 1989), 94.

60 Paul White, 'Ethnic Differentiation among the Kurds: Kurmancî, Kizilbash and Zaza', *Journal of Arabic, Islamic, and Middle Eastern Studies* 2, no. 2 (1995): 67–90. Also see Martin Van Bruinessen, *Agha, Shaikh, and State: The Social and Political Structures of Kurdistan* (Utrecht: University of Utrecht, 1978), 374–5.

61 Martin Van Bruinessen, 'Kurds, Turks and the Alevi Revival in Turkey', *Middle East Report*, no. 200 (1996): 7–10.

62 Nilufer Narli, 'The Rise of the Islamist Movement in Turkey', *Middle East* 3, no. 3 (1999): 38–48.

63 Ahmet Ali̇ş, 'The Process of the Politicization of the Kurdish Identity in Turkey: The Kurds and the Turkish Labor Party (1961–1971)', MA Thesis, Bogazici University, 2009, 55. Also see Kemal Karpat, *Türk Demokrasi Tarihi Sosyal, Ekonomik, Kültürel Temeller (The History of Turkish Democracy: Social, Economic and Cultural Foundations)* (Istanbul: Istanbul Matbaasi, 1967), 244.

64 F. M. Akar, *Abdulmelik Firat* (Istanbul: Avesta, 1996).

65 H. K. Kokce, 'Two Transformative Actors of Turkish Politics: Justice and Development Party and Kurds', MA Thesis, Middle East Technical University, 2010, 89.

66 H. K. Kokce, 'Two Transformative Actors of Turkish Politics', 89.

67 Mustafa Akyol, *Kürt Sorununu Yeniden Düşünmek: Yanlış Giden Neydi? Bun-dan Sonra Nereye? (Revisiting the Kurdish Question. What Went Wrong and Where to Go From Now On?)* (Istanbul: Doğan Kitap, 2006).

68 Kemal Kirişci and Gareth M. Winrow, *The Kurdish Question and Turkey: An Example of a Trans-State Ethnic Conflict* (London: Frank Cass, 1997), 112.

69 Burhanettin Duran, 'Approaching the Kurdish Question via *Adil Düzen*: An Islamist Formula of the Welfare Party for Ethnic Coexistence', *Journal of Muslim Minority Affairs* 18, no. 1 (1998): 111–28.

70 Yigal Schleifer, 'Religious Kurds Become Key Vote in Turkey', *Christian Science Monitor* 101, no. 7 (2009), www.aina.org.

71 Heper, *The State and Kurds in Turkey*, 118.

72 David Hotham, *The Turks* (London: Taylor & Francis, 1972), 180.

73 Gerard Chaliand, *The Kurdish Tragedy*, trans. Philip Black (London: Zed Books, 1994), 47.

74 Kirişci and Winrow, *The Kurdish Question and Turkey*, 131–47.

75 Svante E. Cornell, 'The Kurdish Question in Turkish Politics', *Orbis* 45, no. 1 (2002): 31–46.

76 Mardin Şerif, *Türkiye'de Din Ve Siyaset (Religion and Politics in Turkey)* (Istanbul: Iletisim, 1992), 100.

77 Kirişci and Winrow, *The Kurdish Question and Turkey*, 100.

78 Heper, *The State and Kurds in Turkey*, 113.

79 U. Mumcu, *Kurt-Islam Ayaklanmasi 1919–1925 (Kurdish-Islamic Revolt 1919–1925)* (Ankara: Tekin Yayinevi, 1992).

80 D. Fernandes, *The Kurdish and Armenian Genocides: From Censorship and Denial to Recognition?* (Stockholm: Apec, 2008), 45.

81 Cagaptay, 'Passage to Turkishness', 67.

82 Cagaptay, 'Passage to Turkishness', 68.

83 Chaliand, *The Kurdish Tragedy*, 31.

84 Ibid., 38.

85 Van Bruinessen, *Agha, Shaikh, and State*.

86 A. Cay, *Her Yonuyle Kurt Dosyasi (Kurdish File with Its All Aspects)* (Ankara: Bogazici Yayinlari, 1993), pp. 422–4.

87 I. Tekeli, 'Osmanli Imparatorlugundan Gunumuze Nufusun Zorunlu Yer Degistirmesi Sorunu' ('The Problem of the Forced Resettlement of the Population Since the Ottoman Empire'), *Toplum ve Bilim* no. 50 (1990): 49–71.

88 'The Secret Decision of the Council of Ministers on the Punitive Expedition to Dersim of 4 May 1937' cited in Martin Van Bruinessen, 'Genocide in Kurdistan? The Suppression of the Dersim Rebellion in Turkey (1937–38) and the Chemical War against the Iraqi Kurds (1988)', in G. J. Andreopoulos, ed., *Conceptual and Historical Dimensions of Genocide* (Philadelphia, PA: University of Pennsylvania Press, 1994), 6.

89 S. Selek, *Ismet Inonu Hatiralar (Memoirs of Ismet Inonu)* (Ankara: Bilgi Yayinevi 2006), 528.

90 Tekeli, 'Osmanli Imparatorlugundan Gunumuze Nufusun Zorunlu Yer Degistirmesi Sorunu' ('The Problem of the Forced Resettlement of the Population since the Ottoman Empire'), 49–55.

91 Heper, *The State and Kurds in Turkey*, 107.
92 Van Bruinessen, 'Genocide in Kurdistan?'
93 Konrad Hirschler, 'Defining the Nation: Kurdish Historiography in Turkey in the 1990s', *Middle Eastern Studies* 37, no. 3 (2001): 145–66.
94 B. Simsir, *Kurtculuk 1924–1999 (Kurdism 1924–1999)*, Vol. II (Ankara: Bilgi Yayinevi, 2009).
95 Ismil Besikci, *Dogu Anadolu'nun Duzeni: Sosyo-Ekonomik Ve Etnik Temeller (The Order of Eastern Anatolia: Socio-Economic and Ethnic Foundations)* (Ankara: E Yayinlari, 1969), 220.
96 Tekeli, 'Osmanli Imparatorlugundan Gunumuze Nufusun Zorunlu Yer Degistirmesi Sorunu (The Problem of the Forced Resettlement of the Population since the Ottoman Empire)', 55.
97 Yeğen, 'Prospective-Turks' or 'Pseudo-Citizens'.
98 David McDowall, *A Modern History of the Kurds* (London: IB Tauris, 2000), 412.
99 Ibid., 419.
100 Andrew Mango, *Turkey and the War on Terror: 'For Forty Years We Fought Alone'* (New York, NY: Routledge, 2005), 16.
101 David McDowall, *A Modern History of the Kurds*, 415.
102 Omer Karasapan, 'Turkey and US Strategy in the Age of Glasnost', *Middle East Report* 160 (1989): 4–10.
103 H. Cemal, *Kurtler (The Kurds)* (Istanbul: Dogan Kitap, 2003).
104 Mango, *Turkey and the War on Terror*, 38.
105 Heper, *The State and Kurds in Turkey*, 164.
106 Kirişci and Winrow, *The Kurdish Question and Turkey*, 131.
107 Kurdish villages that did not want to support the struggle for national liberation were attacked by the PKK. A long list of the villages attacked and burned by the PKK is available in Simsir's documentary work. (See Simsir, *Kurtculuk 1924–1999*, 642–648.)
108 'The controversial village guard system was introduced in April 1985 because of the enormous logistical difficulties of ensuring security in the mountains and rural areas of Eastern and South Eastern Turkey. The aim was to enable villages to defend themselves against attacks from the PKK' (Kirişci and Winrow, *The Kurdish Question and Turkey*, 129); however, these village guards were later discovered to have abused their power through brigandage and smuggling. Although this system might be considered as unique to Turkey, Staniland, who analyzes intra-group competition structures in various civil wars, shows that insurgents in fact often defect to fight for the government against their ethnic kin in response to rivalries within their group. (See Paul Staniland. ''Between a Rock and a Hard Place: Insurgent Fratricide and Ethnic Defection in Kashmir and Sri Lanka'. *Journal of Conflict Resolution* 56, no. 1 (2012): 16–40.)
109 M. Hakan Yavuz, 'Five Stages of the Construction of Kurdish Nationalism in Turkey', *Nationalism and Ethnic Politics* 7, no. 3 (2001): 1–24.
110 Nicole F. Watts, 'Activists in Office: Pro-Kurdish Contentious Politics in Turkey', *Ethnopolitics* 5, no. 2 (2006): 125–44.

111 Mehmet Nuri Gültekin, 'Debates on Inter-ethnic Marriages: Assimilation or Integration? The Turkish Perspective'. *Papers: revista de sociologia* 97, no. 1 (2012): 151–166.

112 Sinan Zeyneloglu, Yaprak Civelek, and Ibrahim Sirkeci. 'Inter-regional migration and intermarriage among Kurds in Turkey'. *Economics & Sociology* 9, no. 1 (2016): 143.

113 Leyla Neyzi, 'Zazaname: The Alevi Renaissance, Media and Music in the Nineties', in P. White and J. Jongerden, eds., *Turkey's Alevi Enigma* (Leiden: Koninklikje Brill, 2003).

114 Somer, 'Defensive and Liberal Nationalisms'.

5   When Multiculturalism Does Not Fit
Kurds and Turkey in the 2000s

The heterogeneous nature of the Kurdish minority belies any simplistic characterization of the historical relationship between the Turkish state and the country's Kurds. The persistent use of policies of assimilation and integration has, counterintuitively, facilitated a great deal of fragmentation in terms of the political orientation, social status, and economic power of Turkish citizens across a range of ethnic identities. For example, tension remains between Zaza and Kurmanci, Alevi and Sunni, conciliatory and radical, western and eastern, religious and Marxist Kurds. In these circumstances, contemporary ethnic projects built around the assumption of a simple binary between 'Turks' and other ethnic groups such as the 'Kurds' in Turkey fail to capture the complex and dynamic nature of a nation which is more than the sum of its ethnic components.

In spite of the heterogeneity that marks out Turkey from other multinational countries, Turkey's political discourse perpetuates the idea of this binary, and there is strong pressure to transform the country's central administration by devolving power to separate Turkish and Kurdish blocs. In Turkey, political culture is increasingly being defined by cultural politics, and, in this changing environment, the justifications put forward for the country's transformation have much in common with the arguments put forward in ethnocentric multiculturalist theory.

Turkey's transition from the denial to the recognition of minorities has involved the emergence of multiculturalism as a significant, if limited, discourse in the country. However, as this chapter shows, the politics of recognition and multiculturalism have not been able to accommodate or respond to the in-group differences that exist among the Kurds in contemporary Turkey. Their sole focus on ethnic distinctions is problematic because, as Sandel argues, '[t]e principles of justice that specify our rights do not depend for their justification on any particular conception of the good life of one culture or another',[1] but on the fundamental principles of freedom and equality. In the discussion that follows, the problems that have emerged in Turkey are assessed in order to identify in local and general terms the value and limits of ethnocentric multiculturalist approaches.

As we saw in Chapter 2, two fundamentally different perspectives exist on how to secure positive outcomes for national minorities and the state in the Turkish context. One is the egalitarian perspective which favours the persistent application of a difference-blind approach at the constitutional level; the other is the kind of ethnocentric multiculturalism that stands for cultural freedom and the elevation of particularistic identities to the point where they form part of a decentralized body politic. Whereas the former view yields itself to a type of civic nationalism that inevitably favours the culture of the dominant language, the latter view becomes translated into the kinds of ethno-cultural and often essentialist minority nationalism that can violate the freedoms and equalities of the minority's own population and create further polarization between cultural groups.[2]

Proponents of these competing nationalisms in Turkey try to justify their positions by criticizing each other for having violated the fundamental principles of liberalism. The model of difference-blind egalitarianism/ assimilationism is problematic because, by ignoring cultural differences in public life, it can negatively impact people's enjoyment of their supposedly equal opportunities. It is also highly debatable as to whether the alternative model of ethnocentric multiculturalism can realistically bring equality and/or freedom to Turkey.

The discussion that follows shows that strong ethnocentric multiculturalism leads to further inequalities and limits the freedom of people within the very minority it seeks to empower. It also explains why Turkey actually needs a more moderate multiculturalist politics of recognition that is equally sensitive to the problems generated by equality and cultural freedom. Moderate multiculturalism offers a third way which combines the strengths of the two approaches, which are inadequate when applied on their own.

Part I Multiculturalism in Turkey: From Denial to Recognition

The increase in support for multiculturalism in Turkey has been informed both by the presumption that homogeneity in the public sphere is destructive of ethnic particularities, and by the view that differences cannot be restricted to the private sphere. Turkey's constitution suggests explicitly that differences should be kept within that sphere and should not be reflected, or made subject to regulation, in public life. In these terms, the public domain is understood as a space in which everyone has equality of opportunity and in which people do not have to compete on cultural grounds.

This conventional view of the Turkish situation, adopted in state offices, has been highly criticized by the country's libertarian scholars.[3] Demographic information also suggests that the Kurds represent a large unassimilated minority which has not been integrated into the mainstream in the same absorptive fashion as other ethnicities in Turkey. Sizeable, yet 'not assimilated', the Kurdish minority becomes subject to categorization by multiculturalists in the group of national minorities that they believe should be given self-government rights.

Turkey, as we saw in Chapter 4, is a country in which ethnic differences have been subordinated to the concept of Turkish citizenship in public life, and 'the republic clings to its imagined monolithic identity',[4] despite ongoing expressions of Kurdish identity. Yeğen claims that '[b]etween 1924 and 1990 the Turkish state denied this aspect of the Kurdish question, perceiving it primarily as a social issue generated by the endurance of backward social structures and even occasionally as a security concern posed by foreign rivals'.[5] However, since the 1990s, Turkey has seen a gradual increase in the recognition of Kurdish identity as well as a remarkable change from what was previously known as a denial policy. Moving 'from the culture of politics to the politics of culture' under the pressure of the European Union, Turkey is considered to have 'undergone a remarkable change toward a better liberalism' in the early 2000s.[6] The application of differentiated cultural rights for minority groups was prescribed by the EU as a mechanism for reducing the extent of cultural inequality in Turkey and as part of attempts to develop democracy.[7]

It is important to clarify that the EU does not have a consistent and agreed definition of what constitutes a national minority, and neither does it envisage a standard minority regime that could be applied to all member countries, the minority policies of which vary considerably. Nevertheless, the EU has introduced minority rights as a condition of its enlargement process, and it implicitly accepts the terms and policy advice established by other international organizations such as the Organization for Security and Cooperation in Europe (OSCE) and the Council of Europe: in fact, the conventions and reports of these organizations are referred to as decisive in the European Commission's progress reports on candidate countries. In its 2009 Progress Report on Turkey, the Commission of European Communities – an executive body of the European Union – made its concerns explicit: 'Turkey has not signed the Council of Europe Framework Convention for the Protection of National Minorities or the European Charter for Regional or

Minority Languages. There is a need for a dialogue between Turkey and the OSCE High Commissioner on National Minorities'.[8]

The protection of linguistic minorities in candidate and member countries became more important with the issuing of the Copenhagen OSCE Document in 1990 and the Council of Europe's European Charter for Regional or Minority Languages in 1992. In these documents, members and candidate members of the EU were advised to allow the use of minority languages in public education and services. According to Article Fourteen of the Framework Convention for the Protection of National Minorities, 'states should endeavour to ensure adequate opportunities for being taught in the minority language or for receiving instruction in this language'.[9] Even these linguistic rights were deemed insufficient by Joost Lagendijk, the co-chair of the Turkish-EU Joint Parliamentary Commission when he suggested that 'Turkey should consider regional autonomy to help solve its Kurdish problem'.[10,11]

In compliance with multiculturalist policies, these views have been repeated by many of Turkey's intellectuals. Hirant Dink, an important thinker in Turkey, stated that

Throughout history almost every geography has [this kind of] a multicultural environment in which the cultures have lived together, but it has recently been accepted that multiculturalism requires more than this; since it is vital to recognize the different beings and specific rights derived from such an existence. Indeed it is what the politics of multiculturalism tries to achieve, so in this respect it is different from the concepts of pluralism and difference, which have no historical dimension and can emerge at any time.[12]

Another intellectual, Beyaz, claimed that

the State should recognise the identity, linguistic and cultural rights of the Kurds, take measures for Kurdish children to be taught and educated in their own language and for the promotion of Kurdish culture and by taking into consideration the historical and regional conditions, the state should constitute autonomous self-government regions for the Kurds in places densely populated by Kurds.[13]

In order to meet the minority criteria required for accession to the European Union in 2002, Turkey reformed its policies to allow the teaching of minority languages in private institutions. Moreover, one of the state-funded national television channels, TRT6, today broadcasts on a twenty-four-hour basis solely in Kurdish.[14]

A comprehensive content analysis of the mainstream nationalist Turkish daily newspaper, *Hürriyet*, from 1984 through 2003 (Figure 1) confirms the claim that '[s]ince 1999 mainstream discourse has been undergoing a transformation that prepares a basis for liberal nationalism... Comparison between the periods of 1984–1998 and 2000–2004 shows

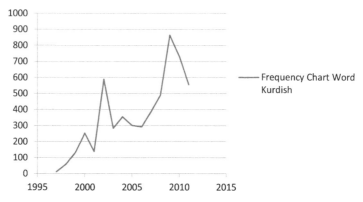

Figure 1. Number of articles using the word 'Kurdish' 1997–2011[16]

that there has been a considerable shift in the mainstream discourse in the sense that non-security (social and identity- and human rights-related) aspects of the Kurdish issue have become considerably more visible'.[15] The following analysis of the articles that appeared in *Hürriyet*'s daily news between 1997 and 2011 also shows that the cultural dimension of the Kurdish question has become more visible than the security concerns that previously dominated the debate on the Kurds in Turkey.

The increasing visibility of the Kurdish question – its cultural dimensions, and possible liberal solutions – in the media and public debates and discourse has been accompanied by a series of policy reforms.

Policy Reforms

First of all, 'the Extraordinary Situation Region (*Olağanüstü Hal Bölgesi*, or OHAL) designation was lifted from the last two provinces of southeastern Turkey where it applied; the death sentence was abolished; and some early, partial steps towards freer broadcasting and education were implemented'.[17] The AKP adopted five laws in 2004 and 2005 to empower regional assemblies and municipalities and introduced a radical shift in the relationships between central and local administration to bring them in line with the standards set out in the European Charter of Local Self-Government (Article Eight).

In 2005, it was clear that the government was planning to change official state policies towards the Kurds in Turkey. In a speech on August 12, 2005, in Diyarbakır, Erdoğan expressed the view that 'The Kurdish problem is my problem too ... we will relax this area. Turkey has always looked through the security window; we will look through a different window'.[18] This was the start of a reform process that then led to the Democratic Opening in 2009.

On July 29, 2009, the Democratic Opening process began with the interior minister Beşir Atalay announcing that a 'broadening and strengthening of our citizens' democratic rights' would take place 'ensuring that each of our citizens, wherever they live, feel themselves to be equal and free individuals of the state'.[19] That same month, the National Unity and Fraternity Project (NUFP) was launched with a view to opening a debate in Turkey that would enable 'the different segments of society to confront their problems and formulate solutions'.[20]

On August 1, 2009, Atalay met up with a group of intellectuals and journalists from different backgrounds to discuss the National Unity and Fraternity Project. They were consulted by the government on how the Kurdish question could be effectively solved and '[t]he optimism that day was reflected by veteran commentator Hasan Cemal, a leading Turkish proponent of a Kurdish compromise, who said that 'this is the first time the Turkish government approaches the Kurdish problem so seriously'.[21]

In April 2010, the bar on the use of all languages other than Turkish in elections was also lifted, invalidating the strict rules introduced by the 1961 Law on the Basic Regulations of Elections and Electoral Rolls, No. 298, which had stressed that 'in principle, political parties and candidates should use Turkish for electoral propaganda'.[22] Several ministers in the government also made declarations in the Kurdish language, and abolished legal barriers that had blocked the foundation of TV channels that would broadcast in Kurdish for twenty-four hours a day. The state allowed places in the southeast region to be renamed with their old Kurdish names, and commercial activities and advertisements conducted in Kurdish are now not uncommon. On April 12, 2012, Erdoğan declared that the Kurdish language and the Ottoman tongue would be taught as elective courses in the curriculum. Sabanci and Bilgi universities now teach elective courses on the Kurdish language, and the Higher Education Institute has even approved the opening of a Kurdish Language and Literature Department in the State University of Mardin Artuklu.

The government made important initial steps in a peace process with the country's Kurdish minority when, at the start of 2013, it announced talks with the captive PKK leader, Abdullah Öcalan, in a bid to end the protracted armed conflict with the PKK. On January 31 of that year, the president signed Law 6411, the Law on the Amendment of Criminal Procedure, which enabled defendants to 'use their preferred language in courtroom testimony during specified segments of their trials . . . That same month, the *Kurdistan Communities Union (Koma Civakên*

Kurdistan – KCK)[23] – the umbrella political organization of the PKK-defendant and former mayor of Batman, Nejdet Atalay, gave the first-ever defense in Kurdish'.[24]

On April 9, 2013, the Grand National Assembly established a Parliamentary Investigation Committee which was charged both with seeking ways to achieve a peaceful society and with assessing the solution process; its work resulted in a final report on its findings and policy advice. Other positive developments at this juncture included the lifting of severe restrictions on the disseminating or reporting of statements by illegal organizations (Article 6/2, Anti-Terror Law), and the scope of the crime of 'making terrorist propaganda', set out in Article 7/2 of the Anti-Terror Law and Article 220/8 of the Turkish Penal Code, was also narrowed.[25]

On July 10, 2014, the Grand National Assembly, Turkey's parliament, adopted Law 6551 on Ending Terror and Strengthening Social Integration. Among its six articles, Article Two sets forth the government's overall responsibilities in terms of how it carries out measures to implement, control, and organize the process. These include:

- determining the steps to be taken in political, legal, socio-economic, psychological, cultural, human rights, security, and disarmament fields and on related issues, in order to end terrorism and strengthen social integration;
- making decisions on such actions as contacting and opening a dialogue with domestic and foreign individuals, institutions, and organizations and appointing the individuals, organization, or institution that will perform this work;
- taking measures to ensure compliance on the part of members of an armed organization who give up their weapons and resume normal life.[26]

However, this transformation, which to some extent complies with the expectations of those who see group rights as a remedy to injustices in diverse societies, did not bring about either peace or equality in Turkey. The *Partiya Karkerên Kurdistan* (Kurdistan Workers' Party or PKK) maintained the conflict at a time when the state had abandoned its policy of forced assimilation, and radical members of the Kurdish cultural group remobilized and increased the extent of ethnic conflict when the state started to recognize their cultural identity within public discourse. Obviously, there are some further levels of recognition which might be accessed, such as the establishment of autonomous regions with legislative powers and the establishment of state-funded education in the mother tongue. The pro-Kurdish HDP, for example, specifies these self-government demands and goals in its 2015 party program/section 'Democratic Autonomy' – *'Demokratik Ozerklik'* – as follows: 'Kurds will govern their internal affairs and assume greater responsibility and control over the decision making that affects their communities. They will use their mother tongue in state-funded education and public offices. Local governments in the Kurdish region will have law making powers, the autonomy and accountability for their own structures and financial arrangements'.[27] It is these levels of recognition that the Kurdish nationalists keep demanding, and in their view the lack of these rights justifies their continued recourse to violence.

Part II In-Group Differences and the Difficult Politics of Recognition

Recognition is undoubtedly a matter of justice, but it cannot be reduced to that alone, since it operates within a more personal psychological domain, and requires the unique bonding of two subjects, which will necessarily be different every time.[28]

The politics of recognition is predominantly informed by a responsive understanding of what recognition entails; that is to say, its proponents tend to assert that there is an authentic self that is waiting to be recognized.[29] To recognize someone in a responsive sense is 'to acknowledge them as they already really are... The demand for recognition in a response-model is produced and justified through pre-existing characteristics of a person... [By contrast,] in the generation-model it is the act of recognition itself which confers those characteristics onto a person through their being recognized as such. The former is a case of person "knowing", whilst the latter is a case of person "making"'.[30] However, any attempt to secure the recognition of identified differences in a responsive way and institutionalize them on these terms is misleading because 'our individual identity is not constructed from within... Rather, it is through dialogue with others that we negotiate [generate] our identity'.[31] There are multiple 'others' that change depending on context, and so there cannot be only one 'self' available to recognize across time and place.

Given that we each have more than one pre-existing characteristic, recognition depends on which characteristics are to be recognized. Like any other form of nationalism, minority nationalism does not only consist of claims to social and cultural identity; it also represents an affirmation of the importance of a certain likeness above all others. We need to ask, then, why a selected likeness has been chosen as the single definition of the political community in question. When the subjects who make up a group have their own differences and conflicting interests, as well as commonalities other than the overarching identity marker, we should understand the reason why these other commonalities among members do not matter, or why all internal distinctions and conflict cannot prevent the binding marker of group identity from becoming singularly and politically relevant. The answer lies in 'the significant other'.[32]

What is distinctive about a group can only be explained in relation to its 'significant other', and, in order to identify this other, our focus needs to move from the 'authenticity' of the group to the contexts within which individuals collectively develop a sense of distinctiveness around one specific difference. This phenomenological understanding of the self encourages us to look at the context and sources of motivation which lead people to prioritize one particular sense of belonging. In applying this dialogic perspective to the Kurdish case, we have to look at the ways in which the 'Kurdish ethnic group' is defined in relation to its significant other. In Chapter 4, an analysis of the historical relationship between Kurds and the state in Turkey showed that the Kurds per se did not represent the significant other of Turkish identity until the 2000s. Turkishness has most often been defined by the dominant social group as a citizenship category that exists on an ideational level; any group formation on the basis of ethnicity was strictly prohibited rather than crystallized and stigmatized. Assimilation was the main method used to promote a homogenization agenda which was deployed with the aim of moulding all differences into the single form of Turkishness.

This process of assimilation is identified in the conventional literature on the Kurdish question as the primary cause for Kurdish nationalist radicalization and the politicization of ethnicity.[33] This view has also been supported by a theoretical account of the ways in which 'the denial of recognition provides the motivational and justificatory basis for social struggles'.[34] The existence of any such relationship between assimilation and social struggle, however, would leave us unable to account for why there was no mass Kurdish struggle at any point between 1938 and 1984. It seems, then, that 'the present paradigm of the assimilation-resistance-assimilation model in respect to ethnic conflict remains less than satisfactory to explain the Turkish case'.[35] The same paradigm also fails to explain the persistent and increasing levels of social struggle and conflict on the part of the Kurds at a time when their identity is being recognized and accommodated by the state.[36]

The 'assimilation-resistance-assimilation' model presumes that the assimilation process poses a challenge to the very existence of the subject's identity, and that therefore the subject who senses the danger of extinction will develop a motivation for social struggle. Not only does this model fail to account for long periods of relative peace in Turkey's past,[37] but it also encourages confusion between additive assimilation and the type of cultural annihilation which can only occur when the culture of origin and the receiving culture into which one is expected to assimilate are mutually exclusive.

Those who want to reverse assimilation policies are often swayed by the erroneous idea that Kurdishness and Turkishness represent mutually exclusive categories and form a binary opposition. Almost all scholars of liberalism in Turkey who think of Kurdish and Turkish identities in this way have advised the government to reverse the assimilation process and recognize ethno-cultural distinctions. Their demand for recognition becomes identical with a demand for a body politic in which each social segment will have its own sphere of authority, allotted on either a territorial or a functional basis. However, this kind of view is not viable on the basis of any analysis of the historical trajectory of assimilation in Turkey. The heterogeneity that it produced both within and across ethnic groups has important implications for the contemporary politics of recognition. There is no such thing as a single overarching category of Kurds, all of whom have been excluded on the basis of their ethnicity per se and have merged around that identity in response to their exclusion. Proponents of 'reverse assimilation' can only interpret its absence as a sign of the supposed immaturity of the minority's societal culture; that immaturity is regarded in turn by so-called liberals in Turkey as the outcome of the unjust historical discourse of assimilation which they think should be reversed. The societal effects of the historical narrative are often dismissed as independent variables when the merits and flaws of liberalism and group rights in Turkey are being discussed. This is because liberalism, in the minds of radical minority members and some liberals in Turkey, is wrongly identified with the opposite of everything done by the state in the past. Their definition of unfairness is informed, dominated, and blinded by their hatred of historical injustices and everything associated with them. It is already a widely accepted fact that state nationalism in Turkey has been illiberal. What follows focuses not on that issue but on the heterogeneity that it has created and what that phenomenon means for multiculturalism's prospects in the country.

The coming section is an account of the heterogeneity in Kurdish societal culture. This part suggests that only by way of showing what these in-group differences are can we go further to explain the injustices that a generative model of recognition is bound to create in Turkey. The data about these differences and the societal order in which we operate is drawn from my fieldwork in eastern cities of Turkey, including Diyarbakir, Mardin, Tunceli, Bitlis, Van, and Hakkari, that I visited twice between 2009 and 2011. I also had less structured informal interviews in the western cities of Istanbul and Izmir during the same period; another important source of information is the broader survey researches done by KONDA research institute in 2006 and 2010. The rest of the chapter visualizes group differences among the Kurds by graphics using data from these other surveys that have a more extensive sample size than my own fieldwork has yielded.[38] More importantly, the outcomes of my ethnographic fieldwork and semi-structured interviews will feed into my critical analysis of these quantitative survey results on the topic. It is not the primary claim of this book to simply provide original demographic data with regard to the Kurdish population in Turkey. The book rather criticizes other quantitative works, some of which have been used to establish misleading correlations between ethnicity per se and political support to the Kurdish movement based on such data. This critical approach is manifested often latently but consistently throughout the book. Nevertheless, what follows will also provide more explicit information about my own fieldwork and response issues I encountered so that it is easier to contextualize the discussions more vividly.

Speaking about politically sensitive issues in the region has always had its difficulties, but the beginning of what was assumed to be a reform process in Turkey as of 2009 seemed to have put the worries of Kurds at ease to some extent back then, and the correspondents who participated in the research themselves explicitly stated that they were now much more enthusiastic to speak about their problems and demands than ever. However, the fieldwork proved that the Kurds, especially the female members of their community, were much more open to talking to me in the company of a female assistant who speaks their own language than other times when I was on my own. They were also much more responsive when I was introduced to them through friends and family than formal connections such as *muhtars* who are state officials in small districts.

These were the lingering signs of distrust to the state and to patriarchy that is still deeply felt by Kurdish women within their own community. For this reason, I promised that the identity of all the correspondents and local people who assisted me during my fieldwork will be kept confidential. I have deliberately avoided talking to the politicians and the militia in the region, whose agendas were already clear to me through their party manifestos, speeches, and publications.

My intention was to speak to a diverse group of ordinary people who self-identify as Kurdish and who experience their ethnic identity in many ways that are different from the one that is dictated and monopolized by either the Turkish state or the political elite (HDP) and militia (PKK) who claim to represent them. This was the motive behind my sampling. As shown in this chapter, the members of the Kurdish community like any other community have multiple identities, and their perception of discrimination and their likelihood of supporting Kurdish nationalist movements depend on how their multiple identities intersect with each other and how they are being treated by different actors, including their own ethnic community leaders as well as the state authorities. Mindful of this, I talked to Kurds from as many different backgrounds as possible and controlled for their identity marks including gender, age, income, religion, education, and marital status. The sample was drawn through stratified and cluster sampling procedures[39] to reflect this diversity. The semi-structured interviews with the participants were intended to understand and document how those multiple and intersectional sources of their identity might be shaping their experiences and expectations from the current political discourse in Turkey. The interviews have also included questions on how those expectations then inform their political behaviour. I conducted semi-structured interviews with 203 people in 2009 and 135 in 2011 in the cities of Diyarbakir, Mardin, Tunceli, Bitlis, Van, and Hakkari, which are predominantly populated by the Kurds. Of the 338 informants, 180 were female, 60 were educated to university level; 135 participants were on minimum wage and 80 were below it, while the rest were financially 'comfortable' in their own terms. Of all the correspondents, 228 said they followed Sunni Islam; 156 of these identified with Shafi Mazhap and the rest said they were Hanafi. Ninety-two correspondents were Alevi, 3 were Yazidi, and the rest – a very small minority – were agnostic. I also talked to the Kurds from LGBTQ community in Istanbul and Izmir who were doubly marginalized by their own ethnic community and the state officials back in their hometowns.

My case selection – why I chose the cities I visited and not others – was also determined by my intention to geographically reflect this complex diversity within the Kurdish community.

For example Tunceli (Dersim) is known to have a big population of Alevi Kurds who are disproportionately represented in the Kurdish Movement. As such, their loyalties are volatile and split between the Kurdish political movement and other secular parties such as the CHP, which got 56.2 per cent of the vote in the city in the 2011 general election. Especially as of 2015, in order to gain popularity among Turkey's Kurdish conservative Muslims, the HDP is promoting a 'Pro-Kurdish democratic Islam'[40] rather than secularism, and this seems to have further alienated Alevi Kurds from the Kurdish movement, leading them closer to other secular parties. When visiting the city of Tunceli (Dersim) it was my intention to account for the voices of the Alevi minority.

The historical tribal (*asiret*) relations in the Kurdish community are also still relevant in modern Turkey. For example, those members of the Barzani *asiret* who are supporting fundamentalist Islamic groups such as the Kurdish *Hizbullah* and the HUDA-PAR (Party of *Allah*) against the Kurdish nationalists – HDP and the PKK – live in and around the city of Hakkari. Although the HDP won the 2011 general elections in the city, these Islamist groups have since prompted worries of intense conflict between the Islamist and nationalist Kurds as well as between different *asirets*. Long after my fieldwork, there were clashes between the supporters of Huda-Par and HDP on October 6 and 7, 2014, which led to the death of 50 people. My aim in visiting Hakkari was to capture those voices and intra-group tensions that got lost in the elections and were evidently driven by factors other than ethnicity in the city.

Similarly, Bitlis is predominantly a Kurdish city where the majority nevertheless voted for the Islamic AKP in the 2007 and 2011 elections. The Kurds of Bitlis are known to have conservative and religious affiliations, which therefore made them supportive of the Islamist parties. This was a sign that the Kurdish identity is multifaceted, and ethnicity is not always and primarily a politically relevant determinant. My visit to the city was intended to explore this complexity.

Mardin is one of the most culturally diverse cities in Turkey, where Kurds live side by side with Arabs, Turks, and Christians. Although it is not predominantly a Kurdish city, the Kurdish movement here is relatively strong and finds political support amongst the residents of the city, no matter what ethnic backgrounds they might belong to. This means that the Kurdish movement is not merely an ethno-cultural phenomenon, as people of other origins have also come to support the Kurdish cause for societal reasons that are not necessarily or merely about ethno-cultural rights. My visit to Mardin was to expose those circumstances in light of which the Kurdish struggle was clearly not only a fight for cultural freedom. It was also a quest for equality that matters to all and not only to those who are ethnically Kurdish.

The Kurds in Contemporary Turkey: Additive Assimilation and a Conflict of Interests

As Chapter 4 established, Turkishness has been defined by the constitution as a category of citizenship and, as such, it has been internalized by a huge number of minority citizens in the country. Most people from different ethnic groups have refused to be identified as a

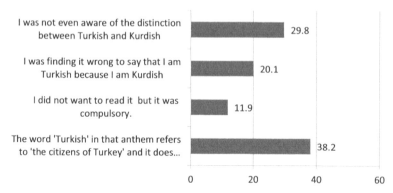

Figure 2. Q: You know it is compulsory in elementary schools to read an anthem every day, which starts as follows: 'I am Turkish, I am honest and I am hardworking'. How did or does it make you feel?

minority because of their clear understanding that a minority in Turkey must refer to a group of second-class citizens who are deprived of fundamental rights on the basis of their differences from the majority. In fact, 38.2 per cent of Kurds in the southeast and in central-east Anatolia claim that their ethnic Kurdishness is in no conflict with their Turkishness, as long as the latter is defined as a category of citizenship; 29.8 per cent of them implied that their Kurdishness and Turkishness form a binary opposition which has only recently been inaugurated (Figure 2): it is not a binary they understood to exist during their childhoods. Only 32 per cent of eastern Kurds refuse to accept Turkish identity in any form, while 68 per cent of eastern Kurds do not see their ethnicity and Turkishness by citizenship as mutually exclusive categories.

The Kurds' varying perceptions of Turkishness are also reflected in the variety of demands that they have in relation to education in their mother tongue. Of Kurds, 82.1 per cent want education in their mother tongue,[41] but what they understand by this varies considerably. Fifty-six per cent of the Kurds who demand this type of education think of it in terms of an optional language course which would be offered alongside Turkish, while Turkish would remain the medium of instruction in all taught courses (Figure 3). Only 19 per cent of Kurds in the region claim that all grades of education should be taught in Kurdish.

I had many open-ended conversations with Kurdish people in the region, and these discussions revealed that, while they believe that their demand for cultural recognition is represented by the BDP (Pro-Kurdish Peace and Democracy Party), its leaders' insistence on education in Kurdish for children in all grades does not, in fact, represent the interests of

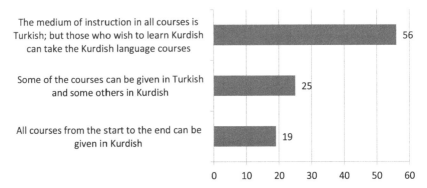

Figure 3. Q: What do you think is meant by 'education in mother tongue' when Kurdish politicians refer to it in their speeches?

the majority of Kurds who think that a positive future for their children will depend on their ability to use Turkish well. Gültekin suggests that '[m]ost Kurdish couples speak Kurdish between themselves but the communication process in Kurdish is cut off when they communicate with their children at home; they speak Turkish with their children in order to support their school life and future interests'.[42] Among the many like-minded people (especially women) I spoke to, one explained that

Most of the children in the region already speak Kurdish as it is their mother tongue. Those Kurds who want education of all grades in Kurdish desire to develop a societal culture in Kurdish; their wish is not to be recognized as such; they want to live in that language and for this reason they need to institutionalize the language in a way that everyone here in the southeast can ultimately live without a need to speak and write in Turkish at all. I believe that majority of the Kurds think that their children need to learn Turkish as well so that they can have equal chances in education and job market all over the country.

The discourse which wrongly claims that Kurds all have the same demands in relation to issues of autonomy and education also claims that all Kurds are financially worse off than their Turkish neighbours. However, the picture is not as clear-cut as it looks. Kurds are diverse in terms of their economic positioning, and those of them who are in worse-off groups are not directly disadvantaged because of their ethnicity but because of other systematic injustices they have been exposed to, such as regional disparity, armed conflict, and forced migration.

Ahmet Icduygu, David Romano, and Ibrahim Sirkeci argue that 'economic disparities can cause people to develop a heightened awareness of their class or regional identity. But because the southeast of Turkey is both the poorest region and the only predominantly Kurdish part of the

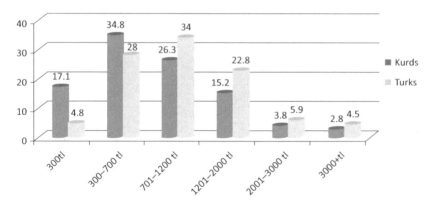

Figure 4. Distribution of ethnic groups by income per month (Turkish lira)

country, economic disparities lend themselves particularly well to heightened, politicized ethnic identity formation'.[43] According to statistics, 29 per cent of Kurds live under the poverty line, whereas the figure for Turks is around 20 per cent.[44] The reason why this sense of economic disadvantage is felt more deeply among Kurds than Turks is that the majority of those Kurds who live under the poverty line are concentrated in the southeast region. This strongly suggests that the economic dimension of the problem is regional rather than ethnic, but the discourse of differentiation and the politics of grievance erroneously suggest that there is a causal relationship between ethnicity and economic deprivation.

It is important to note that economic deprivation is not purely a regional problem for the Kurds living in the southeast; it is also relevant for the millions of Kurds who live in the poorest neighbourhoods of the big cities in the western parts of Turkey. Their problems, too, are more attributable to armed conflict and forced migration than ethnicity per se. Another key factor is the fact that most Kurds had to leave their hometowns when they were not fully prepared to survive in new urban settings. As a result, they have often had to take on low-skilled jobs upon their arrival in the west, and, in most cases, their children could not even attend schools. Many of those Kurds who were forced to leave their hometowns and migrate to the west were therefore left economically vulnerable for generations to come.

The survey results illustrated in Figure 4 reveal that there is an economic disparity between Turks and Kurds, but the disparities between them as ethnic groups are smaller than those that emerge when different income groups within the same ethnicity are compared. Wealthier members of the Kurdish population, regardless of their ethnicity, have

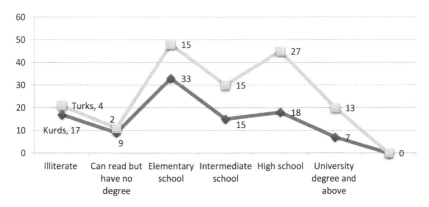

Figure 5. Education by ethnicity (per cent)

quite often managed to climb to positions of influence and affluence in Turkey. It is worth remembering that economic disparity cannot be explained in terms of Kurdish ethnicity alone because none of the country's categories of better-off people are populated exclusively by members of the dominant Turkish ethnic group.

In fact, research on education and income inequality in Turkey suggests that the income disparity between Turks and Kurds can best be explained by their differentiated access to education:

There is a wide gap between the educational levels of the poorest and richest socioeconomic groups in Turkey. For example, in 1987, 53% of the lowest income quintile had a primary school leaving certificate while this ratio was less than 40% for the richest quintile. Only 0.75% of households with a university degree belonged to the lowest quintile in the same year. These ratios got even higher over the years as the share of households with primary school completion, which is in the poorest segment, rose over 56% whereas the ratio of university graduates in the same category declined to 0.5%. Within the richest portion, households with university educations started to have a share of almost 28% in 2005. The numbers suggest that higher educational levels are associated with higher incomes.[45]

This argument is also supported by research based on different levels of educational attainment. The percentage of illiterate Kurds is almost identical to the percentage of Kurds in the lowest income bracket (see Figures 4 and 5). Figures also suggest that educational opportunities, such as income and material sources, have not been available exclusively to one ethnic group or another. It is, however, true that those who could not secure equal access to education also made up the lowest income group, and this in turn made them less likely to invest in the education

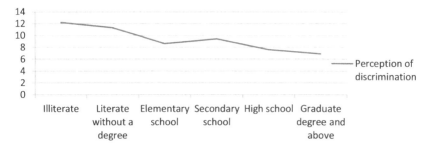

Figure 6. Perception of discrimination and education level amongst Kurds (per cent)

of their own children. Those Kurds stuck in this vicious cycle of injustice were also found to be the group with the deepest sense of being discriminated against in Turkey (Figure 6).

The recognition of linguistic differences by the state is a matter of justice because it affects equal access to education. It is, however, misleading to depict the problem as being only to do with ethnicity and then to formulate solutions on the basis of that criterion alone in order to promote the ethnic character of the body politic. Any such approach is problematic because it overlooks the fact that equal access to education is obstructed by factors other than ethno-linguistic differences. As research has shown, access to education seems to be associated more closely with family income and class differences than with ethnicity.

As Figure 7 shows, 37.8 per cent of Kurds think that improvement in their economic conditions is the most important remedy required to make things better for all Kurds in the region.

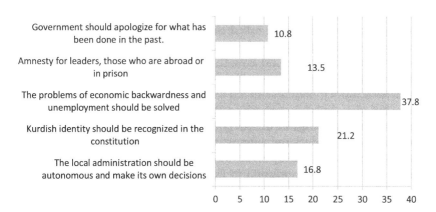

Figure 7. Q: What should the state do to satisfy the Kurds?

Freedom of Exit for the Kurds

No authority should impose cultural membership on a person with reference to where he or she is born. It also means that a person must be totally free to leave his or her cultural group and to join any group of his or her own choice, i.e. the 'freedom of exit and association'.[48]

Education in the mother language represents a very problematic issue for multiculturalism in Turkey because of questions about its capacity to provide children from different ethnicities with equality of opportunity to exit from their ethnic communities. Scholars who stress the importance of 'freedom of exit' assert that decisions about the language of education should not be left solely in the hands of parents. This is because freedom of exit is only possible if people who want to exit a minority group are well equipped to use that option. As education is the only means to attain the qualifications that open the exit door, the state should make sure that education is provided in the language that gives the largest number of people access to the largest range of the opportunities available in the body politic.

It is not uncommon to come across the legal opinion that the state may, and indeed should, step in when the autonomous parents' cultural interests limit the capacity of their children to enjoy their liberty.[49] This view is usually rebuffed by minority groups whose members argue that parents' decisions on educational issues cannot limit their children's freedom because children can leave the community of their mother language when they become mature enough to do so. However, as has been noted in earlier chapters, the parents' interest in sending children to schools where the medium of instruction is in the mother language, and their freedom to direct their children's education in this way, would realistically decrease the children's subsequent opportunities to leave.

Given that the societal culture of the Kurdish community is not yet developed to the extent expected and required by ethnocentric theories of multiculturalism, the experience of a full education in all subjects through Kurdish would prevent children from enjoying the opportunities made available within Turkey's broader society. As this problem is contingent on the lack of a full societal culture and one might be developed over time, this might not be a problem in the future, but, to make this possible, there must be a gradual implementation of multiculturalism with the minority language first becoming available as an elective course on Turkish curricula. While this is indeed what is currently happening in Turkey, this approach creates other difficulties because radical nationalists in the minority group react to moderate multiculturalism as just another manipulative way in which the state is seeking to integrate Kurds into the mainstream community.

Radical minority nationalists have a tendency to exacerbate a conflict in their bid to gain what they ultimately want, and language is one issue around which they can organize their efforts. Evidence shows that the 56 per cent of Kurds who want to have Kurdish only as an elective course far exceeds the 19 per cent who insist that education should be provided at all grades in Kurdish. Even if everyone is given what they want in this context, the development of a societal culture of the kind necessary for the foundation of a stronger multicultural regime is less likely when such a small number of people are willing to use the Kurdish language at every stage and in every part of their lives.

The only strategy that radical nationalists can follow is to try to win the support of minority members, and any means they use to this end involves them in promoting an environment of insecurity, fostering a sense of injustice, or increasing the minority's alienation from the broader society. The next chapter returns to this point in order to assess the feasibility of moderate multiculturalism; it also considers the possibility that the current situation in Turkey could evolve into a more positive one under a more robust multiculturalist regime. First, however, it is important to explain two remaining ways in which ethnocentric multiculturalism limits freedom in Turkey.

The Stigmatization of Kurds and Diminishing Self-Respect

Social Identity theory argues that individuals choose to affiliate with social groups primarily because such affiliation serves to enhance their self-esteem.[50] From the inter-subjective perspective, self-esteem cannot be generated from within because '[i]t is through dialogue we negotiate our identity'.[51] What dignity Kurds can derive from political recognition will be dependent on the image of Kurdishness which is generated by that politics in the eyes of the majority. If the recognition and prioritization of Kurdish ethnic particularity in the political sphere creates inequalities and injustices as noted earlier in this chapter, then the idea that Kurds can derive self-respect from this collective image becomes seriously questionable.

The politics of recognition may be more likely to create new stereotypes about the minority than to liberate its members. There is evidence of the emergence of these new stereotypes in the increasingly popular Turkish view that Kurds are responsible for escalating the conflict, and, as an outcome of this stigmatization, the military conflict between the PKK and Turkish armed forces has almost turned into a civil war.

In October 2011, thousands of civilians attacked the pro-Kurdish BDP centers in Bursa, Eskisehir, Konya, and Erzincan to protest against the PKK's killing of twenty-four soldiers in Hakkari. At the present time, most of the Kurds in Turkey's western cities complain that they are increasingly stigmatized in daily life just because people tend to think that any Kurd who is proud of being Kurdish must necessarily support the PKK. This might not be a problem in an ideal context where members of different groups live in their own societal cultures under territorially concentrated self-governments, but, given that almost 40 per cent of Kurds are scattered across the country, this seems to be quite a problem.

It is important to acknowledge that stigmatization is not merely a consequence of the assumption that all Kurds support the PKK. Although members of the lowest income groups in Turkey are a mix of Turkish and Kurdish people (see Figure 4), the discourse of differentiation means that a correlation between income and ethnicity is generally assumed to exist. The politics of recognition has produced as one of its side effects a general presumption that the majority of Kurds are poorer than their Turkish counterparts. Some Turks blame 'the poor' Kurds for increasing crime rates, and this whole discourse fuels increased ethnophobia.[52]

Stigmatization of the Kurds has also been heightened by some of the television series which have been made since the early 2000s. Although they were not long-running, *The Valley of Wolves Terror* (*Kurtlar Vadisi Teror*, 2007), *Code Name* (*Kod Adi*, 2006), and *Deaf Room* (*Sagir Oda*, 2006–2007) all focused on the state's intelligence activities and on the organization and activities of paramilitary groups. '*One Turkey* [*Tek Turkiye*, 2007–2011], *Sakarya Firat* (2009–2013), and *Sefkat Hill* [*Sefkat Tepe*, 2010–] featured soldier-heroes fighting against Kurdish guerrillas in defence of Turkey ... thus depicting the Kurdish question from a militarist perspective'.[53] In such series, armed Kurdish groups and their supporters are portrayed as uncivilized and rural and are associated with brutal practices such as forced marriages and honour killings. Although in reality such things happen all around the country and are carried out by people from all ethnicities, these TV series are misleadingly creating the impression that only Kurds perpetrate these kinds of crimes.

The Essentialism and Reification of Kurdish Identity in Modern Turkey

Multiculturalism involves a reductive sociology of culture that risks essentializing the idea of culture as the property of an ethnic group or race; it risks reifying cultures as separate entities by overemphasizing the internal homogeneity of

cultures in terms that potentially legitimise repressive demands for cultural con-
formity; and by treating cultures as badges of group identity, it tends to fetishize
them in ways that put them beyond the reach of critical analysis.[54]

As was argued in the previous chapter, state nationalism in Turkey has
been informed by ideas like equal citizenship, patriotism, and rights on
the one hand and by a resort to religion as a source of mobilization on
the other. Over time, a secular, ethnicity-blind, civic and French formu-
lation of nationhood in Turkey has been supplanted by religion, which
offers a surer way to mobilize support. The Kurds, who belong to the
same religion as the rest of the population, have always been incorporated into the system on the basis of this commonality. The outcome
of their inclusion can be observed in a survey completed in 2010 which
shows that the most important source of identity that binds people, and
especially the Kurds, to Turkey is now religion; according to the same
survey, almost half of all Kurds tend to identify with Islam before their
ethnicity. This figure is reflected in the fact that almost half of all Kurds –
even those in the southeast region and those scattered across the country – vote for the AKP, which is a pro-Islamic party. Its program strongly
resonates with religious Kurds, and the party had seventy-five Kurdish
MPs in its cabinets in 2007. After the AKP's electoral victory in 2007,
Emine Ayna, who was a Kurdish nationalist DTP MP, commented that
'Whoever becomes an AKP candidate is not a Kurd, even if she says "I
am a Kurd"'.[55]

It is not only nationalist activists who get to determine who is, or is
not, a Kurd; the dominant narrative also shapes answers to this question.
Zaza people, who assert that they are not Kurds, are treated as traitors
by radical Kurdish nationalists, and when I made a visit to the city of
Tunceli this narrative was affirmed by the Zaza people I spoke to who
stated in the strongest terms possible that their Zazaki (Alevi Kirmanci)
identity is distinct from a Kurdish one. This assumption of difference
was also evident when the city of Elazig, which has a large Zaza population, organized a very well-attended protest against 'PKK terrorism' on
October 24, 2007. The participants, many of whom were Zaza Kurds,
shouted, '"We are all Turks, we are all Mehmets" [a generic name given
to soldiers of the Turkish Army]'.[56]

Theories of multiculturalism cannot in themselves be accused of
encouraging essentialism, and it is true that political actors hold most
of the responsibility for the practices and consequences that arise from
their adoption. Yet the problems inherent in multiculturalist theory are
deeper than is often suggested, and they do not only concern the ways
that political actors arbitrarily interpret and use multiculturalism in

practice. The contexts in which decisions are made about the constitution of specific ethnic groups are hugely important. In situations
where a group's definition and boundaries have not been established by
group members themselves from an inter-subjective perspective, external
actors, for the sake of expediency, create the group they set out to serve,
and the decisions they make about group composition, identity, needs,
and solutions have far-reaching implications. As Jennings points out,
'[t]he question of who has the right to self-determination complicates
the principle. On the surface, it [self-determination] seemed reasonable:
let the people decide. It was in fact ridiculous because the people cannot
decide until somebody decides who are the people'.[57] We must, however,
accept that some groups are defined by their members having a deeper
sense than other groups of togetherness, consent, and willingness to be
recognized as a coherent whole. As I have argued before, people's sense
of collectivity is entrenched as strongly as, and for as long as, they are
defined as 'the other' by their significant collocutor.[58]

Ethnocentric multiculturalism is more likely to result in the essentialization of ethnicity when the 'group' at stake has not already
been defined as 'the other' by the system. Phillips explains that
'[m]ulticulturalism . . . solidifies differences that are currently more fluid,
and makes people from other cultures seem more exotic and distinct than
they really are. Multiculturalism then appears not as a cultural liberator
but as a cultural straitjacket'.[59] This is clear in the Kurdish case, where
multiculturalists reduce the multiple identities of the Kurdish minority's
members to one single identity in order to further their political aims.
According to their view, members of the Kurdish group are seen as Kurdish before anything else. Kurdishness is understood to come before religion, sex, profession, ideology, family position, or any role around which
they might define themselves. Of course, this need not be a barrier to the
other things that they can be, but if the creation of their group identity is
primarily dependent on the prioritization of this ethnic distinction, the
discourse that arises means that people are primarily represented by their
ethnicity. For example, a meeting of intellectuals in this kind of culture
becomes more likely to be referred to in an ethnically marked way as a
meeting of 'Turkish and Kurdish intellectuals'.[60]

This trend can be observed in surveys in which the opinions of Kurdish and Turkish respondents about discrimination are attributed to their
ethnicities. Those Kurds who think that they cannot live their identity
because legal barriers restrict them comprise less than one quarter of
all Kurdish people in places where Kurds represent the majority. Half
of the Kurdish respondents in the region think that they either can live

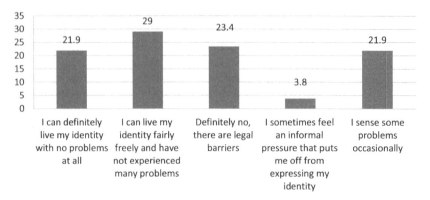

Figure 8. Q: Can you live out your identity freely?

their identity in fair circumstances or do not have any problem in living it at all.

Survey outcomes like those shown in Figure 8 are shaped by the discourse of division and often lead us to think that respondents who say that they cannot live out their identities fully are saying so because they are Kurdish. A more accurate analysis requires us to develop an awareness that people attributed to the Kurdish group are not only Kurds but also hold other identities that might be subject to discrimination in society. LGBT people and Alevis form some of Turkey's other marginalized groups, and a Kurd's sense of deprivation might be informed by an additional affiliation to any one of the other identities that are subject to exclusion and marginalization in the country. Identity has multiple components, and the definition of the 'self' changes depending on contexts in which one particularity becomes more relevant than others in relation to the 'significant other' that 'the self' is constructed around.

The opposite case is also true: if we only look at those Kurds who say that they can live without any problem, we cannot infer that these Kurds are not stigmatized or that they are fairly free to live out their 'Kurdish' identity. The information they provide can be interpreted as evidence of the existence of Kurds who define their identity primarily with the Sunni form of Islam, which has always been financed, maintained, and promoted by the state. These people may well feel that they can live their identity freely. What is important in either case is the point that not everything a person does or says should be attributed to their Kurdishness or Turkishness. This is an especially important issue in Turkey where 'Turks', who have been indoctrinated since the foundation of the

Republic with the idea that Turkishness is a category of citizenship, are now forced to define that citizenship in ethnic terms in relation to Kurds. The feasibility of multiculturalism is complicated, then, not only by Kurds who resist it, but also by Turks who refuse to acknowledge an ethnic interpretation of their identities. Emina Ayna, who is a hard-line politician in the faction led by Öcalan (the PKK's founder and now its honorary leader), insists that the constitution should use a language in which the country's people are referred to as the 'citizens of Turkey' but not 'Turkish'. This claim yields itself to the suggestion that Turkishness is a category of ethnicity and not of citizenship. Apparently, minority activists are not only dictating who is Kurd and who is not; they are also seeking to define who is a Turk. In refusing this ethnic conceptualization of their identity, the majority of the people in Turkey blame the nationalist Kurds for creating false categories and fuelling psychological warfare.

Part IV Can Multiculturalism Bring About Equality in Turkey?

Ethnocentric multiculturalism is not only problematic for minorities who want their freedoms and dignity to be respected. The politics of recognition it promotes also has the potential to create further inequalities for members of the Kurdish community as well as for other citizens in Turkey. People's understanding of injustice is informed by their sense of discrimination, which in turn derives from inequalities, and people who feel discriminated against will tend to fight against the systematic injustice that affects them. Equity theory suggests that 'people strive for justice in their relationships and feel distressed when they perceive an injustice'.[61] According to this view, the main motivation for human action and conflict is fairness rather than self-interest, which is often perceived to be a primary motive. Even those people who prioritize freedom over equality use the rhetoric of justice in the sense that they claim to be 'equally' free to live their culture with the same freedoms as everyone else in their society. If multiculturalism is not able to promote equality, then – it is argued – people's demands to be free from the system that generates these inequalities will persist and intensify. Calls for freedom will gain momentum because ongoing inequality will serve as a source of motivation and as a means of justifying conflict. An egalitarian analysis of multiculturalism in Turkey needs to be undertaken, not just so that equality can be promoted as a good in itself, but because it is vital to leverage equality as a source of motivation for people to opt into Turkey's political system.

The slow transition from the denial of minorities to their recognition in Turkey has added new inequalities to the ones it has failed to resolve. The following section uses empirical evidence to explore inequalities that have the potential to exacerbate the worsening conditions and problems faced by the Kurds in Turkey.

Multiculturalism, Kurds and Intra-group Inequalities

Multiculturalist theory is most commonly interpreted in practice through the granting of self-government rights to national minorities in the form of regional autonomy. Article Ten of the European Charter for Regional or Minority Languages, which concerns administrative authorities and public services,[62] also indicates that minorities should be able to use their mother tongue within the borders of their local or regional authorities, as recommended by Article 2 (1) of *the Draft European Charter of Self-Government* drawn up by the Council of Europe's Congress of Local and Regional Authorities of Europe (CLRAE).[63]

As noted earlier, the AKP adopted five laws in 2004 and 2005 to bring the dynamics between central and local administrations in line with the standards set out in the European Charter of Local Self-Government (Article Eight). However, they did not succeed in addressing the issues related to the inequality faced by Kurds for several reasons.

First of all, self-government rights in the form of regional autonomy (legislative or administrative) cannot provide all Kurds in Turkey with the same opportunities to maintain their cultural identity while they engage in public discourse. The strategy of granting regional autonomy does not succeed in giving people proper representation because it fails to recognize that '[c]ultural groups are not undifferentiated wholes but associations of individuals with interests that differ to varying extents'.[64] In Turkey, 52.1 per cent of 'Kurds' choose not to prioritize regional autonomy and believe that 'the only way (of solving the problem) is to end terrorism'. No Kurdish leader can represent the interests of all of a minority group's members. This was made clear by the reaction of Kurdish people when members of the DTP refused to condemn the PKK, a radical organization that used to demand a separate homeland for Kurds in southeastern Turkey.

The PKK was involved in a fight against armed state forces that caused the deaths of more than 30,000 people through guerrilla attacks. Most ethnic Kurds in Turkey did not vote for the DTP because it was seen to be supporting the PKK's violent tactics, and '[i]n 2007's parliamentary elections ... the AKP (Justice and Development Party) managed to collect 56 percent of the Southeast's votes. Even in Diyarbakır, considered

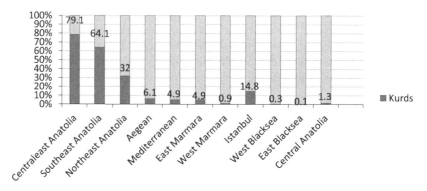

Figure 9. The ratio of Kurds to other groups by region

a DTP stronghold, the AKP took 41 percent of votes, up from only 16 percent in the previous general elections in 2002'.[65] Clearly, the Kurdish leadership in Turkey does not always represent the majority of Kurdish citizens, and any move to grant that leadership the right of veto in relation to the whole minority group may constitute a violation of the rights of conciliatory Kurds to make decisions about their futures.

Another reason why the ethnocentric approach and the regional autonomy solution it entails cannot work in Turkey is because of the dispersed demography of Kurds. Through its assimilationist or acculturative government policies, the Turkish state intended not to exclude but to integrate the Kurdish population into the rest of the community. Kurds themselves were willingly moving to the western provinces from the 1950s onward in order to secure better employment opportunities and better economic conditions. After the armed fighting between the PKK and military forces started, a large number of villages inhabited by Kurds were vacated for security reasons. The exact number of Kurds who were internally displaced is not known with certainty, but the official estimate produced by the Turkish government in 1998 suggests that about 350,000 people were affected.[66] As a result of this evacuation process, the Kurdish population became relatively dispersed, and, although some cities are still intensively populated by Kurdish people, the overall population in Turkey is quite mixed (Figure 9); therefore it is not possible to assume that there is a clear distinction between cities dominated by different ethnic groups.

According to the social structure surveys conducted by the KONDA Research and Consultancy Institute in 2006 and 2010, 1,571,000 Kurds live in Istanbul compared with 618,000 in Diyarbakır. It is clear then, that the greatest number of Kurds live in Istanbul, not in Diyarbakır:

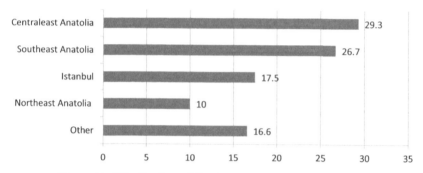

Figure 10. Distribution of Kurds by region

'The level of the Kurdish population in Istanbul is striking, demonstrating the high percentage of ethnic mixing among society and how inseparable ethnic groups are'.[67] The survey shown in Figure 10 also calculated that 66 per cent of Kurds live in northeastern, central-eastern, and southeastern Turkey, while 34 per cent are dispersed across the country.

The distribution of Kurds by region and their ratio to people of other ethnicities in their region of residency show that, even in areas where they comprise the majority, approximately 30 per cent of the population is still made up by people from non-Kurdish ethnic groups.

This suggests that regional autonomy in southeastern Turkey would give its Kurdish residents rights that could not be enjoyed by Kurds who live in other areas. If regional autonomy was granted, Kurds who lived under the authority of the new regional administration would be able to use their mother tongue in public life and schools, while Kurds elsewhere would be prevented from enjoying those same rights. Moreover,

Map 1. Turkey – map by region[68]

Table 1. *The tendency of Kurds to move away permanently, by region*

	Istanbul	Aegean	Eastern Marmara	Western Anatolia	Mediterranean	Neareast Anatolia	Centraleast Anatolia	Southeast Anatolia
Yes	19.1	18.5	6.9	25.0	8.3	10.3	13.0	10.1
Depends on conditions	35.1	25.9	17.2	25.0	33.3	51.7	53.2	26.1
No	41.5	51.9	72.4	47.2	52.8	37.9	31.2	60.3
Have no idea	4.3	3.7	3.4	2.8	5.6	0.0	2.6	3.5

(Column header spanning: Would you like to move away from this city or village for good?)

the KONDA survey indicated that, unlike those Kurds who could not integrate into the socio-economic life of the cities to which they moved years ago, more than half of Kurds now feel settled in western cities and would not be willing to move away from them.

As Table 1 illustrates, the percentages of Kurds who answered 'no' to the question, 'Would you like to move away from this city or village for good?' were 41.5 per cent in Istanbul, 51.9 per cent in the Aegean, 72.4 per cent in Eastern Marmara, 47.2 per cent in Western Anatolia, and 52.1 per cent in the Mediterranean.[69] This raises the issue about what would happen to these people if regional autonomy was to be declared in the southeast. Kurds who already live there would benefit from the advantages of the federal solution at no cost, while Kurds with good jobs and homes in the west would have to move away and risk losing their jobs in order to enjoy the advantages of regional autonomy. Autonomy does not represent an equal opportunity for all Kurds, some of whom are already integrated into the socio-economic life of the country.

Regional autonomy is an ill-advised proposal because it is arguably likely to create further inequalities among the Kurds. In economic terms, those Kurds who are already integrated into the community are unlikely to need or seek regional autonomy as much as Kurds who do not currently have equal access to socio-economic opportunities. Meanwhile, the educational and vocational opportunities that many Kurds lack are more likely to emerge from the targeted use of state investment than from regional autonomy.

Socio-economic disparities represent the biggest inequality problem that Turkey faces. Demographic studies show that southeastern and eastern Anatolia are the country's most underdeveloped regions, and consequently local Kurds living in these lands have been most affected by material difficulties and illiteracy. There is no doubt that the state should increase the extent of its investment in underdeveloped regions in order to increase equality among citizens who live in different areas of the country, but the multiculturalist solution offered by self-government is unlikely to enable the state to remedy this regional inequality. Granting such public rights to a distinct cultural group in a deeply diverse society would erode any sense of solidarity among communities. If the sense of solidarity disappears, democracy cannot function properly. This problem is convincingly explained by Stilz, who draws on Rousseau's view of freedom in an egalitarian state:

Rousseau offers us one kind of controversial answer to these problems: he claims that in order to legislate generally and impartially on one another's behalf, the citizens of a democratic state must share a special bond of identity, one that motivates them to show concern for the freedom and welfare of their compatriots. In Rousseau's view, in order to legislate impersonal laws – laws that will truly protect each citizen's freedom equally – each citizen must be capable of taking up the viewpoint of the general interest or common good, a perspective that requires solidarity with her fellow citizens.[70]

A common language is an important mechanism for developing this feeling, but the use of that mechanism is challenged by ethnocentric multicultural discourse which diminishes any sense of solidarity by placing subgroups in their autonomous regions, separated along the lines of ethnicity. Further problems arise because of the fact that the state needs the majority's support to increase the budget it has available for rectifying regional disparities. When members of the majority lack fellow feeling for separatists, they are unlikely to have any inclination to help meet the needs of self-governing minority groups and regions.[71]

A striking example of this problem was evident in the aftermath of the destructive earthquake which struck the Turkish city of Van in 2011. The city was densely populated by Kurds, and the earthquake struck just after twenty-four soldiers had been killed by the PKK. The public outrage which was generated by the increasing cost of terrorist attacks spurred hostility towards the Kurds, even at a time when they were in desperate need of help in the recovery phase. The aid transferred to the region was immense, but an increasing number of anti-Kurdish groups openly expressed contempt for the tragic event and the damage it caused in Van.

The Kurds who live in Turkey's eastern cities appear to be much more vulnerable to humanitarian crises than their contemporaries in Turkey's western cities, but the kind of social solidarity they require may well be diminished if ethnic distinctions are emphasized and used to promote the autonomy of different groups within the state. Furthermore, the inequalities that exist between Kurds who live in different regions of Turkey help to undermine fellow feeling even within the Kurdish ethnic group. Those Kurds who live in the western parts of the country are not as vulnerable to or affected by the economic implications and disadvantages of the autonomy solution as their counterparts who live in the east.

The intra-group inequalities which can arise from differentiated multicultural rights are not limited to the unjust consequences of the ethnocentric regional autonomy proposal. Multiculturalists and the pro-Kurdish HDP also propose the permanent use of minority languages in public services, and egalitarians believe that if this solution was applied in Turkey it would also cause intra-group inequality within those minorities that accommodate linguistic, religious, or racial subgroups. These subgroups should ideally have an equal opportunity to represent and shape their cultural community, but, in practice, cultural communities are usually dominated, recognized, and identified by the characteristics of the subgroup(s) that has or have the greatest power in terms of size and capacity. This tendency is evident in the Kurdish community where the rights of the Zaza-speaking minority are overlooked while the Kurmanci-speaking majority is treated as if it represents an undivided and organically whole Kurdish cultural identity.

The exact number of Zaza people in Turkey is not known because the last census which noted ethnic affiliation was conducted in 1965 and people who declared their ethnic language as Zaza were recorded as Kurds. Since then, different surveys have provided some idea of the approximate number of Zaza people in Turkey. The most detailed social structure surveys, performed by the KONDA Research Company in 2006 and 2010, indicated that 8.6 per cent of the 50,000 respondents who were randomly interviewed across the country in 2006 identified themselves as Kurdish, while 0.41 per cent defined themselves as Zaza. This data suggests that Zaza speakers constitute at least 5 per cent of the Kurdish-speaking population in Turkey. The 2010 survey suggested that this ratio might be higher by as much as 10 per cent.

As an outcome of assimilative policies in Turkey, Kurds who already speak different dialects of the Kurdish language would not be in a position to generate a common understanding of belonging. Today, the Zaza- and Kurmanci-speaking groups in the Kurdish community can barely communicate with each other because '[t]here are substantial differences between Zaza and other Kurdish dialects'.[72] This fact became evident when a remarkable number of DTP parliamentarians from a Zaza background failed to understand the speech of their leader Ahmet Turk when he spoke in the Kurmanci dialect. A Zaza member of parliament,

Ayse Tugluk from Diyarbakır, stated that 'I could hardly understand the speech; some of us do not even know Kurdish at all'.[73] Sellahattin Demirtaş from Diyarbakır, Ayla Akat Ata from Batman, Şerafettin Halis from Tunceli, and Sabahattin Tuncel from Istanbul experienced the same difficulty. This is a clear indicator of the substantial differences that exist between the Zaza and Kurmanci subgroups of the Kurdish community in Turkey, and it proves that it would be unjust to equate the linguistic identity of the Kurds with the dominant dialect of Kurmanci speakers, although they are more numerous and better represented than the Zazas in public discourse.

When the state-owned channel TRT6 broadcast most of its programs in the Kurmanci dialect, the Zaza group understandably complained on the grounds that their right to media access in their mother tongue had been ignored and their dialect was becoming extinct.[74] However, their demand for a separate TV channel in the Zaza language raised important questions about the viability of providing all subgroups with differentiated cultural rights in public life. The case of the Zaza people, whose culture and language were subordinated to the broader Kurdish cultural community in a multicultural discourse, illustrates that the protection of one cultural minority may inadvertently perpetuate inequality between subgroups within that minority. In this respect, 'the state also indirectly partakes in the ongoing process of redefining the established traditions that constitute a group's nomos',[75] and thereby loses its neutrality.

Multiculturalism and Inter-group Inequalities in Turkey

Inequalities associated with the adoption of multiculturalist policies are not only about the intra-group dynamics of the Kurdish population in isolation from other groups. As Güleç notes, 'Irrespective of the discourses of democracy and human rights that the different groups use, they fight for their own political interests and concerns, not for the general interests of the society. This is a general weakness of identity politics and has its own reflections in Turkey, too'.[76]

The multicultural paradigm supported by the EU and the Council of Europe requires states to provide their minorities with certain linguistic rights.[77] Public education and public services in minority languages are among those requirements, and in Turkey there are about sixteen distinct linguistic groups which have been settled for centuries. Table 2[78] shows the percentages of these groups in the whole population of Turkey, as they stood in 2006.

Although there are many different linguistic groups in Turkey, the EU only recommended that Turkey provide the Kurds with the right to

Table 2. *Population by native language in 2006*

Language	Per Cent as Mother Tongue	Language	Per Cent as Mother Tongue
Turkish	84.54	Balkan languages	0.23
Kurdish	11.97	Caucasian languages	0.07
Zazaki	1.01	Laz	0.12
Arabic	1.38	Circassian	0.01
Armenian	0.07	Turkic languages	0.28
Greek	0.06	Romani language	0.1
Jewish languages	0.01	Other	0.12
Western European languages	0.03	Total	100

public education in their own language. No other linguistic groups were mentioned in negotiations,[79] and this clearly raises questions about the conditions under which a cultural group is entitled to the special rights advocated by multicultural discourse.[80]

One may think the criterion for deciding whether a minority is entitled to receive public services in the mother language is its size. This would, however, undermine the premise of multicultural discourse, which is to secure equal rights for all disadvantaged minority groups. According to the theory of multiculturalism, all national minorities of adequate size (i.e. more than 10 per cent of the whole population)[81] that are capable of developing a societal culture should be given the right of self-government.[82] However, the implementation of this proposal violates the equal opportunities of people whose cultural group is too small to develop an institutionally complete societal culture. Even if the claims and grievances of a particular group warranted the application of special rights, there would nevertheless be a potential inequality between groups with a greater or lesser capacity to voice their claims. In effect, as Brian Barry points out, 'Multiculturalism (understood as normative policy implying the recognition of identity groups) is only a formula for manufacturing conflict, because it rewards the group that can most effectively mobilize or make claims on the polity'.[83]

This has certainly been the case in Turkey, where culturally distinct groups such as the Lazes, Roma, Arabs, Kurds, and Circassians are assumed by the state to have an equal right to promote their cultural identities in the private sphere. However, the Kurds – who are greater in number than the other cultural groups – have been able to mobilize most effectively to claim public recognition, and the EU's support of linguistic minorities in Turkey has only been extended to the Kurdish group.[84] After Turkey launched state television broadcasting in Kurdish, Laz, Arabic, and Georgian cultural groups demanded the same treatment.[85]

Multicultural discourse is unable to explain why certain groups are or are not entitled to differentiated rights and on what basis. This failure emerges as the root cause of the inter-group inequalities which arise when differentiated rights are awarded to members of cultural minorities. The politics of multiculturalism seems to ignore the fact that 'the liberal state should take no interest in these interests or attachments – cultural, religious, ethnic, linguistic or otherwise – which people might have. It should have no collective projects; it should express no group preferences. Its only concern ought to be with upholding the framework of law within which individuals and groups can function peacefully'.[86]

Official language policy can limit the ability of minorities to gain the benefits they would derive if public services were available in their own languages. Noting this problem, '[multiculturalist] liberals – who see this policy as unfair – often align themselves with national demands raised by 'underdogs', be they indigenous peoples, discriminated minorities or occupied nations, whose plight can easily evoke sympathy'.[87] In line with this ethnocentric multicultural logic, minorities are also understood to have the right to receive public education in their own languages. Implementation of this proposal would not necessarily prevent minority pupils from having equal access to jobs that involve use of the majority language because 'minority language speakers may be able to learn the dominant language and generally equip themselves for success in the modern economy even while receiving a significant portion of their schooling in their home language'.[88] However, it is unfair to assume that members of linguistic minorities who undergo public education in their mother tongues will have the opportunity to become as fluent in the majority language as native speakers; any such lack of fluency would constitute a disadvantage in a state where the majority language is the medium of business.

In the Turkish education system, students are required to take a central exam to enter university, and the grades achieved in this exam are the only decisive factor for admission. The exam is conducted in Turkish and requires extensive knowledge of grammar. It would be absurd to expect that seventeen-year-old Kurdish students, with no motivation other than their own will and a partial requirement in public education to learn Turkish, could be as successful in this exam as native speaker candidates.

Indeed, statistics show that, even in countries where instruction in the official language is compulsory, students from linguistic minorities are less successful than native speakers.[89] The reason for this is that there is usually no additional programme to help minority pupils when they face the official language for the first time in school. In Germany, where a similar situation sees most children of naturalized Turkish families barely speaking German at all in elementary school, the educational attainment of children educated in a minority language has been found to be relatively low: 'In 2006, out of the 12,258 students successfully graduating from gymnasium in Berlin, there were only 165 Turks, i.e. a total of less than 1.5 percent'.[90] This research concluded that additional language courses should be provided within the public education system, with teachers who are experts in both the official and the minority language helping children from non-majority language communities to improve their official language skills. This bilingual education facility, the report argued, should also be open to any other citizens who required it. This approach would be equally applicable to Turkey, where Kurdish children require extra assistance to learn Turkish when they begin their schooling.[91] However, most minority nationalists overlook the need for additional programs at the elementary-school level.

In fact, minority nationalists propose that public education should be provided in the minority language for children in all grades, despite the fact that the availability of education in the child's first language would not increase their chances of success but would rather damage their educational and economic opportunities by, for example, leaving them unprepared for college admission exams in the majority language. This outcome would constitute the liberal state's failure to deliver on its primary responsibility, which is to provide students from different backgrounds with equality of opportunities in relation to access to higher education and subsequent employment.[92] Howe suggests that the state should be concerned with the promotion of equal opportunity on a much broader scale than that recommended by multiculturalist scholars who confine their concerns to equality of cultural identity in public life.[93] 'Education is, no doubt, valuable in its own right', Howe suggests, 'but it also is *enabling* in the sense that it serves (however imperfectly) as the gateway for obtaining other societal goods, such as desirable employment, adequate income, and political power. For this reason, equal *educational* opportunity is related to equal opportunity more generally because it serves as an important link in what might be termed an opportunity chain'.[94]

Egalitarian liberalism is more concerned with equality of opportunity than with equality of identity. In Turkey's case, that goal can best be achieved if children have the opportunity to learn the official language, which gives them their best chance of achieving educational distinction and becoming fully equipped for the job market.[95] An emphasis on multiculturalism is unlikely to generate such long-term opportunities in Turkey. It is possible to argue that 'some language minorities are sufficiently large and institutionally complete [that] they constitute their own societal culture so that individual members can find a relatively full range of economic, social and cultural options and opportunities in their own language'.[96] This was exactly the case in Quebec and Flanders. However, this argument hardly applies to Turkey. Using Kurdish as the main language of education in minority public schools might seriously impact the ability of minority pupils to benefit from full participation in the country's socio-economic network. This is because the Kurdish population cannot, in present circumstances, develop its own network to the extent that it could act as a counterweight to the opportunities available in the majority language.

There are two clear indicators that Kurdish societal culture has this insufficiency. Firstly, the dispersed demography and fragmented cultural structure of the Kurdish community would make it difficult to develop an institutional network sufficiently broad to accommodate the Kurdish population's lives and careers in their mother tongue. It is striking that half of the Kurdish group leaders in parliament cannot communicate with each other, and that MPs from the DTP, such as Akin Birdal and Emine Ayna, cannot speak in the Kurdish dialect at all.[97]

Another indicator of the institutional incompleteness of the Kurdish national minority group is the low level of industrialization and of recruitment opportunities in the southeast region where some local Kurds have claimed self-government rights. Geographic and climatic hardships,[98] and the insecurity of the region following the PKK's radical activities, are among the reasons why industrial progress and employment opportunities have stagnated there.[99] These factors clearly indicate that the Kurdish community in Turkey could not develop a societal culture capable of providing a full range of socio-economic opportunities for its members in their own language. This conclusion is not adopted in order to patronize a minority; instead it arises from a careful assessment of the minority's capacity to support the full range of its members' needs and aspirations. The question as to 'whether a cultural group can be thought of as a societal culture whose practices and institutions cover a full range of human activities, is certainly a matter of degree, rather than the either/or distinction'.[100] Under current circumstances, the provision of public education in Kurdish at all grades might give Kurds some cultural freedom, but in the long term it might also prevent their children from integrating into the Turkish-speaking network which at present offers the best way for them to access a wide range of socio-economic opportunities.

Conclusion

The imposition of one official language in public education can be justified on the grounds that everyone should have sufficient knowledge of the official language to be able to communicate with public authorities, benefit equally from public services, and compete on an equal footing for education or for employment opportunities. However, even if everyone in the country is given an equal opportunity to learn the official language, there is still an older generation of people who cannot learn Turkish and so need to use their mother tongue in relations with the public authorities. 'A semi-official survey on internally displaced persons (IDPs) conducted by Hacettepe University Institute of Population Studies shows that "not speaking Turkish" ranks third among reasons for IDPs' lack of access to health services; 27.4 per cent of IDPs, the vast majority of whom are Kurds, responded positively to this question'.[101] To ensure that such people are accorded equal citizenship rights, they should be provided with services in their own language, at least on the basis of their ad hoc needs. This arrangement would not violate individual equality, as long as all citizens from different linguistic groups within the country could benefit from it.

The same logic – which ensures that difference does not become a barrier to accessing equal opportunity – has already been discussed here with reference to minority pupils who need help in their own language in order to be able to learn the official language when they first face it in elementary school. Those minority pupils who do not learn the official language at home suffer from disadvantages in the initial years of their education if they are encountering the official language for the first time. Their educational success and motivation are seriously affected by this unfair experience at the beginning of their formal education. They frequently score badly in examinations, study at worse colleges than they might otherwise have accessed, and take up unqualified and more poorly-paid jobs than their majority group peers. Kurds with poorly paid jobs subsequently have less money to invest in their children's education than those peers, and so injustice is passed on systematically to the next generation, creating a vicious cycle that perpetuates inequality between Turks and Kurds.

There are, of course, many Kurds in Turkey who break this cycle, manage to access the best educational opportunities, and reach positions of influence that many Turks cannot. However, their opportunities are often secured at the expense of their parents' freedom to speak to their own children in Kurdish. Many Kurds think they must speak to their children in Turkish to support their education in school and so slowly surrender to the domination of the majority culture in private as well as public realms. An extreme interpretation of equality is not only destructive of cultural diversity but also creates systematic inequality for those who value their cultural freedom to speak to their children in Kurdish.

The liberty of people belonging to minority national ethnic groups is violated when they are forced by the state into a civic project that is not their own. Violent assimilationist policies also have other negative effects in that they marginalize and radicalize members of minority groups, some of whom go on to become combatants who threaten the state. Research shows that those who support the violent tactics of the PKK in Turkey tend to have low levels of education and income, and a concomitant sense that they are discriminated against.[102] Denial of difference in the public realm effectively marginalizes people, then, not only because it limits their cultural freedom but also because it creates systematic injustice and a sense of discrimination. It is this injustice that most Kurds want to defeat in Turkey.

A significant number of Kurds who resist assimilation have never had a sense of belonging to the same public as the majority. Egalitarians are incapable of accounting for this reality, and their views are positively inflammatory to those Kurds whose understanding of injustice is primarily informed by their experiences of historical suppression in Turkey. They prioritize cultural freedom over equality and reject the very premises of difference-blind egalitarianism/assimilationism. The situation in Turkey offers a clear example of this dynamic at work. As in most cases where a great accumulation of historical baggage is combined with strong memories of violent conflict, it is next to impossible to find a common legitimate public objective which can serve as the single and widely shared basis for the laws that govern equality.

However, the lack of common purpose does not justify the implementation of ethnocentric multiculturalism by default. The denial of difference is not an option, but recognition, as defined by ethnocentric multiculturalism, is equally problematic in Turkey's current circumstances. Ethnocentric multiculturalism is dependent on an erroneous definition of societal culture and restricts individual freedom because it essentializes, reifies, and stigmatizes the identity it purports to defend.

In Turkey, any granting of autonomy to an ethnically defined group seems more likely to limit individuals' autonomy than to enable it. The emphasis on Turkey here might be criticized on the grounds that the fluidity of societal culture is not exclusive to one case or another. Certainly the Turkish case provides a particularly striking illustration of the idea that every group contains members who are individuals with dynamic interests and changing motivations shaped by non-ethnic particularities and contextual factors. However, what is crucial in every case is the willingness of people to put their differences aside and merge around one ethnic particularity. Multiculturalist theory's strong inclination to prioritize an ethno-cultural approach to identity seems to be derived from the observation that, most of the time, most national minority members are simply unwilling to relegate their ethnic particularity to a private discourse. Such willingness is vital to the delivery of the outcomes promised by multiculturalist theory, and therefore its absence deserves attention.

As was shown in the case of Turkey and is suggested by the theoretical literature, we cannot take for granted Kurds' consent for the ascription of meaning and value to the use of their first language in public. When it is an option, learning, using, and living in another language may be even more liberating than learning, using, and living in the language we were given by accident of birth and through our parents' choices. Yet this argument's strength depends totally on the way the receiving, assimilating culture engages with a minority. In Turkey, Kurds are accepted as peers in a society in which they are equal not only by citizenship but also in terms of the religious characteristics which are the primary differentiating factor used to define the symbolic boundary of the Turkish nation. In this context, it is quite possible for a person to preserve her Kurdish identity within private discourse and assimilate into Turkish identity in public situations.

This chapter has brought together two different types of approach to national minorities (one prizes the fluidity of societal culture, while the other values a willingness to assimilate). An inter-subjective understanding of identity, according to which the autonomous self is primarily informed by its relation to the significant other and the space that surrounds it, helps draw out the problems that each of these approaches generates. By applying this understanding of the 'self' to group psychology, the chapter has shown that when binarized categories of distinction are not readily available, any claim for recognition based on a binary has first to generate a key distinction and its meanings in a process that transforms this collection of individuals into a group. In Turkey the only difference that is readily available between Kurds and others is language, and so it has been of primary concern for elements in the Kurdish minority who claim their autonomous right to use their language freely.

The existence of a notable distinction does not by itself create a binary opposition, however. Kurdishness and Turkishness are not mutually exclusive categories, and individuals can be both Kurdish and Turkish, as long as they speak both languages, especially because Turkishness is generally defined as a broad and inclusive category of citizenship. Moreover, the level of significance attributed to the use of the mother tongue in public life is only a matter of individual choice that may be informed by many independent variables other than the value of the language as a good in itself. What is complex about the language question is that those who prioritize the use of their mother tongue in public life are dependent on the participation of others. This is because the language has a function only in a dialogical environment where one needs another person to speak to. One's freedom to use a language in public is, therefore, wholly dependent on the participation of others. As I have argued in theory and illustrated in the case of Turkey, a person's freedom to use their first language in public is wholly dependent on their ability to generate an awareness or belief that it is crucial for all Kurds to use their mother tongue in relation to the state.

This chapter has shown the ways in which the generative model of recognition associated with ethnocentric multiculturalism is bound to limit individual autonomy and exacerbate disparity. The progressive implementation of a balanced, moderate multiculturalism that is simultaneously sensitive to the cultural freedoms of groups and to the equal opportunities of the individuals within them seems to be the ideal solution in Turkey. After all, it is the primary role of the liberal state to provide an impartial system that gives individuals freedom to follow their own understanding of what is good to the utmost extent, insofar as that does not contravene someone else's freedom to do the same.

Moderate multiculturalists believe that individual freedom and equal citizenship will be enhanced further if the state adds bilingual education to its impartial system. Unlike strict egalitarians, they support the recognition of culture in the public sphere because they believe that 'formal equality in the enjoyment of the rights, do[es] not guarantee the equality of respect, access to labour markets on an equal footing or making use of the welfare measures like free health and education services ... The combination of all these factors marginalises the minorities and blocks the formation of extensive and inclusive concept of citizenship'.[103] Culture is a source of difference, and we need to take this into account in order to assess if a person can really enjoy the opportunities guaranteed by the principle of formal equality.[104]

Although this approach seems ideal, it is highly impractical at the present time. This impracticality seems to arise from the reaction of radical groups to newly introduced multiculturalist policies that liberals believe offer the most likely route to an optimal solution. The problems that have arisen after the introduction of these policies in Turkey pose an important challenge to the orthodoxy that nurturing democracy will lead to the resolution of ethnic conflict. It is still a matter of debate as to 'why the insurgent PKK (*Partiya Karkerên Kurdistan*), which was militarily defeated, which renounced the goal of secession, and whose leader was under the custody of the Turkish state, remobilized its armed forces in a time when opportunities for the peaceful solution of the Kurdish question were unprecedented in Turkey'.[105] The next chapter elaborates on this matter and uses a comparative perspective to examine the role of multiculturalism as a conflict-solving mechanism in Turkey.

Notes

1 Michael J. Sandel, *Liberalism and the Limits of Justice* (Cambridge: Cambridge University Press, 1998), 185.
2 Murat Somer, 'Defensive and Liberal Nationalisms: The Kurdish Question and Modernization and Democratization', in E. F. Keyman, ed., *Remaking Turkey: Globalization, Alternative Modernities, and Democracies* (Oxford: Lexington Books, 2007).
3 Baskin Oran, 'Linguistic Minority Rights in Turkey, the Kurds and Globalization', in G. Gurbey and F. Ibrahim, eds., *The Kurdish Conflict in Turkey: Obstacles and Chances for Peace and Democracy* (New York, NY: St. Martin's Press, 2000).
4 Omer Taspinar, *Kurdish Nationalism and Political Islam in Turkey: Kemalist Identity in Transition* (London: Routledge, 2005).
5 Mesut Yeğen, 'The Kurdish Question in Turkey: Denial to Recognition', in M. Caiser and J. Jongerden, eds., *Nationalism and Politics in Turkey* (New York, NY: Routledge, 2011), 72.
6 Hasan Bulent Kahraman, 'From Culture of Politics to Politics of Culture: Reflections on Turkish Modernity', in Keyman, *Remaking Turkey*.
7 Durukan Kuzu, 'A Self-Governing Group or Equal Citizens – Kurds, Turkey and the European Union', *Journal on Ethno-politics and Minority Issues* 9 (2010): 32–65.
8 Commission of the European Communities, 'Turkey 2009 Report', European Commission, http://ec.europa.eu/.
9 The Council of Europe, 'Framework Convention for the Protection of National Minorities, Article 14', Council of Europe, https://rm.coe.int/.
10 The commission is composed of an equal number of members from the Turkish Grand National Assembly and the European Parliament.
11 EU Turkey Civic Commission, 'EUTCC Welcomes Joost Lagendijk's Statement Regarding Regional Autonomy', EU Turkey Civic Commission, www.eutcc.org/articles/7/document366.ehtml.
12 Asli Güleç, *The Problem of Multiculturalism in Turkey within the Context of European Integration* (Ankara: METU, 2003), 163.

13 Ibid.
14 Abubakar Siddique, 'Turkey's New Kurdish TV Hopes to Win Hearts and Minds', Radio Free Europe Radio Liberty, www.rferl.org/.
15 Murat Somer, 'Defensive and Liberal Nationalisms: The Kurdish Question and Modernization and Democratization', in Keyman, *Remaking Turkey*, 123.
16 In this analysis, articles with the word 'Kurdish' have been counted. It should be emphasized that the word 'Kurdish' refers to the language of Kurds, and all the articles analyzed here focused on the linguistic dimension of the problem.
17 International Crisis Group, 'Turkey: Ending the PKK Insurgency', in *Europe Report* (Brussels: International Crisis Group, 2011), 5.
18 Ibid., 6.
19 Ibid., 7.
20 Wendy Zeldin, 'Turkey: Adoption of New Law Aimed at Ending Terrorism and Achieving Social Integration', *Global Legal Monitor*, www.loc.gov.
21 Hugh Pope, 'Turkey and the Democratic Opening for the Kurds', in F. Bilgin and A. Sarihan, eds., *Understanding Turkey's Kurdish Question* (Lanham, MD: Lexington Books, 2013), 122.
22 International Crisis Group, 'Turkey: Ending the PKK Insurgency'.
23 The Kurdistan Communities Union (*Koma Civakên Kurdistan – KCK*) is a political organization that brings together various Kurdish movements scattered across the Middle East including the PKK (Kurdistan Workers' Party), PYD (Democratic Union Party), PJAK (Kurdistan Free Life Party), and PÇDK (Kurdistan Democratic Solution Party). The organization follows and represents the views of Abdullah Ocalan – the founder and honorary leader of the PKK.
24 US Department of State, '2013 Human Rights Reports: Turkey', US Department of State, www.state.gov.
25 Ibid.
26 Zeldin, 'Turkey: Adoption of New Law Aimed at Ending Terrorism and Achieving Social Integration'.
27 Halklarin Demokratik Partisi Programi (The HDP Party Program), www.hdp.org.tr/tr/parti/parti-programi/8.
28 Eimear Wynne, 'Reflections on Recognition: A Matter of Self-Realization or a Matter of Justice?' Paper presented at the Thinking Fundamentals. IWM Junior Visiting Fellows Conferences, Vienna, 2000, www.iwm.at/wp-content/uploads/jc-09-06.pdf.
29 Cressida J. Heyes, 'Can There Be a Queer Politics of Recognition?' in Robin N. Fiore and Hilde Lindemann Nelson, eds., *Recognition, Responsibility, and Rights: Feminist Ethics and Social Theory* (Washington, DC: Rowman & Littlefield, 2003): 59–71.
30 Paddy McQueen, 'Social and Political Recognition', *Internet Encyclopedia of Philosophy*, www.iep.utm.edu/recog_sp/.
31 Ibid.
32 Alex Gillespie and Flora Cornish, 'Intersubjectivity: Towards a Dialogical Analysis', *Journal for the Theory of Social Behaviour* 40, no. 1 (2010): 19–46.

33 Welat Zeydanlıoğlu, 'The White Turkish Man's Burden: Orientalism, Kemalism and the Kurds in Turkey', in G. Rings and A. Ife, eds., *Neo-Colonial Mentalities in Contemporary Europe: Language and Discourse in the Construction of Identities* (Newcastle upon Tyne: Cambridge Scholars Publishing, 2008).

34 McQueen, 'Social and Political Recognition'.

35 Metin Heper, *The State and Kurds in Turkey: The Question of Assimilation* (Houndmills, UK: Palgrave Macmillan, 2007), 2.

36 Güneş Murat Tezcür, 'When Democratization Radicalizes: The Kurdish Nationalist Movement in Turkey', *Journal of Peace Research* 47, no. 6 (2010): 775–89.

37 Güneş Murat Tezcür, 'Kurdish Nationalism and Identity in Turkey: A Conceptual Reinterpretation', *European Journal of Turkish Studies*, no. 10 (2009): 1–18.

38 Unless noted otherwise the graphs in this chapter are based on data from the Konda Research and Consultancy 2010 survey for which the sample population is 10,393 people from 59 cities, 374 boroughs, and 902 villages of Turkey. *A Survey on Social Structure: Perceptions and Expectations in the Kurdish Question* (Istanbul: Iletisim, 2011).

39 Cluster sampling is used when the target population can be categorized easily in relation to other external groups but when the selected population itself is internally heterogeneous. For example, it is easy to establish that the Kurds living in the southeast of Turkey constitute a distinct group, because they evidently face peculiar problems that others do not experience in the rest of the country. However, the Kurdish residents in different southeastern cities also differ from each other in some respects. This sampling method is normally associated with quantitative research. However, geographical clustering was important for my qualitative fieldwork because the population I worked with was highly dispersed. Adopting this quantitative sampling rationale gave direction to my fieldwork and made my qualitative research more resource intensive than it would have otherwise been. This method is more effective where clusters are associated exclusively with some certain characteristics. However, in the case of Kurds it was not possible to associate each cluster I visited exclusively with one characteristic or another. For example the Alevi Kurds in the city of Tunceli (Dersim) generally differ from most Sunni Kurds in terms of their worldviews, but they also differ from each other within their own cluster as well as having some characteristics in common with other Kurds from across the country. I needed to reflect the diversity and breadth of the sample population. For this reason I additionally adopted the rationale of stratified sampling, which is another technique mostly used in quantitative research. This allowed me to divide the sample population into nests within each cluster by selecting particular units or cases that vary according to a key dimension such as income, education, or gender.

40 Sanem Vaghefi. 'Turkey's Kurdish Movement: in Search of 'Real Islam', *Open Democracy* (6 June 2015) www.opendemocracy.net/sanem-vaghefi/turkey%E2%80%99s-kurdish-movement-in-search-of-%E2%80%9Creal-islam%E2%80%9D.

41 Konda Research and Consultancy, *A Survey on Social Structure: Perceptions and Expectations in the Kurdish Question* (Istanbul: Iletisim, 2011), 124.

42 Mehmet Nuri Gültekin, 'Debates on Inter-Ethnic Marriages: Assimilation or Integration? The Turkish Perspective', *Papers: Revista de Sociologia* 97, no. 1 (2012): 151–66.

43 Ahmet Icduygu, David Romano, and Ibrahim Sirkeci, 'The Ethnic Question in an Environment of Insecurity: The Kurds in Turkey', *Ethnic and Racial Studies* 22, no. 6 (1999): 991–1010.

44 Konda Research and Consultancy, 'A Survey on Social Structure', 96.

45 Anil Duman, 'Education and Income Inequality in Turkey: Does Schooling Matter?' *Financial Theory and Practice* 32, no. 3 (2008): 369–85.

46 Konda Research and Consultancy, 'A Survey on Social Structure', 96.

47 There is no reliable data about the exact number of those Kurds who live in western Turkey because the census in Turkey does not include information on ethnicity. Therefore it is almost impossible to say how many of them speak the Kurdish language and how well they speak it. However my informal conversations with the people of Kurdish origin in the cities of Izmir and Istanbul revealed that most of those western Kurds who supported the BDP in the 2011 election either speak no Kurdish at all or they have very limited knowledge of the language. There is an increasing language shift within the Kurdish minority. Some analysts such as O' Driscoll even show that the Kurdish language might be on the road to extinction in Turkey, just like the Gaelic language in Ireland. See Dylan O'Driscoll, 'Is Kurdish Endangered in Turkey? A Comparison between the Politics of Linguicide in Ireland and Turkey'. *Studies in Ethnicity and Nationalism* 14, no. 2 (2014): 270–88.

48 Seyla Benhabib, *The Claims of Culture: Equality and Diversity in the Global Era* (Princeton, NJ: Princeton University Press, 2002), 19.

49 Brian Barry, *Culture and Equality* (Cambridge: Polity Press, 2001).

50 Terence Turner, 'Anthropology and Multiculturalism: What Is Anthropology That Multiculturalists Should Be Mindful of It?' *Cultural Anthropology* 8, no. 4 (1993): 411–29.

51 McQueen, 'Social and Political Recognition'.

52 Durukan Kuzu, 'The Politics of Identity, Recognition and Multiculturalism: The Kurds in Turkey', *Nations and Nationalism* 22, no 1 (2016): 123–142.

53 Kumru Berfin Emre Cetin, 'The 'Politicization' of Turkish Television Dramas', *International Journal of Communication* 8 (2014): 22.

54 Benhabib, *The Claims of Culture*, 4.

55 Tezcür, 'Kurdish Nationalism and Identity in Turkey', 5.

56 Ibid., 7.

57 Ivor Jennings, *The Approach to Self-Government* (Cambridge: Cambridge University Press, 2011).

58 Kuzu, 'The Politics of Identity, Recognition and Multiculturalism'.

59 Anne Phillips, *Multiculturalism without Culture* (Princeton, NJ: Princeton University Press, 2009), 14.

60 Somer, 'Defensive and Liberal Nationalisms', 105.
61 Melvin J. Lerner, 'The Justice Motive: Some Hypotheses as to Its Origins and Forms', *Journal of Personality* 45, no. 1 (1977): 1–52; Donald M. Taylor and Fathali M. Moghaddam, *Theories of Intergroup Relations: International Social Psychological Perspectives* (Westport, CT: Greenwood Publishing Group, 1994), 97.
62 The Council of Europe, *European Charter for Regional or Minority Languages*, Strasbourg, 5.XI.1992, Art. 10(2).
63 The Council of Europe, 'Draft European Charter of Self–Government', June 5, 1997, Art. 2(1), Centre Virtuel de la Connaissance sur l'Europe, www.cvce.eu.
64 Chandran Kukathas, 'Are There Any Cultural Rights?' *Political Theory* 20, no. 1 (1992): 105–39.
65 Yigal Schleifer, 'Religious Kurds Become Key Vote in Turkey', *Christian Science Monitor* 101, no. 7 (2009), www.aina.org.
66 Human Rights Watch Report, 'Turkey 'Still Critical': Assessing the Scale of the Problem', Human Rights Watch, www.hrw.org/.
67 KONDA Research and Consultancy, *A Survey on Social Structure: Who Are We? Turkey* (Istanbul: KONDA, 2006).
68 Nations Online Project, 'Turkey Map', Nations Online, www.nationsonline.org.
69 KONDA Research and Consultancy, *A Survey on Social Structure: Who Are We? Turkey.*
70 Anna Stilz, *Liberal Loyalty: Freedom, Obligation, and the State* (Princeton, NJ: Princeton University Press, 2009), 23.
71 Brian Barry, 'Self-Government Revisited', in D. Miller and L. Siedentrop, eds., *The Nature of Political Theory* (Oxford: Clarendon Press, 1983).
72 Mary Lou O'Neil, 'Linguistic Human Rights and the Rights of Kurds', in Zehra Arat, ed., *Human Rights in Turkey* (Philadelphia, PA: University of Pennsylvania Press, 2007).
73 Show News, 'DTP de Kürtçe Bilmeyen Kaç Milletvekili Var?' ('How Many MPs in the DTP Do Not Know Kurdish?'), Showhaber.com, www.showhaber.com.
74 Radikal Newspaper, 'Meclise Zaza, Laz ve Gürcü Dillerinde TV Kurulsun Dilekcesi' ('Petition to the Turkish Parliament to Demand TV Channels in Zaza, Laz and Georgian Languages'), Radikal, www.radikal.com.tr.
75 Ayelet Shachar, 'On Citizenship and Multicultural Vulnerability', *Political Theory* 28, no. 1 (2000): 64–89.
76 Güleç, *The Problem of Multiculturalism in Turkey*, 14.
77 See the *European Charter for Regional or Minority Languages.*
78 KONDA Research and Consultancy, *A Survey on Social Structure: Who Are We? Turkey.*
79 Commission of the European Communities, 'Recommendation of European Commission on Turkey's Progress Towards Accession', Commission of the European Communities, http://ec.europa.eu.

80 Rainer Forst, *Contexts of Justice: Political Philosophy Beyond Liberalism and Communitarianism*, Vol. 9 (Berkeley, CA: University of California Press, 2002), 133.
81 Will Kymlicka, *Multicultural Citizenship: A Liberal Theory of Minority Rights* (Oxford: Clarendon Press, 1995), 111.
82 Kymlicka, *Multicultural Citizenship: A Liberal Theory of Minority Rights*.
83 Barry, *Culture and Equality*, 21.
84 K. Yildiz, *The Kurds in Turkey: EU Accession and Human Rights* (London: Pluto Press, 2000).
85 Council of Europe, 'European Charter for Regional or Minority Languages', Council of Europe, www.coe.int/.
86 Chandran Kukathas, 'Liberalism and Multiculturalism: The Politics of Indifference', *Political Theory* 26, no. 5 (1998): 686–99.
87 Yael Tamir, *Liberal Nationalism* (Princeton, NJ: Princeton University Press, 1995), 11.
88 Will Kymlicka and Alan Patten, *Language Rights and Political Theory* (Oxford: Oxford University Press, 2003), 40.
89 Erica Black Grubb, 'Breaking the Language Barrier: The Right to Bilingual Education', *Harvard Civil Rights–Civil Liberties Law Review* 9 (1974): 52–94.
90 Björn Jungius, 'Aziz Nesin Grundschule, Berlin: A Bilingual Turkish–German Public Elementary School', Migration Online: Language and Integration, http://migrationonline.cz.
91 Grubb, 'Breaking the Language Barrier'.
92 John Rex, 'Equality of Opportunity and the Ethnic Minority Child in British Schools', in S. Modgil, G. Verma, K. Mallick and C. Modgil, eds., *Multicultural Education* (London: Falmer Press, 1988).
93 Kenneth R. Howe, 'Liberal Democracy, Equal Educational Opportunity, and the Challenge of Multiculturalism', *American Educational Research Journal* 29, no. 3 (1992): 455–70.
94 Howe, 'Liberal Democracy, Equal Educational Opportunity'.
95 Barry, *Culture and Equality*, 107.
96 Kymlicka and Patten, *Language Rights and Political Theory*, 40.
97 Zaman, '1/3 of MPs from the DTP did not understand speech in Kurdish', Haber7, haber7.com, www.haber7.com.
98 Baycan-Levent Tuzun, 'The Demographic Transition and Urban Development in Turkey', in H. S. Geyer, ed., *International Handbook of Urban Systems: Studies of Urbanization and Migration in Advanced and Developing Countries* (Cheltenham, UK: Edward Elgar, 2002).
99 A. S. Albayrak, S. Kalayci, and A. Karatas, 'Examining with Principal Components Analysis the Socio-Economic Development Levels of Provinces in Turkey According to Geographical Regions', *Suleyman Demirel University, Journal of Economics and Administrative Sciences Faculty* 9 (2004): 101–30.
100 Iris Marion Young, 'Polity and Group Difference: A Critique of the Ideal of Universal Citizenship', in Ronald Beiner, ed., *Theorizing Citizenship* (Albany, NY: New York University Press, 1995), 51.

101 Minority Rights Group, *A Quest for Equality?: Minorities in Turkey* (London: Minority Rights Group, 2007), 19.

102 Necati Alkan, 'Youth and Terrorism: Example of Turkey' presented at the International Workshop: Political Violence, Organized Crime, Terrorism and Youth, Hacettepe University, Ankara, 13–14 September 2007.

103 Güleç, *The Problem of Multiculturalism in Turkey*, 45.

104 Nancy Fraser, *Scales of Justice: Reimagining Political Space in a Globalizing World* (New York, NY: Columbia University Press, 2009).

105 G. M. Tezcür, 'When Democratization Radicalizes', 775.

6   Can Multiculturalism Really End Ethnic Conflicts?

> Multiculturalism is a set of policies designed to accommodate ethnic minorities in an equitable fashion. Another virtue of multiculturalism, as many have suggested, is that it will also bring peace.[1]

Kurdish and Turkish scholars and activists frequently draw on examples from situations across the globe in which the policies of multiculturalism have solved ethnic conflict under all sorts of different circumstances. The so-called lessons learned approach is very popular, and solutions for Turkey are most often sought through examination of Northern Irish and Basque case studies that are seen to exemplify strategies that could be used to end the armed conflict in Turkey; both case studies are generally interpreted in ways that suggest that the politics of recognition offer the best prospect for change in the Turkish situation. Most international organizations, including the European Union, concur with this approach and suggest that ethnic minorities including the Kurds should be recognized and granted self-government rights. This step, it is believed, will rectify historical injustices between national minorities and lead to the eventual resolution of a violent conflict that arises from differences in ethnicity.

It is less common for interested parties to pay attention to case studies from other situations like that in Corsica, where the policies of multiculturalism have failed to induce peace. The Irish and Basque cases draw more attention because their problems were home-grown in western Europe, have lasted longer, and have cost more lives than the Corsican situation. The fact that these conflicts have been pacified gives the impression that they are more relevant and that their solutions are more likely to be effective than the Corsican one in solving the problems that Turkey faces. The Corsican conflict was comparatively short, cost fewer lives than the situations in Northern Ireland and the Basque country, and was still causing problems as late as 2008.[2] In June 2014, the National Liberation Front of Corsica declared a permanent and unconditional ceasefire,[3] but '[a]lthough political violence has almost vanished, the murder rate remains nine times higher than in France as a whole'.[4]

The Corsican example is mostly ignored by scholars of the Kurdish question in Turkey because any points of comparison seem unlikely to yield workable suggestions for conflict resolution. However, the Kurdish armed conflict, like that in Corsica, has continued to escalate despite the government's attempts to recognize the Kurdish minority's identity in the 2000s. The presumption that the politics of recognition can end violent conflicts failed in France and has so far failed to prove valid in Turkey. This chapter explains these outcomes in detail, but it also compares the Kurdish and Corsican cases, in both of which policies of multiculturalism were accompanied by long-term ongoing conflict. The comparison reveals the circumstances that create similarities between the Kurds and the Corsicans, who actually differ greatly in many other respects.

The discussion illustrates that 'the politics of recognition' inadvertently promotes the further growth of the conflicts it is designed to settle in both Turkey and France. These countries have not been able to replicate Northern Ireland's relatively successful use of that politics to resolve a violent conflict. The analysis that follows illustrates the peculiarities of the Kurdish-Turkish conflict from a comparative perspective, and it also reflects on the bigger question about the situations in which ethnocentric multiculturalism can and cannot offer realistic opportunities for ending violent ethnic disputes.[5]

Multiculturalism and Ethnic Conflict in Turkey

In earlier chapters, we have seen that the AKP government tried to work out a peaceful and gradual settlement of the chronic conflict in Turkey by pursuing the politics of recognition in the period until 2015. The transformation the government looked for complied to some extent with the expectations of normative theorists who see group rights as a remedy to the injustices that exist in diverse societies. However, the process did not bring about either peace or equality. The PKK escalated the conflict at a time when the state had abandoned its policy of forced assimilation; radical members of the Kurdish cultural group remobilized and increased the extent of ethnic conflict when the state started to recognize their cultural identity within public discourse. Casualties increased markedly, and during the ceasefire that ran from 1999 to 2004 figures rose from 368 to 467, while in the period from 2004 to 2012 they rose from 2,728 to 4,188.[6]

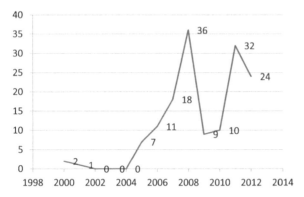

Figure 11. PKK conflict graphic 2000–2012[7]

As Figure 11 shows, PKK-inspired incidences of conflict steadily increased from 2004 onwards, and their rise was simultaneous with a period in which the AKP government continuously initiated reform policies.[8] Although there were several attempted truces, none of them could make significant progress. The PKK declared a ceasefire on April 13, 2009, but ended it on May 1, 2010. On August 12, 2010, a Ramadan ceasefire was declared by the PKK, but this ended on February 28, 2011.[9]

The conflict between the PKK and the state's armed forces persisted despite the introduction of reforms from the early 2000s onwards, and so the multiculturalist policies adopted by the AKP have hardly served as a panacea for the ethnic conflict in Turkey. It is not this chapter's aim to explain the causes of the country's ethnic conflict. Political oppression and many other factors, including the strength of the effort made by the political elite, financial resources, and geopolitics, can be of help in explaining the occurrence and endurance of the ethnic insurgency; yet none of these can fully explain why the ethnic conflict in Turkey continued in such a violent fashion at a time when there was a real chance of success for political deliberation and when the politics of recognition were closer to fruition than ever before.

It is useful to acknowledge at the outset of this discussion that the correlation between reform and radicalization in Turkey does not suggest a direct or definitive causal relationship between the two. The escalation of ethnic conflict can be attributed to many and varied causes which might well include the PKK's interests as an organization. The PKK's organizational interests and the party's commitment to its own survival have often dominated and subordinated their agenda on freedom and equality.[10] The PKK prolonged the conflict at times when reforms were being pushed forward because those reforms were offered in the context of the government's continued efforts to counter terrorism.

While members of the AKP government often expressed sympathy towards the Kurds and explicitly recognized their distinct identity in public during their reforms, their sympathy did not extend to the PKK, and during the reform period many supporters of the PKK, including politicians and activists from the Kurdish community, were subjected to a wide range of prosecutions.[11] This approach is not exclusive to Turkey; as Cunningham notes, states may accommodate the demands of some factions within divided minority groups and suppress or combat others, making it difficult to find a solution that will satisfy all parties to the conflict at the same time.[12] As of 2015, military forces claim to have killed at least 771 PKK militants in southeast Turkey and in northern Iraq; the police have also arrested around 1,600 people in nationwide operations to detain suspected militants involved in the PKK and the Revolutionary People's Liberation Party-Front (DHKP-C).[13] Both the PKK and DHKP-C are still listed as terrorist groups in Turkey, the United States, and the European Union.

It is clear that the PKK will not be supportive of the AKP-led reforms if they are not given any credit for their outcomes. This issue and any other potential causes for the escalation of conflict in Turkey between 2004 and 2009 are beyond the scope of this chapter. Instead, the sections that follow analyze the political diversity and fragmentation of the Kurdish minority that arose from its members' constant involvement in processes of assimilation; they also assess the extent to which the PKK has had to engage in the political mobilization of its own ethnic constituency in order to justify its cause. As will become clear, the politics of recognition have made an urgent and absolute priority of the need to create political cohesion within the Kurdish community.

Any presumption that political cohesion automatically exists amongst the Kurds themselves is problematic, and, at times when the state is promoting reform and cooperation, radicals often resort to conflict in order to generate intra-group cohesion around a shared sense of insecurity. One of the functions of inter-group conflict is its ability to create that kind of intra-group cohesion.[14] In such cases, a radical organization's own survival depends on a sustained level of recruitment, and so the radical movement requires popular support in order to equip itself with the human resources its organization requires.[15] As we have seen, this popular support can be guaranteed by strengthening the salience of causes that justify the radical organization's existence.[16] Mindful of this fact, radical organizations use violence as a tool to make their cultural identity a constant target for state repression. In the process, they create a strong sense of separation,[17] and they are able to whip up strong anti-state feeling among new generations and members of the minority group who, in the atmosphere created by reform, might otherwise have been likely to compromise with the central administration for various reasons shaped by their group-based and personal interests.[18] This is also in line with the findings of Kidd and Walter, who show that negotiations with the state often fuel conflicts between "moderates" and "radicals" within the insurgent groups.[19]

This mobilization strategy is explicitly endorsed in the PKK's founding declaration (1978) which states that, 'The PKK considers that cultural and social development is possible only through war. The PKK's goal is to create a people which struggle in the name of independence and freedom. Therefore, it prefers to be born in war instead of disappearing in peace'.[20] Öcalan, who was the founder of the PKK in 1978 and now serves as its honorary leader, also stated that war could serve the additional purpose of eliminating cultural and social divisions within Kurdish society. With these aims in mind, radical factions deliberately create instability in order to provoke government repression. The increasing number of PKK-related incidents in Turkey since 2004 is certainly consistent with the argument that '[government] repression on ethnic group [sic] increases disadvantages for ethnic group [sic]. The existence of collective disadvantages creates opportunities for ethnic leaders to mobilize the ethnic group for their movement'.[21]

The implementation of stronger anti-terrorism policies by the AKP government from April 2009 onwards gave the Kurds a further reason to escalate their mobilization around the radical nationalist cause after a period of reforms. It may therefore seem reasonable on some level to blame the Turkish state for the persistence of violence and ethnic insurgency; however, it is important to remember that the continuing operations of the PKK, despite reforms, and their mobilizing impact on the insurgency have cast a shadow over efforts to progress a solution process.

One example of the effects they have produced can be found in the unfortunate series of events that took place in October 2009 when '[t]he Turkish authorities and the PKK leadership had negotiated the arrival of 34 Kurds as an initial step toward the PKK's "coming down from the mountains", that is, ending their insurgency'.[22] Eight PKK fighters and twenty-six people from the PKK refugee camp in northern Iraq came and were welcomed by a group of officials from the Democratic Society Party (DTP), then the major pro-Kurdish political party, and hundreds of people marched and shouted slogans to celebrate. Their ostentatious celebrations were broadcast in the media and interpreted by the majority as the victory for the PKK. The PKK's killing of twenty-four troops near the Iraqi border on the very same day confirmed and strengthened this message.[23]

This had different implications for both Turks and Kurds but they were equally damaging to the reform process. The continuation of ethnic terror and the increase in the number of casualties despite reforms provoked nationalistic sentiments among the majority community, and this in turn damaged the feasibility of progressing multiculturalist projects. Furthermore, 'a poll showed 51 per cent of the population opposed to the Democratic Opening and . . . the AKP's popularity plunged 7.1 percentage points between August and November 2009'.[24]

Having lost support amongst nationalist Turks, the AKP drastically changed its policies towards the Kurdish question. The pro-Kurdish political party DTP was closed down on the grounds that it was associated with the PKK, and its hawkish leaders were barred from politics for ten years. The US State department noted that '[i]n 2010 the government began trying thousands of persons alleged to be members or supporters of the Kurdistan Communities Union (KCK)'.[25] The BDP (Peace and Democracy Party) succeeded the DTP, adopting the same set of goals and the same party program. Despite its name, the party has gone on to contribute to the continuous circle of provocative relationships between activists and the state. According to a BDP announcement, '7748 party executives and employees were taken into custody and 3895 were arrested between 14 April 2009 and 6 October 2011'.[26] This hostile state of affairs obstructed, at least for a while, democratic strategies for negotiating towards a pluralist democracy in Turkey.

Democratic Opening and the Rekindled Conflict

The BDP then morphed into the HDP in preparation for its bid to represent a larger constituency than the ethnic Kurds living in the southeast region. During the same period, the government was also in negotiations with the jailed rebel leader, Öcalan. It was hoped that the ongoing talks between Öcalan and the government would mark the start of a new era, named at first as the 'Solution Process' (*Çözüm Süreci*) in public. Finally, on March 21, 2013, after a series of long negotiations with the Turkish government, Öcalan's public statement calling off the armed struggle was delivered both in Turkish and Kurdish during the Newroz celebrations in Diyarbakır. On April 25, 2013, the PKK announced that its soldiers would withdraw from Turkey to northern Iraq in early May as part of a peace deal with Ankara.[27]

Yet even while peace talks were ongoing, both sides were simultaneously preparing to fight in case negotiations failed. In February 2013, one month before a number of PKK fighters withdrew from Turkey, the pro-PKK media had already proclaimed the foundation of the Patriotic Revolutionary Youth Movement (YDG-H). This transformed swiftly into an armed, urban youth militia with the capacity to lure police forces into indiscriminate street battles in the southeast. Meanwhile, the government was continuing to empower its police forces in the region and construct military outposts, dams, and roads.

During this period, the HDP won 13.1 per cent of the total vote in the elections of June 2015, an unexpectedly high result that secured them eighty members in parliament. Their success, unprecedented in the history of modern Turkey, represented an exceptional opportunity for the Kurds to move their battle to the political arena while the peace talks continued.[28] However, on July 11, just four days after the HDP's electoral victory which marked the Kurds' best opportunity for representation in parliament, the PKK declared it was ready 'to mobilise all means necessary, including the guerrilla forces' to stop the building of Turkish military outposts and dams.[29] The International Crisis Group notes that 'Since the summer of 2015, the urban conflict has been defined by street clashes; YDG-H has dug trenches and built barricades, pledging to bar police from entering "autonomous" cities and districts . . . The government interpreted this as an end to the PKK's ninth unilateral ceasefire'.[30] The YDG-H urban youth militia established its presence further and went on to declare 'autonomy' in several districts of the southeastern cities of Diyarbakır and Sirnak. In response, the government announced a regional security law that authorized and massively expanded the police force's rights to detain protesters and employ lethal force against them if necessary.[31]

Since the end of the ceasefire, most of the conflict's violent battles have taken place in urban centers in the southeast where the security forces have also issued more than sixty curfews. When negotiations to arrange a coalition government proved futile, Erdoğan called new elections for November 1 and '[t]he inter-election period was one of the most violent periods in Turkey's modern history. Between July and December 15, violence claimed the lives of 194 security officials, at least 221 PKK insurgents, and as many as 151 civilians'.[32] The increasing violence took observers by surprise because it all happened at a point when the pro-Kurdish political party had crossed the electoral threshold and had been negotiating with the ruling government for a peaceful solution.

Arwa indicates that the PKK's increasing violence was aimed in part at weakening the hand of the pro-Kurdish HDP in the eyes of Kurdish voters and showing them that future success depended on the PKK's popular support.[33] This suggests that the PKK has not just felt threatened by the AKP, but has also felt pressured by the strong emergence of the pro-Kurdish HDP. Since the HDP crossed the 10 per cent threshold in the parliamentary elections of June 2015, a deepening rivalry has become evident between the two groups. Both the HDP and the PKK have claimed credit for the electoral victory, and, according to reports in the Turkish newspaper *Yeni Safak*, 'PKK leader Duran Kalkan lashed out at HDP co-chair Selahattin Demirtas saying: "Who is he, what has he accomplished?"'[34]

The HDP's election success has been contingent on votes coming from supporters of the PKK because both groups appeal to the same constituency. However, Demirtas (the leader of the HDP) has challenged the PKK, asking the party to put down its arms and work toward a ceasefire: 'From wherever it is coming and whoever is doing it, violence must stop', he said, while also referring to the soldiers killed by the PKK as 'our sons'.[35] While both the PKK and the HDP similarly demand regional autonomy in the southeast which is predominantly populated by the Kurds, the methods they use to achieve this ultimate goal are different. The HDP, having won seats in the parliament, wants to use democratic means within the present political system, whereas the PKK uses force and violence to form de facto self-governing areas.

The legitimacy of the PKK has been debatable in the eyes of the majority of Kurds in Turkey, particularly since Kurds have seen HDP MPs making progress in pursuing Kurds' democratic rights. People have begun to question the presence of an armed group when the case for violent tactics has essentially been weakened. This trend illustrates the validity of the idea that escalating violence and a reactionary state response were necessary for the PKK to 'justify' the ongoing existence of its armed struggle.

An interviewee from Diyarbakır, Ibrahim (38), suggested that 'the support to the HDP during the June 7 elections caused a panic in the PKK because they thought their power and influence would decrease. That is why they increased the level of violence and cut the path toward legal politics'.[36] According to Çandar, a journalist who has been working on the Kurdish matter for years, 'PKK wanted the HDP to be weakened just as much as the government'.[37] One of the Kurdish interviewees in *Diyarbakır*, Welat (25), stated that the PKK's insincerity ended the process: 'They [the PKK] wanted to continue the war strategy, which is the reason for their existence and sovereignty. However, the government's wrong policies during the elections were a chance for the PKK to increase its legitimacy among people'.[38]

By provoking government repression, but also by directly attacking health and education facilities in the region, the PKK situated the Kurds in an environment characterized by insecurity and danger: the '5219 citizens, 1330 village guards, 325 public officials, and 123 teachers that the PKK killed – in Kurdish regions' are proof of this fact.[39] These developments demonstrate how 'the creation of new political spaces can threaten insurgent groups' survival and – at least in the short run – lead to insurgent violence against civilians'.[40] The climate of terror in the southeast also discourages medical doctors and teachers from taking up posts in the region because of their fear of intimidation and murder. As a consequence, the quality of the services people can benefit from in the region is reduced while the Kurds' sense of discrimination is increased. This increasing sense of discrimination in return feeds into a more aggressive approach towards the state. Minority nationalists generate this atmosphere, just as the PKK did, by accelerating an environment of insecurity and increasing the sense of victimization among their supporters.[41]

People who feel victimized are motivated to further support the ethno-nationalist cause.[42] Many Kurds are genuinely convinced that the government's approach to the Kurdish issue has changed little from that taken by its predecessors. In this climate, Kurds increasingly start to think that it is impossible to have a democratic peace agreement with the Turkish state. Indeed, research in 2016 discovered that more than half of Kurdish respondents (54%) think that the Turkish state discriminates against Kurds, and around 60 per cent of Kurdish respondents believe that Kurds in Turkey are not equal with Turks in terms of the rights, freedoms, and socio-economic status they can enjoy.[43] The same research also showed that the increasing perception of discrimination amongst the Kurds feeds their predisposition towards conflict. There is, therefore, a new trend emerging in stark contrast to those indicated in the results of the earlier surveys in 2006 and 2010, which showed that the majority of Kurds were positive about the democratic initiatives of the AKP government and felt more positive about their freedoms.[44]

There is a growing public fury towards the government in the southeast, but there is no huge sympathy towards the PKK for introducing urban warfare tactics either. On the contrary, the Kurds seem increasingly likely to hold the PKK jointly responsible for their anguish. The escalation of violence immediately after the electoral success of the HDP has reversed the discourse once again, moving its emphasis from democratization and reform to securitization. One interviewee, Mehmet (34), gave voice to the widely-held idea that the actions of the PKK have destroyed the hopes that the HDP created.[45]

In a recent research study conducted in 2016, seventy-eight out of 187 Kurds interviewed in the southeast region thought that the government's attitude was the fundamental cause of the end of the peace process, while the remainder of the respondents held the PKK somehow responsible for escalating the violent conflict.[46] Only thirty-two per cent of the respondents from *Diyarbakır* suggested that entrenchments were being carried out as a result of the need for self-defense, whereas the majority of the respondents (67.6 per cent) thought that the PKK's strategy of establishing autonomous units by forming entrenchments and barricades in urban areas was essentially wrong. Fatma (43), an interviewee from Diyarbakır, stated that 'this entrenchment policy hurts the people of the region the most. This brings more tears, suffering, deportation and exile rather than freedom'.[47]

Civil society organizations and ordinary civilians think that their voices are not being heard by either the state or the rebel groups which claim to represent them. Whereas the public has already decided on where to direct its resentment, it is yet to reach conclusions about where to turn to for help to ameliorate its predicaments. It seems reasonable to say that the Kurdish population is living, during this recent spate of urban fighting, in a state of emotional flux.[48]

Why the IRA's Success in the UK Should Not Be a Model for the Kurds in Turkey

Attempts to follow a multiculturalist agenda have so far failed to end or mollify the ethnic conflict in Turkey. However, it is still very common for scholars and journalists to make recourse to examples from other situations in which the transition to multiculturalism has brought about an end to terrorism. The devolution of power to authorities along ethnic lines has been accepted as a form of multiculturalism that can be used to end ethnic conflicts for national minorities. The 1998 Good Friday Agreement in Northern Ireland is usually seen as an exemplar of this kind of process at work and is often referred to when people look to identify an ideal solution for the Kurdish question in Turkey.[49] The Good Friday Agreement established the basis for power-sharing in Northern Ireland following decades of bloody dispute over the rights of the large Catholic minority and the Protestant majority. Parties on all sides of the religious and political divide in Belfast reached an agreement on Friday, April 10, 1998, which was designed to formulate a nationalist (Catholic) and unionist (Protestant) power-sharing government in Northern Ireland. Progress since the agreement was signed has been irregular, and

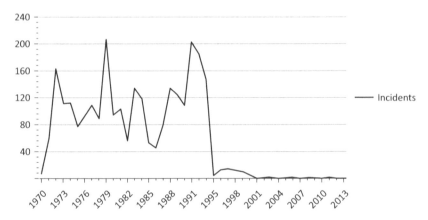

Figure 12. IRA incidents (1970–2013)[50]

many discrepancies persist, but the Belfast of today is almost unrecognizable from the violent place it used to be three decades ago.

The case of Catholic minority nationalists in Northern Ireland – unlike that of the Kurds in Turkey – exemplifies a context in which the minority's members were effectively differentiated, discriminated against, and systematically excluded from the mainstream community: Leopold observes that '[t]hroughout the existence of devolved government in Northern Ireland there were allegations of discrimination against Roman Catholics in all areas of life'.[51] The solidarity that existed within the Catholic community in Northern Ireland had been facilitated by the historical boundary that state discourse maintained between the mutually exclusive categories of Catholicism and Protestantism. John McGarry and Brendan O'Leary argued that '[f]or over a century, historic Ulster, and then the Northern Ireland that was carved from it, has been divided electorally into two rival ethno-national blocs . . . [and] there has been no swing voting between the two ethno-national blocs over the last three decades'.[52] The kinds of internal fragmentation and assimilationism experienced by the Kurdish population in Turkey were not experienced by Catholic republicans in Northern Ireland.

Once parity of esteem was guaranteed by the Good Friday Agreement, and the boundary between these ethno-national blocs was accepted as shaping the working of the body politic, the IRA no longer needed to further the violent conflict (Figure 12). In cases like Northern Ireland where autonomy is introduced as a solution, separatist nationalists do not need to continue their violent tactics as a means of mobilization. In such cases, the majority of minority members have already been mobilized by the exclusion they suffered in the past, and so any possible compromise with the state does not undermine their support for their community's nationalist leadership. It would appear that ethnic conflict situations where groups need to be mobilized from scratch are more volatile than those where the communities involved are already mobilized and co-ordinated.[53]

Sinn Féin, generally treated as the political wing of the IRA, agreed to shift the violent battle to the political level when the opportunity arose because they knew that their nationalist leadership in the political arena could not be challenged by the possibility of cooperation between its constituency and the Protestant majority. This was not the case in Turkey, where the majority of Kurds cooperated with and voted in the 2007 elections for the AKP government which had started a reform process. Feeling threatened by this development, the PKK struck again to provoke government repression and produce a heightened sense of insecurity amongst the Kurds who would, it was hoped, eventually distance themselves from the government. This pattern also explains the PKK's actions when it was threatened by rivalry from within the Kurdish movement after the HDP's success in the 2015 elections.

Many scholars remain reasonably certain that the conflict would have been solved through the kind of power-sharing and multiculturalism adopted in Northern Ireland if the Turkish state had been determined to solve the problem democratically. The situation there has arguably been durable and rewarding thanks to the strong tradition of democracy in the United Kingdom.[54] Many regard the central government's dedication to initiating self-government rights and power-sharing mechanisms for Catholic republicans as the key to success in the case of Northern Ireland. The rights granted to Catholics there have not been given to the Kurds in Turkey, and Kurds, whose group rights have not so far been addressed in the constitution, therefore still continue to fight.

It is true that Turkey has not yet achieved the status of a democratic country, and group rights have still not been introduced into a Turkish constitution that persistently places emphasis on the individual rights of its citizens. Yet, as this book has established, the introduction of multiculturalist policies has surely marked a turning point for what used to be an overly centralized state which historically secured its domination through a long series of military interventions. The AKP government, which has been conservative in terms of its use of religion in regulating social relations, has somehow been open to the idea of recognizing ethnic differences under its rule and began a transition process that has so far been nothing but a failure.

The failure of Turkey's endeavours suggests that the limited capacity of multiculturalist policies to solve ethnic conflicts might be a sociological problem as well as an ideological one. The difficult case of the Corsicans in France illustrates that a transition from centralism to multiculturalism might pose problems no matter how democratic the country in which this transition takes place. France has a strong democratic tradition, yet, as in the Kurdish situation, it is possible to see that attempts to give more autonomy to Corsica have failed in many respects to satisfy the radicals; the conflict in Corsica has continued to be a major problem in the politics of both the island and the mainland, despite attempts to increase Corsica's autonomy in a gradual process that has been ongoing since 1982.

The FLNC and Corsicans in France

During the heyday of socialist power between 1981 and 1986, the aim in Corsica was to promote ethno-cultural pluralism by protecting and developing the cultures and languages of regional minorities.[55] In 1991, further action was taken and a bill was passed to establish a regional Corsican assembly on the island. This assembly was given the authority to define and implement policies on fiscal matters and education. Although the local Corsican government has been increasingly empowered in ways that indicate compliance with the European Union's multiculturalist agenda and freedom of association, 'ethnic violence [has] increased in both quantity and intensity' during times of reform and apparent progress on the island.[56]

The historical relationship between Corsicans and France, just like that between the Kurds and Turkey, shows that political systems which have historically favoured assimilation present deep problems for the solution of ethnic conflict. Corsica is the region which has expressed the most solid resistance to French centralism for the last thirty years, and in fact represents the only other case of long-running violent separatism outside Ulster and Euskadi.

Despite the enforcement of polices of forced assimilation in France, which marginalized and radicalized a huge number of ethnic dissidents, a consistent discourse of integration there generated a high number of hyphenated identities and mixed marriages that cross ethnic and cultural boundaries between the Corsicans and French mainlanders. In France, as in Turkey, the extremely centralized state discarded both institutional and ethno-cultural pluralism in politics for a long period until the 1980s. It seems fair to say that the 'British tradition of liberal pluralism which accords places to social orders, classes, and particularistic communities, has been opposed by the unitary French conception of citizenship'.[57] Assimilation has been the fundamental method used to secure progress in Corsica for a century.[58] As a result, throughout the nineteenth and twentieth centuries most Corsicans identified with the French state. They joined the army, the police force, customs units, and other branches of the French civil service. Corsican's identification with France reached its apex during the First and Second World Wars, when thousands of islanders gave their lives for *la patrie*.[59]

In cases like those in Corsica and Turkey, it is not uncommon to see minority members cooperating with the state that has assimilated them and treated them on a par with everyone else in the country. Radical groups emerged from the 1950s onwards and fought against the French state, especially at times of economic crises, but the majority of people on the island supported none of the radical Corsican factions, the last of which was the *Fronte di Liberazione Naziunale Corsu* (FLNC). There are outstanding difficulties, but as Sanchez points out, '[w]hat complicates the situation is the divorce between the Corsican population and the separatists. The latter, along with policy makers in Paris, want to separate France and Corsica (to what degree is still a disagreement nevertheless), but the Corsican people wish to maintain strong ties with the mainland. France, being as unique as it is, has the awkward situation where both the government and a group of separatists (most of them criminals in disguise who run the island with a "mafia-style" system) want a similar objective, and it is the civilian population that resists it'.[60]

There are similarities here with the opinion held by 62.5 per cent of Kurds in Diyarbakır who described as banditry the violent actions of the Kurdish Patriotic Revolutionary Youth Movement (Kurdish: *Tevgera Ciwanen Welatparêz Yên Şoreşger*, Turkish: *Yurtsever Devrimci Gençlik Hareket*, YDG-H), which is closely affiliated with the PKK.[61] Like the Zaza Kurds in Turkey, who aligned with the Turkish state and marched in protest against the PKK, '25,000 Corsicans marched through the streets in favour of French unity in December of 1984. Their banners read: 'No to Separatism, No to Terrorism'.[62] In the election which was held immediately after the establishment of the Corsican Assembly, the separatist candidate was able to secure less than 13 per cent of the vote.[63] The Corsican minority nationalists, like their radical Kurdish counterparts, constantly need to make ethnicity a politically relevant distinction, especially in times when relative liberalization threatens to render cultural boundaries less problematic for most members of the minority community.

For example, in December 1999 and January 2000 the main Corsican separatist groups agreed to a 'ceasefire' in order to let elected Corsican officials hold a dialogue with the government. In July 2000, the government and Corsican officials reached an agreement that would give more legislative power to Corsica's elected officials, and although the ceasefire was still in effect there were several bombings in Corsica after the July agreement was reached. The Global Security Organization notes that 'On 18 June 2003, in Yvelines, France, militants from the Corsican National Liberation Front (FLNC) detonated explosive charges. In 2004, the Ministry of Interior reported that 154 people were arrested in connection with the steady number of low-level explosions that have occurred on the island of Corsica since the 1950s. In general, the explosions target symbols of French government authority. Attacks on the French island of Corsica were up approximately 38 percent in 2006, totalling over 225'.[64]

It is possible to argue that the gradual transition from a centralized government structure to power-sharing between Corsica and the mainland could not end ethnic violence in France (Figure 13) because the level of recognition offered to the Corsicans was rather weak and thus unsatisfactory. In Turkey too it could be said that the failure of multiculturalist policies to subdue ethnic conflict was because the cultural recognition given to the Kurds has never translated into political and legislative autonomy in their homelands. Kymlicka suggests that

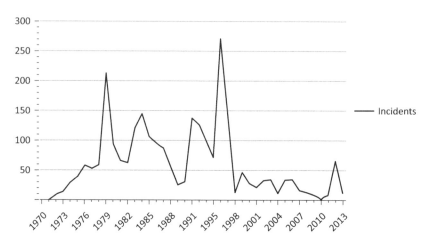

Figure 13. FLNC incidents in Corsica (1970–2013)[65]

multiculturalism in the extensive form of self-government rights and legislative autonomy was successfully established in case of the UK and Northern Ireland and that this was the only reason why they were able to bring violent conflict to an end. In his view, this was not the case in France, where the constitutional court has constantly prevented a similar agreement from emerging and Corsican nationalist demands have remained unaddressed. However, this account of centralized and weak French multiculturalism versus pluralist and strong UK multiculturalism is overly simplistic.

The Good Friday Agreement ensured that any constitutional changes regarding Northern Ireland's autonomous decisions, including those shaped by Catholic republicans, would be subject to the consent of the majority (in this case, the Protestant Unionists). The limited legislative autonomy given to the Northern Ireland Assembly by the UK's central government therefore only had symbolic value for Catholic republicans, whose absolute cultural autonomy at the constitutional level is still dependent on the consent of the Protestant majority. Catholic republicans in Northern Ireland do not have exclusive power of jurisdiction in Northern Ireland, and it is worth noting that they have never had the full complement of self-government rights idealized in multiculturalist theory. Instead, the Northern Irish situation resembles more properly a version of moderate multiculturalism similar to that experienced by Corsicans in France.

Corsica has an executive council and a regional assembly with decision-making powers, and it is guaranteed to have four deputies and two senators at the National Assembly.[66] This limited autonomy, granted on the basis of freedom of association, protects the rights of the majority of the island's population who voted against a higher level of autonomy for Corsica in the 2003 referendum.[67] Catholic republicans have remained controlled by the consent of the Protestant majority, and so their position is like that of the Corsicans in France. Although the powers they possess seem very different on paper, these two national minorities are similar in terms of the levels of autonomy they enjoy in practice.

In spite of their similarity, the Northern Irish and Corsican cases differ from each other in terms of how their similar levels of autonomy have impacted on the conflicts that they were designed to resolve. Whereas the Irish Republican Army (IRA) in Northern Ireland agreed to a ceasefire, the FLNC conversely increased its operations in response to the limited autonomy solution. Like the Kurds in Turkey, Corsicans in France have also shown that policies of multiculturalism and their capacity to end violent conflict are complicated above all else by the internal dynamics and fragmentation of the ethnic groups in question.

Conclusion

Ethnocentric multiculturalism is unable to induce the adoption of liberalism's fundamental principles of equality and freedom in Turkey, but it is also unhelpful when it comes to ending ethnic conflict under many circumstances. The introduction of cultural recognition, limited autonomy, or power-sharing solutions is helpful in moving a violent conflict into the political democratic arena in cases like the one involving Northern Ireland and the UK. However, the success of multiculturalist policies is context dependent, and it is important to understand in what circumstances the politics of recognition and ethnocentric multiculturalism can actually work to end conflicts.

This chapter has shown that in contexts where deep-rooted exclusion and the marginalization of particular groups exist, ethnic constituencies may be supportive of violence against the 'out-group', but a shift towards multiculturalist policies is genuinely likely to bring an end to violence. In such cases, the majority of people in the ethnic group are supportive of policies which appear to address the problems of their past marginalization. In Northern Ireland, Catholics were already mobilized along the lines of ethnicity by historical exclusion and direct discrimination, for example. However, in contexts where there is a history of forced assimilation and integration into the majority society, the ethnic group is likely to be more fragmented and far less politically cohesive. In such cases, support for inter-group violence is not as strong and there are prominent intra-group conflicts over how to resolve key issues; when weak forms of multicultural policy are adopted, some of the group will be content, but others will not and are likely to carry out terrorist acts aimed at creating fear within the group, as well as a continuation of violence between the group and the state. This is also in line with the findings of Cunningham, who observed that conflicts regarding the claims to self-determination of divided minorities are often prolonged and intractable particularly because individual factions within divided minorities have conflicts of interest between each other, and when one of the factions is on the road to making commitment to a settlement, others might renew the challenge to the state if that commitment is not in their best interest.[68] This pattern was very much evident in the Corsican and Kurdish cases, which involve communities deeply fragmented by the policies of forced assimilation and civic state-building that they were exposed to in their respective countries.

In cases like this, radical organizations such as the PKK and the FLNC find themselves with an increasing need to mobilize their ethnic constituencies, which are far too fragmented in terms of their political orientations and interests to leverage change. The durability of the Kurdish insurgency after its military defeats and the capture of its leader in 1999 were also a function of its strategy which aimed to create collective threat perceptions and mobilize new recruits to combat these threats, as Tezcür has argued.[69] The PKK is unlikely to abide by a truce during which its attempts to mobilize a majority of the Kurds in Turkey in peacetime would coincide with the reforming government implementing changes that would meet the needs of some minority group members and draw them into the mainstream.

The possibility that governments may have authoritarian motives in these situations is illustrated by the AKP's recently evident intolerance of any critiques regarding the ways in which the Kurdish question is being dealt with. The politics of recognition and multiculturalism in Turkey have been shaped solely by the AKP's one-sided views of diversity and by the heavy-handed decision-making powers the government uses to manage it. As time goes on, the solution process that the AKP initiated seems to be getting further and further away from the liberal promises implicit in true multiculturalism. The increasing use of state violence against the PKK and its supporters in 2015 has damaged the reform process that started a decade ago.

More significantly, the process is also damaged by the PKK's total domination of the Kurdish movement, which runs counter to the kind of optimal multiculturalist solution that would guarantee the equal representation of many voices in and between the cultural blocs it is proposed to accommodate. For the time being, any transition to the politics of recognition and multiculturalism in Turkey is likely to work against the PKK's organizational interests and its attempts to monopolize Kurdish politics in the country. For this very reason, the politics of multiculturalism and recognition are, in current circumstances, only serving to escalate the conflict they were actually meant to resolve.

Notes

1 Will Kymlicka, 'Testing the Liberal Multiculturalist Hypothesis: Normative Theories and Social Science Evidence', *Canadian Journal of Political Science* 43, no. 2 (2010): 257–71. Also see Walker Connor, 'National Self-Determination and Tomorrow's Political Map', in A. Cairns, John C. Courtney, Peter MacKinnon, Hans Michelmann, David E. Smith, eds., *Citizenship, Diversity and Pluralism: Canadian and Comparative Perspectives* (Montreal, QC: McGill-Queen's University Press, 1999), 163–76.
2 W. Alejandro Sanchez, 'Corsica: France's Petite Security Problem', *Studies in Conflict & Terrorism* 31, no. 7 (2008): 655–64.

3 Michael Day, 'Corsican Terror Group Lays Down Arms in Battle for Independence from France'. *The Independent*, www.independent.co.uk.

4 John Lichfield, 'Corsica: Installation of Nationalist Government Sparks Concern in Paris amid Renewed Calls for Independence', *The Independent*, www.independent.co.uk.

5 The case selection beyond Turkey in this comparative chapter is also based on a systematic qualitative comparative methodology. The chapter explores why multiculturalism and administrative autonomy with limited legislative powers can be a solution to violent conflict in cases such as Northern Ireland in the UK while the approach only rekindles radicalism amongst Corsicans in France and Kurds in Turkey. The chapter uses the mixed method of difference and agreement. It explores the difference between mobilization strategies of the IRA in Northern Ireland and the FLNC in Corsica and explains the reason why they react differently to the similar policies of multiculturalism in the UK and France, countries that are also similar to each other in many other respects. The chapter uses the method of difference to analyze this. This reveals that ethnic conflict is more complicated and will last longer in France, Corsica, because the minority constituency itself is deeply fragmented by the policies of forced assimilation and civic-state building. Another part of the analysis in this chapter is aimed at verifying this by comparing the FLNC in France to the PKK in Turkey, which similarly increased its operations at times of reform and multiculturalism between 2002 and 2009. In this part the chapter uses the method of agreement to explain how and why this similarity occurs between France and Turkey despite all the other political, cultural and geographical differences observed between the two.

6 Uppsala Conflict Data Program, 'Turkey: Kurdistan – Entire Conflict', Uppsala Conflict Data Program, http://ucdp.uu.se.

7 The chronological account of PKK attacks used in generating this graph is available from the PKK Terrorism blog, 'Articles about Terrorist Activities', www.pkkterrorism.org, and Ihsan Bal and Emre Ozkan, 'PKK Chronology 1976–2006', Uluslararası Stratejik Araştırmalar Kurumu, www.usak.org.tr.

8 International Crisis Group, 'Turkey: Ending the PKK Insurgency', International Crisis Group, www.crisisgroup.org.

9 Mehmet Ümit Necef, 'Who Started the War between the Turkish State and the PKK – Erdoğan or the PKK?' Researchgate, www.researchgate.net.

10 Güneş Murat Tezcür, 'Kurdish Nationalism and Identity in Turkey: A Conceptual Reinterpretation', *European Journal of Turkish Studies*, no. 10 (2009): 1–18.

11 Marlies Casier, Joost Jongerden, and Nic Walker, 'Fruitless Attempts? The Kurdish Initiative and Containment of the Kurdish Movement in Turkey', *New Perspectives on Turkey* 44 (2011): 103–27.

12 Kathleen Gallagher Cunningham, *Inside the Politics of Self-Determination* (New York, NY: Oxford University Press, 2014), 6.

13 Arwa Ibrahim, 'Turkey's Regional Policy and the Kurdish Peace Process', Middle East Eye, www.middleeasteye.net.

14 Terence Turner, 'Anthropology and Multiculturalism: What Is Anthropology That Multiculturalists Should Be Mindful of It?' *Cultural Anthropology* 8, no. 4 (1993): 411–29.

15 Ignacio Sánchez-Cuenca and Paloma Aguilar, 'Terrorist Violence and Popular Mobilization: The Case of the Spanish Transition to Democracy', *Politics & Society* 37, no. 3 (2009): 428–53.

16 Jack L. Walker, 'The Origins and Maintenance of Interest Groups in America', *American Political Science Review* 77, no. 2 (1983): 390–406.

17 Christopher C. Sonn and Adrian T. Fisher, 'Identity and Oppression: Differential Responses to an In-Between Status', *American Journal of Community Psychology* 31, no. 1–2 (2003): 117–28. Also see Edison J. Trickett, Roderick J. Watts and Dina E. Birman, *Human Diversity: Perspectives on People in Context* (San Francisco, CA: Jossey-Bass, 1994).

18 Daniel Byman, 'The Logic of Ethnic Terrorism', *Studies in Conflict & Terrorism* 21, no. 2 (1998): 149–69. Also see John L. Sullivan, *ETA and Basque Nationalism (RLE: Terrorism & Insurgency): The Fight for Euskadi 1890–1986* (New York, NY: Routledge, 2015).

19 Andrew Kidd and Barbara F. Walter, 'Sabotaging the Peace: The Politics of Extremist Violence'. *International Organizations* 56, no. 2 (2002): 263–96.

20 Mehmet Orhan, *Political Violence and Kurds in Turkey: Fragmentations, Mobilizations, Participations & Repertoires*, Vol. 77 (New York, NY: Routledge, 2016), 101.

21 Bahadir K. Akcam and Victor Asal, 'The Dynamics of Ethnic Terrorism'. Paper presented at the 23rd International Conference of the System Dynamics Society, Boston, 2005.

22 International Crisis Group, 'Turkey: Ending the PKK Insurgency', 8.

23 Fevzi Bilgin and Ali Sarihan, *Understanding Turkey's Kurdish Question* (Westport, CT: Lexington Books, 2013).

24 Zeynep Aydogan, 'The Symbolic Politics of the Kurdish Democratic Opening', Unpublished Thesis, San Francisco State University, 2011. See also International Crisis Group, 'Turkey: Ending the PKK Insurgency', 9.

25 US Department of State, '2013 Human Rights Reports: Turkey', US Department of State, www.state.gov.

26 E-Kurd Daily, '7748 Kurds in Turkish Custody – 3895 Arrested in 30 Months in the Scope of KCK Operations', E-Kurd Daily, http://ekurd.net.

27 Cagil Kasapoplu, 'Murat Karayilan Announces PKK Withdrawal from Turkey', *BBC World News*, www.bbc.co.uk.

28 Nigar Goksel and Berkay Mandiraci, 'New Turkey-PKK Peace Talks: An Inevitability Postponed', *Turkish Policy Quarterly*, www.turkishpolicy.com.

29 World Bulletin, 'Kurdish Militants Threaten to Attack Turkish Dam Sites', World Bulletin, www.worldbulletin.net.

30 International Crisis Group, 'A Sisyphean Task? Resuming Turkey-PKK Peace Talks', International Crisis Group, www.crisisgroup.org.

31 Ibid.

32 Ibid.

33 Arwa Ibrahim, 'Inter-Kurdish Tensions Point toward HDP-PKK Divide', Middle East Eye, http://middleeasteye.net.

34 Ibrahim, 'Inter-Kurdish Tensions Point toward HDP-PKK Divide'.
35 Ibid.
36 Mehmet Yanmis, *The Resurgence of the Kurdish Conflict in Turkey: How Kurds View It* (Washington, DC: Rethink Institute, 2016), 14.
37 Cansu Camlibel, 'Both PKK and AKP Want HDP to Be Weakened', *Hurriyet Daily News*, www.hurriyetdailynews.com.
38 Yanmis, *The Resurgence of the Kurdish Conflict in Turkey*, 14.
39 Bal and Ozkan, 'PKK Chronology 1976–2006'.
40 Claire Metelits, *Inside Insurgency: Violence, Civilians, and Revolutionary Group Behavior* (New York, NY: New York University Press, 2009), 150.
41 Fernando Reinares, 'Nationalist Separatism and Terrorism in Comparative Perspective', in T. Bjorgo, ed., *Root Causes of Terrorism: Myths, Reality and Ways Forward* (New York, NY: Routledge, 2005), 119–30.
42 Akcam and Asal, 'The Dynamics of Ethnic Terrorism'.
43 Zeki Sarigil and Ekrem Karakoc, 'Who Supports Secession? The Determinants of Secessionist Attitudes among Turkey's Kurds', *Nations and Nationalism* 22, no. 2 (2016): 325–346.
44 Konda Research Consultancy, *A Survey on Social Structure: Perceptions and Expectations in the Kurdish Question* (Istanbul: Iletisim, 2011).
45 Yanmis, *The Resurgence of the Kurdish Conflict in Turkey*, 25.
46 Ibid., 11.
47 Ibid., 17.
48 Galip Dalay, 'PKK's War of Choice Lacks Kurdish Public Support in Turkey', Middle East Eye, www.middleeasteye.net.
49 Kerim Yildiz, 'Turkey's Kurdish Conflict: Pathways to Progress', *Insight Turkey* 14, no. 4 (2012): 151.
50 Global Terrorism Database, 'IRA Incidents (1970–2013)', Global Terrorism Database, www.start.umd.edu/gtd.
51 P. M. Leopold, 'Autonomy and the British Constitution', in M. Suksi, ed., *Autonomy, Applications and Implications* (The Hague: Kluwer Law International, 1998).
52 John McGarry and Brendan O'Leary, 'Consociational Theory, Northern Ireland's Conflict, and Its Agreement 2. What Critics of Consociation Can Learn from Northern Ireland', *Government and Opposition* 41, no. 2 (2006): 249–77.
53 Jóhanna Kristín Birnir and Molly Inman, 'Ethnic Mobilization, Parties and Violence', in *Working Group on Political Parties and Civil Peace* (Oslo: Centre for the Study of Civil War, Peace Research Institute Oslo (PRIO), 2010), 23–4. Also see Edward D. Mansfield and Jack Snyder, *Electing to Fight: Why Emerging Democracies Go to War* (Cambridge, MA: MIT Press, 2005).
54 Adam Przeworski, 'Minimalist Conception of Democracy: A Defense', in I. Shapiro and C. Hacker-Cordon, eds., *Democracy's Values* (Cambridge: Cambridge University Press, 1999), 23. Also see Christian Davenport, 'State Repression and the Tyrannical Peace', *Journal of Peace Research* 44, no. 4 (2007): 485–504.
55 William Safran, 'Pluralism and Multiculturalism in France: Post-Jacobin Transformations', *Political Science Quarterly* 118, no. 3 (2003): 437–65.

56 John Loughlin and Francisco Letamendía, 'Lessons for Northern Ireland: Peace in the Basque Country and Corsica?' *Irish Studies in International Affairs* 11, (2000): 147–62.

57 Safran, 'Pluralism and Multiculturalism in France', 439.

58 Alec G. Hargreaves, 'Half-Measures: Antidiscrimination Policy in France', *French Politics, Culture & Society* 18, no. 3 (2000): 83–101. Also see Farimah Daftary, 'Experimenting with Territorial Administrative Autonomy in Corsica: Exception or Pilot Region?' *International Journal on Minority and Group Rights* 15, no. 2 (2008): 273–312.

59 Loughlin and Letamendía, 'Lessons for Northern Ireland', 155.

60 Sanchez, 'Corsica: France's Petite Security Problem', 663.

61 Yanmis, *The Resurgence of the Kurdish Conflict in Turkey*, 25.

62 Walker, 'Success with Separatism? Brittany, Corsica, and the Indivisible French Republic'. Paper presented at the 40th Annual Meeting of the Alabama Political Science Association Conference Tuscaloosa, May 2, 2013, 25.

63 Patrick Hossay, 'Recognizing Corsica: The Drama of Recognition in Nationalist Mobilization', *Ethnic and Racial Studies* 27, no. 3 (2004): 403–30.

64 Global Security Organization, '*Front De La Liberation Nationale De La Corse* [FLNC]', Global Security Organization, www.globalsecurity.org.

65 Global Terrorism Database, 'FLNC Incidents in Corsica (1970–2013)', Global Terrorism Database, www.start.umd.edu/gtd.

66 Loughlin and Letamendía, 'Lessons for Northern Ireland', 157.

67 I. Serrano, 'France: The End of the Corsican Question', in *Annual ASEN Conference 2007* (LSE, London, 2007), 1–33. Also see Alessandro Michelucci, 'Rebel Island: Corsica's Long Quest for Autonomy', in Thomas Benedikter, ed., *Solving Ethnic Conflict through Self-Government: A Short Guide to Autonomy in Europe and South Asia* (Bolzano: EURAC, 2008), 35–9.

68 Kathleen Gallagher Cunningham, 'Divide and Conquer Or Divide and Concede: How Do States Respond to Internally Divided Separatists', *American Political Science Review* 105, no. 2 (2011): 275–97.

69 Güneş Murat Tezcür, 'Violence and Nationalist Mobilization: The Onset of the Kurdish Insurgency in Turkey', *Nationalities Papers* 43, no. 2 (2015): 248–66.

7   Conclusion

Turkey inherited a cultural mosaic from the Ottoman Empire where cultures from Sumer, Babylon, and Assyria interacted with each other for centuries. The society it inherited was a mix of ethnic groups, languages, and cultures that successfully co-existed. After the foundation of the modern republic in 1923, the Muslim population, including the Kurds, was forced to assimilate into Turkishness and its cultural differences were oppressed. What once was a cultural mosaic soon transformed into the kind of assimilationist melting pot associated with the often-idealized state of affairs in the United States. This assimilationist model has been successful in creating an extremely complex and intersectional societal structure through mixed marriages, equal opportunities, and religious brotherhood for the predominantly Muslim population in Turkey.

However, the transformation it occasioned also caused injustices for those who resisted this process in Turkey. Kurds who played an important role in this resistance also pushed hard to change the system back to a less homogenized cultural structure in which they could freely and publicly enjoy their culture and self-government rights. Their demands have gained more credibility thanks to Turkey's candidacy for the European Union, which entailed, as a condition of accession, the protection of minority groups. In the twenty-first century, Turkey has begun a journey towards multiculturalism which has led to Kurds making significant progress towards gaining their rights. A series of reforms have been introduced since 2004, and the EU's 2013 progress report on Turkey concluded that 'Turkey made progress on cultural rights. Steps in the right direction were made on minorities and on cultural rights but further efforts are needed'.[1] Although a transformation from the denial to the recognition of cultural rights has taken hold for the first time in the country's history, the Kurds have been increasingly marginalized. Social polarization and tensions between them and Turks have reached new peaks, and violent conflict has escalated since 2004, when multicultural reforms were introduced. It has been my aim to explain why the newly begun transition to a so-called multiculturalist discourse in Turkey has failed to create a more peaceful and liberal country and has instead actually rekindled radicalism and polarization.

At the time of writing this book, there is a general lack of academic research focusing on the failure of multiculturalism for two reasons. First of all, the virtues of multiculturalism are usually taken for granted by minority nationalists, some scholars, and international institutions such as the EU; they do not question its viability in Turkey because multiculturalism is assumed to offer a fundamentally valuable approach. There is a general sense too that a critical approach would be discouraging of positive changes that are not yet established and are believed to be essential to Turkey's liberalization. Other scholars make a simple distinction between Western and Eastern communities to suggest wrongly that multiculturalism is not applicable in Eastern countries like Turkey which have not adopted liberal principles.[2] When these assumptions are held, it becomes nonsensical to begin questioning why multiculturalism is not working in Turkey: either it is understood to be on its way to working, or it is thought not to be workable there at all.

The discussion here has shown that multiculturalism is not only problematic in Eastern communities; it has also led to difficulties in liberal democracies like France. The problem of how best to deal with minorities is universal, but its nature and solutions to it vary. Throughout the chapters here, I have demonstrated that this variety is due to the types of relationships that exist between any given minority and the state in which it exists, and no hard and fast geographical categorization can account for those differences. Multiculturalism is not practiced exclusively in Western communities which have already internalized liberalism to some extent and in different forms; it is also a potential model for some countries in transition in both the East and the West. Liberalism is not a dichotomous variable but a matter of degree in countries – often simplistically labelled as either 'liberal' and 'illiberal' – where individuals are striving for more freedom and equality. Problems arise because of the tension that exists between approaches which choose to prioritize either equality or freedom over each other, breaking the important linkage between the two fundamental principles of liberalism itself. The question we need to face therefore is not about whether liberal pluralism can be exported to 'illiberal' countries, but about which interpretation of liberalism one should adopt under certain circumstances if the goal is to advance both of those values in effective ways.

This book's exploration of the conundrum about the best way to accommodate national minorities has been very sensitive to context. The use of a comparative methodology to explore the Kurds' situation has shown that there is no universal 'best' solution available for application to the diverse range of problems faced by national minorities across the world. Ethnocentric multiculturalism might produce positive outcomes in places like Canada and Belgium where there is, in many respects, a clear-cut line between ethno-cultural blocs. However, it is not effective when this kind of certainty is absent – as is the case in Turkey, where the Kurdish community has been too politically, socially, culturally and economically fragmented to be represented by a single discourse that predominantly focuses on ethnic differences. In-group differences as well as conflicts of interests between Kurds have been facilitated by assimilationist policies of integration in Turkey, which brought some advantages but deprived Kurds of the opportunity to develop a cohesive societal culture.

Any attempt to counter that fragmentation by retroactively installing ethnocentric multiculturalism has been shown to be problematic. In Turkey, a form of ethnocentric multiculturalism that involves promoting an 'authentic' ethnic Kurdish identity can be seen to have hampered the very diversity it sought to promote. There is no unanimous Kurdish group which can be recognized and elevated to act on behalf of all of its minority's members, and, as this book has made clear, any attempts to contain all Kurds in one cultural bloc violate individuals' freedom of exit, essentialize culture, and further marginalize Kurds in Turkish society. If ethnocentric multiculturalism is rejected in favour of the difference-blind treatment of minorities, the situation is not improved. As this book as shown, an overemphasis on equality and assimilation has also been problematic in Turkey because it cannot come to terms with or respond adequately to the systematic injustices and conflict that the policies of forced assimilation have created.

If neither ethnocentric multiculturalism nor difference-blind assimilationism are viable options, then what might serve as a viable liberal approach to the problems faced by the Kurds and Turkey? This discussion has shown that many strands of liberal thought offer insights which can be incorporated into a nuanced strategy for accommodating the Kurds. Institutional reform in Turkey should be carried out in a manner which ensures that no one model of liberalism will dominate the process as a whole. As neither ethnocentric multiculturalism nor difference-blind assimilationism are viable options with respect to the Kurds, it is now important to focus on developing an alternative liberal view in which there is no need to sacrifice either the equality of opportunity that can be produced through assimilation or the ethno-cultural freedoms that can be secured using multicultural approaches.

It has not been my aim to offer a rigorous overview of what should be done with regard to the Kurdish question in Turkey. This book has not made claims about the institutions that should be developed or about how power should ultimately be distributed. Instead, I have shown that the success of any multiculturalist or egalitarian/assimilationist project is conditional and that any attempts to reach a future solution solely by recourse to abstract principles cannot do justice to Turkey's changing socio-political environment. There are forms that liberal solutions simply should not take in current circumstances. Whatever the shape a workable process might take, it can safely be asserted, from a liberal perspective, that a moderate version of multiculturalism is more suited to Turkey than the kind of strong ethnocentric multiculturalism which blindly claims that ethno-cultural distinctions are the only source of political legitimacy. The cultural boundary between the Turks and the Kurds in Turkey is very fluid, and institutional arrangements and any redistribution of power must be carried out in ways that take this into account. The current focus is on the provision of legislative autonomy with an exclusive power of jurisdiction that derives from membership of Kurdish or Turkish ethnicities; this should be replaced with a new approach, one which concentrates on territorial needs and empowering local administrations with key competencies in education, finance, and security.

Modern Turkey's current circumstances expose the flaws of multiculturalist discourse, and political actors have exacerbated its problems by implementing multiculturalist precepts in ways that have destroyed hopes for a better democracy in the country. The AKP government insists it will not extend further administrative powers to the predominantly Kurdish regional authorities; it has monopolized the transformation process and developed an authoritarian stance towards everyone who challenges its hegemony. Meanwhile, the PKK, which insists on its right to legislative autonomy and exclusive power of jurisdiction over Kurds, has continued to invest in conflict during times of reform at the expense of freedoms and equality for the very Kurds that the PKK claims to represent.

As of 2016, the Turkish state and the PKK are locked in their deadliest violent conflict to date, and while this does not mean that an ethnocentric multicultural scenario will not emerge in Turkey, its delivery depends on many factors. Turkey's government has a religious vision which it believes will be able to unite Muslim Kurds and Muslim Turks, even if Kurds are granted regional autonomy. Others argue that the government, in its attempt to bring a presidential system to Turkey, needs the support of nationalist Kurds in parliament and so might soon need to compromise with radical Kurds on many issues that have recently dragged the country to the verge of civil war. Kurds might eventually mobilize, and a majority of them might choose separation over integration if this choice is presented to them as an option through a referendum.[3] Domestic politics are also affected by changing international dynamics in the Middle East and increasing tensions with neighbouring countries such as Syria and Iran. It is possible that the Kurds in Iraq, Iran and Syria will play an important role in the region and that this will affect the government's considerations as it takes future steps to tackle the Kurdish question. For all of these reasons, ethnocentric multiculturalism can become a reality in Turkey, but it is another question altogether as to whether or not this change will be a liberal one. In order for a genuinely liberal outcome to be achieved, a wide range of political actors need to engage with the kind of critical and comparative thinking about multiculturalist approaches that this book has undertaken.

Notes

1 The Commission to the European Parliament and the Council, 'Turkey 2013 Progress Report', European Commission, http://ec.europa.eu.
2 Yasutomo Morigiwa, Fumihiko Ishiyama and Tetsu Sakurai, *Universal Minority Rights?: A Transnational Approach: Proceedings of the Fifth Kobe Lectures, Tokyo and Kyoto, December 1998* (Stuttgart: Franz Steiner, 2004).
3 Ethno-nationalism is most often triggered at times of socio-economic and political crises. This is what Billig refers to as 'hot' nationalism, 'which arises in times of social disruption'. See Michael Billig, *Banal Nationalism* (London: Sage Publications, 1995), 44. We witness the rise of right-wing ethnocentric nationalism today all over the world, and there is no reason why the increasingly marginalized Kurds, too, might not choose separation along the lines of ethnicity over integration, especially if this choice is presented to them as an option through a referendum. However, this would not reflect fairly the deep-rooted conflict of interests between the Kurds themselves. 'Referendum voting can select an overall Condorcet loser or an outcome that is Pareto-dominated by every other possible outcome. This is indeed a perversion of majority rule, and it undermines claims that a referendum will reflect "what the people want"'. See Dean Lacy and Niou Emerson, 'A Problem with Referendums', *Journal of Theoretical Politics* 12 (1998): 5–31.

Bibliography

Adamou, Evangelia. 'Bilingual Speech and Language Ecology in Greek Thrace: Romani and Pomak in Contact with Turkish', *Language in Society* 39, no. 2 (2010): 147–71.

Akar, F. M. *Abdulmelik Firat.* Istanbul: Avesta, 1996.

Akcam, Bahadir K., and Victor Asal. 'The Dynamics of Ethnic Terrorism', paper presented at the 23rd International Conference of the System Dynamics Society, Boston, 2005.

Akkoc, Raziye. 'Ankara Explosion: Turkish President Vows War on Terror as Officials Say One Bomber Was "Female Kurdish Militant"', *The Telegraph*, www.telegraph.co.uk.

Akyol, Mustafa. *Kürt Sorununu Yeniden Düşünmek: Yanlış Giden Neydi? Bundan Sonra Nereye? (Revisiting the Kurdish Question. What Went Wrong and Where to Go from Now On?).* Istanbul: Doğan Kitap, 2006.

Alba, Richard, and Victor Nee. 'Rethinking Assimilation Theory for a New Era of Immigration', *International Migration Review* (1997): 826–74.

Albayrak, A. S., S. Kalayci, and A. Karatas. 'Examining with Principal Components Analysis the Socio-Economic Development Levels of Provinces in Turkey According to Geographical Regions'. *Suleyman Demirel University, Journal of Economics and Administrative Sciences Faculty* 9 (2004): 101–30.

Alexandris, A. 'Religion and Ethnicity: The Identity Issues of Minorities in Greece and Turkey', in R. Hirshchon, ed., *Crossing the Aegean: An Appraisal of the 1923 Compulsory Population Exchange between Greece and Turkey.* New York, NY: Berghahn Books, 2003.

Aliş, Ahmet. 'The Process of the Politicization of the Kurdish Identity in Turkey: The Kurds and the Turkish Labor Party (1961–1971)'. MA Thesis, Bogazici University, 2009.

Alkan, Necati. 'Youth and Terrorism: Example of Turkey' presented at the International Workshop: Political Violence, Organized Crime, Terrorism and Youth, Hacettepe University, Ankara, 13–14 September 2007.

Anagnostou, Dia, and Anna Triandafyllidou. 'Regions, Minorities and European Integration: A Case Study on Muslims in Western Thrace, Greece'. *Romanian Journal of Political Sciences* 6, no. 1 (2007): 100–25.

Andrews, Peter A., and Rüdiger Benninghaus. *Ethnic Groups in the Republic of Turkey.* L. Wiesbaden: Reichert, 1989.

Ankara Arastirma Merkezi. *Atatürk'ün Söylev Ve Demeçleri (Atatürk's Speeches and Declarations)*, Vol. III. Ankara: Türk Tarih Kurumu Basımevi, 1997.

Appiah, Anthony K. 'Identity, Authenticity, Survival: Multicultural Societies and Social Reproduction', in A. Gutmann, ed., *Multiculturalism: Examining the Politics of Recognition*. Princeton, NJ: Princeton University Press, 1994.

Arslan, Abdurrahman. *Samsun'dan Lozan'a Mustafa Kemal Ve Kürtler (1919–1923)*. Vol. 4. Istanbul: Doz Basım ve Yayıncılık Limited Şti., 1991.

Aslan, Senem. '"Citizen, Speak Turkish!": A Nation in the Making'. *Nationalism and Ethnic Politics* 13, no. 2 (2007): 245–72.

Aydogan, Zeynep. 'The Symbolic Politics of the Kurdish Democratic Opening'. Unpublished Thesis, San Francisco State University, 2011.

Baer, Marc. 'The Double Bind of Race and Religion: The Conversion of the Dönme to Turkish Secular Nationalism'. *Comparative Studies in Society and History* 46, no. 4 (2004): 682–708.

Bahceli, Tozun. 'The Muslim-Turkish Community in Greece: Problems and Prospects'. *Journal Institute of Muslim Minority Affairs* 8, no. 1 (1987): 109–20.

Bal, Ihsan, and Emre Ozkan. 'PKK Chronology 1976–2006'. Uluslararası Stratejik Araştırmalar Kurumu, www.usak.org.tr/dosyalar/dergi/z6UFq2LoFkdiuzBbZSt9qHMi7u4Ke2.pdf.

Barkey, Henri J. 'The Struggles of a "Strong" State'. *Journal of International Affairs* 54, no. 1 (2000): 87–105.

Barkey, Henri J., and Graham E. Fuller. 'Turkey's Kurdish Question: Critical Turning Points and Missed Opportunities'. *The Middle East Journal* (1997): 59–79.

Barry, B. 'Equal Treatment and Same Treatment', paper presented at The New York University Department of Politics Seminar Series, 2009, www.politics.as.nyu.edu, 1–20.

Barry, Brian. *Culture and Equality*. Cambridge: Polity Press, 2001.

Barry, Brian. 'Self-Government Revisited', in D. Miller and L. Siedentrop, eds., *The Nature of Political Theory*. Oxford: Clarendon Press, 1983.

Bassino, Jean-Pascal, and Jean-Pierre Dormois. 'Were French Republicans Serious About Equality? Convergence in Real Wages, Literacy, and the Biological Standard of Living in France 1845–1913'. Paper presented at the third Economics and Human Biology Conference, Strasbourg, June 22–24, 2006.

Battiste, Marie. 'Enabling the Autumn Seed: Toward a Decolonized Approach to Aboriginal Knowledge, Language, and Education'. *Schooling in Transition: Readings in Canadian History of Education* (2012): 275–86.

Bauböck, Rainer. 'The Crossing and Blurring of Boundaries in International Migration. Challenges for Social and Political Theory'. *Public Policy and Social Welfare* 23 (1998): 17–52.

Bayar, Yesim. 'In Pursuit of Homogeneity: The Lausanne Conference, Minorities and the Turkish Nation'. *Nationalities Papers* 42, no. 1 (2014): 108–125.

Bayar, Yesim. 'The Trajectory of Nation-building through Language Policies: The Case of Turkey during the Early Republic (1920–38)'. *Nations and Nationalism* 17, no. 1 (2011): 108–28.

Baysal, Mustafa. 'National Minorities in the Turkish Law', Tribunal Constitucional, http://tribunalconstitucional.ad.

Becquelin, Nicolas. 'Criminalizing Ethnicity: Political Repression in Xinjiang'. Paper presented at the China Rights Forum, 2004.

Benedikter, Thomas. *Solving Ethnic Conflict through Self-Government: A Short Guide to Autonomy in Europe and South Asia* (Bozen/Bolzano: Eurac, 2009).

Benhabib, Seyla. *The Claims of Culture: Equality and Diversity in the Global Era*. Princeton, NJ: Princeton University Press, 2002.

Berlin, Isaiah. 'Two Concepts of Liberty', in Isaiah Berlin, ed., *Four Essays on Liberty*. New York, NY: Oxford University Press, 1970.

Besikci, Ismail. *Dogu Anadolu'nun Duzeni: Sosyo-Ekonomik Ve Etnik Temeller (The Order of Eastern Anatolia: Socio-Economic and Ethnic Foundations)*. Ankara: E Yayinlari, 1969.

Bilgin, Fevzi, and Ali Sarihan. *Understanding Turkey's Kurdish Question*. Westport, CT: Lexington Books, 2013.

Billig, Michael. *Banal Nationalism*. London: Sage Publications, 1995.

Birnir, Jóhanna Kristín, and Molly Inman. 'Ethnic Mobilization, Parties and Violence', in *Working Group on Political Parties and Civil Peace*. Oslo: Centre for the Study of Civil War, Peace Research Institute Oslo, 2010.

Borou, Christina. 'The Muslim Minority of Western Thrace in Greece: An Internal Positive or an Internal Negative "Other"?' *Journal of Muslim Minority Affairs* 29, no. 1 (2009): 5–26.

Bozarslan, Hamit. 'Kurdish Nationalism in Turkey: From Tacit Contract to Rebellion (1919-1925)', in A. Vali, ed., *Essays on the Origins of Kurdish Nationalism*. Costa Mesa, CA: Mazda, 2003.

Brancati, Dawn. 'Decentralization: Fueling the fire or dampening the flames of ethnic conflict and secessionism?'. *International Organization* 60, no. 3 (2006): 651–85.

Brubaker, R. *Ethnicity without Groups*. Cambridge, MA: Harvard University Press, 2004.

Brubaker, R. 'Immigration, Citizenship, and the Nation-State in France and Germany: A Comparative Historical Analysis'. *International Sociology* 5, no. 4 (1990): 379–407.

Brubaker, R. *Nationalism Reframed: Nationhood and the National Question in the New Europe*. New York, NY: Cambridge University Press, 1996.

Brubaker, R. 'The Return of Assimilation? Changing Perspectives on Immigration and its Sequels in France, Germany, and the United States'. *Ethnic and Racial Studies* 24, no. 4 (2001): 531–48.

Bulloch, John, and Harvey Morris. *No Friends but the Mountains: The Tragic History of the Kurds*. London: Penguin Books, 1992.

Byman, Daniel. 'The Logic of Ethnic Terrorism'. *Studies in Conflict & Terrorism* 21, no. 2 (1998): 149–69.

Cagaptay, Soner. 'Passage to Turkishness: Immigration and Religion in Modern Turkey', in H. Gunalp, ed., *Citizenship and Ethnic Conflict: Challenging the Nation State*. London: Routledge, 2006.

Calhoun, Craig. 'Nationalism and Ethnicity'. *Annual Review of Sociology* 19, no. 1 (1993): 211–39.

Camlibel, Cansu. 'Both PKK and AKP Want HDP to Be Weakened'. *Hurriyet Daily News*, www.hurriyetdailynews.com.

Canefe, Nergis. 'Turkish Nationalism and Ethno-Symbolic Analysis: The Rules of Exception'. *Nations and Nationalism* 8, no. 2 (2002): 133–55.

Carens, Joseph H. *Culture, Citizenship, and Community: A Contextual Exploration of Justice as Evenhandedness*. Toronto, ON: Oxford University Press, 2000.

Carillet, J. B., and M. Roddis. *Corsica*. London: Lonely Planet Publications, 2007.

Casier, Marlies, Joost Jongerden and Nic Walker. 'Fruitless Attempts? The Kurdish Initiative and Containment of the Kurdish Movement in Turkey'. *New Perspectives on Turkey* 44 (2011): 103–27.

Cay, A. *Her Yonuyle Kurt Dosyasi (Kurdish File with All Its Aspects)*. Ankara: Bogazici Yayinlari, 1993.

Cemal, H. *Kurtler (The Kurds)*. Istanbul: Dogan Kitap, 2003.

Cetin, Kumru Berfin Emre. 'The 'Politicization' of Turkish Television Dramas'. *International Journal of Communication* 8 (2014): 2462–83.

Chaliand, Gerard. 'The Kurdish Tragedy'. Trans. Philip Black. London: Zed Books, 1994.

Choudhry, Sujit. 'Does the World Need More Canada? The Politics of the Canadian Model in Constitutional Politics and Political Theory'. *International Journal of Constitutional Law* 5, no. 4 (2007): 606–38.

Claude, Inis L. *National Minorities: An International Problem*. Cambridge, MA: Harvard University Press, 1955.

Commission of the European Communities. 'Recommendation of European Commission on Turkey's Progress Towards Accession'. Commission of the European Communities, http://ec.europa.eu.

Commission of the European Communities. 'Turkey 2009 Report'. European Commission, http://ec.europa.eu/.

Connor, Walker. 'National Self-Determination and Tomorrow's Political Map', in A. Cairns, John C. Courtney, Peter MacKinnon, Hans Michelmann, and David E. Smith, eds., *Citizenship, Diversity and Pluralism: Canadian and Comparative Perspectives*. Montreal, QC: McGill-Queen's University Press, 1999.

Connor, Walker. 'Nation-Building or Nation-Destroying?' *World Politics* 24, no. 3 (1972): 319–55.

Constitutional Court of the Republic of Turkey. 'The Constitution of the Republic of Turkey (1982): Chapter Four, Political Rights and Duties. Article 66'. Türkiye Büyük Millet, www.tbmm.gov.tr.

Cornell, Svante E. 'The Kurdish Question in Turkish Politics'. *Orbis* 45, no. 1 (2002): 31–46.

Corson, David. *Language Diversity and Education*. New York, NY: Routledge, 2000.

Council of Europe. 'Details of Treaty No.122- European Charter of Local Self-Government'. www.coe.int/en/web/conventions/full-list/-/conventions/treaty/122.

Cunningham, Kathleen Gallagher. 'Divide and Conquer or Divide and Concede: How Do States Respond to Internally Divided Separatists?'. *American Political Science Review* 105, no. 2 (2011): 275–97.

Cunningham, Kathleen Gallagher. *Inside the Politics of Self Determination* (New York, NY: Oxford University Press, 2014).

Cunningham, Kathleen Gallagher, Kristin M. Bakke, and Lee J. M. Seymour. 'Shirts Today, Skins Tomorrow: Dual Contests and the Effects of Fragmentation in Self-Determination Disputes'. *Journal of Conflict Resolution* 56, no. 1 (2012): 67–93.

Daftary, Farimah. 'Experimenting with Territorial Administrative Autonomy in Corsica: Exception or Pilot Region?', *International Journal on Minority and Group Rights* 15, no. 2 (2008): 273–312.

Dalay, Galip. 'PKK's War of Choice Lacks Kurdish Public Support in Turkey'. Middle East Eye, www.middleeasteye.net.

Dallaire, Christine, and Claude Denis. '"If You Don't Speak French, You're Out": Don Cherry, the Alberta Francophone Games, and the Discursive Construction of Canada's Francophones'. *Canadian Journal of Sociology* (2000): 415–40.

Davenport, Christian. 'State Repression and the Tyrannical Peace'. *Journal of Peace Research* 44, no. 4 (2007): 485–504.

Day, Michael. 'Corsican Terror Group Lays Down Arms in Battle for Independence from France'. *The Independent*, www.independent.co.uk/.

Demir, M. T. *Nurcu Movement in Turkish Political System and 'Fetullahcilar' as a By- Product: Advanced Issues in Turkish Politics*. Izmir: Dokuz Eylul University Press, 2005.

Donnelly, Jack. 'Human Rights, Individual Rights and Collective Rights', in J. Berting, ed., *Human Rights in a Pluralist World: Individuals and Collectivities*. Westport, CT: Meckler, 1990.

Duman, Anil. 'Education and Income Inequality in Turkey: Does Schooling Matter?' *Financial Theory and Practice* 32, no. 3 (2008): 369–85.

Duran, Burhanettin. 'Approaching the Kurdish Question Via Adil Düzen: An Islamist Formula of the Welfare Party for Ethnic Coexistence'. *Journal of Muslim Minority Affairs* 18, no. 1 (1998): 111–28.

Edrisnha, R. 'Multination Federalism and Minority Rights in Sri Lanka', in W. Kymlicka and B. He, eds., *Multiculturalism in Asia*. New York, NY: Oxford University Press, 2005.

Eisenberg, Avigail, and Jeff Spinner-Halev. *Minorities within Minorities: Equality, Rights and Diversity*. Cambridge: Cambridge University Press, 2005.

E-Kurd Daily. '7748 Kurds in Turkish Custody – 3895 Arrested in 30 Months in the Scope of KCK Operations'. *E-Kurd Daily*, http://ekurd.net.

Entessar, N. *Kurdish Ethno-Nationalism*. London: Lynne Rienner, 1992.

Ercan, Yavuz. 'Türkiye'de Azınlık Sorununun Kökeni (Osmanlı'dan Cumhuriyet'e Gayrimüslimler)'. *OTAM-Ankara Üniversitesi Osmanlı Tarihi Araştırma ve Uygulama Merkezi Dergisi* 20 (2006): 1–15.

Espiritu, Y. L. *Asian American Pan-Ethnicity*. Philadelphia, PA: Temple University Press, 1992.

EU Turkey Civic Commission. 'EUTCC welcomes Joost Lagendijk's statement regarding regional autonomy'. EU Turkey Civic Commission, www.eutcc.org/articles/7/document366.ehtml.

European Commission against Racism and Intolerance. *Third Report on Turkey.* Strasbourg: ECRI, 2005.

Fernandes, D. *The Kurdish and Armenian Genocides: From Censorship and Denial to Recognition?* Stockholm: Apec, 2008.

Forst, Rainer. *Contexts of Justice: Political Philosophy Beyond Liberalism and Communitarianism,* Vol. 9. Berkeley, CA: University of California Press, 2002.

Fottrell, D., and B. Bowring, eds. *Minority and Group Rights in the New Millennium.* The Hague: Kluwe Law International, 1999.

Fraser, Nancy. *Scales of Justice: Reimagining Political Space in a Globalizing World.* New York, NY: Columbia University Press, 2009.

Galenkamp, Marlies. *Individualism Versus Collectivism the Concept of Collective Rights.* Deventer, The Netherlands: Gouda Quint, 1998.

Gellner, Ernest. *Nations and Nationalism.* Oxford: Basil Blackwell, 1983.

Gillespie, Alex, and Flora Cornish. 'Intersubjectivity: Towards a Dialogical Analysis'. *Journal for the Theory of Social Behaviour* 40, no. 1 (2010): 19–46.

Global Security Organization. 'Front De La Liberation Nationale De La Corse [FLNC]'. Global Security Organization, www.globalsecurity.org.

Global Terrorism Database. 'FLNC Incidents in Corsica (1970–2013)'. Global Terrorism Database, www.start.umd.edu/gtd/.

Global Terrorism Database. 'IRA Incidents (1970–2013)'. Global Terrorism Database, www.start.umd.edu/gtd/.

Goksel, Nigar, and Berkay Mandiraci. 'New Turkey-PKK Peace Talks: An Inevitability Postponed'. *Turkish Policy Quarterly,* www.turkishpolicy.com.

Grubb, Erica Black. 'Breaking the Language Barrier: The Right to Bilingual Education'. *Harvard Civil Rights–Civil Liberties Law Review* 9 (1974): 52–94.

Guérard, Stéphane. 'Local Referendums in France: A Disappointing Experience', in Theo Schiller, ed., *Local Direct Democracy in Europe.* Wiesbaden: Springer, 2011.

Guerra, Lillian. *Popular Expression and National Identity in Puerto Rico: The Struggle for Self, Community, and Nation.* Gainesville, FL: University Press of Florida, 1998.

Güleç, Asli. *The Problem of Multiculturalism in Turkey within the Context of European Integration.* Ankara: METU, 2003.

Gültekin, Mehmet Nuri. 'Debates on Inter-Ethnic Marriages: Assimilation or Integration? The Turkish Perspective'. *Papers: Revista de Sociologia* 97, no. 1 (2012): 151–66.

Gunter, Michael. 'Reopening Turkey's Closed Kurdish Opening?' *Middle East Policy* 20, no. 2 (2013): 88–98.

Gurr, Ted Robert. *Minorities at Risk – A Global View of Ethnopolitical Conflicts.* Washington, DC: United States Institute of Peace, 1995.

Gutmann, Amy, and Charles Taylor. *Multiculturalism and 'the Politics of Recognition': An Essay.* Princeton, NJ: Princeton University Press, 1992.

Gyurcsik, Ivan, and James Satterwhite. 'The Hungarians in Slovakia'. *Nationalities Papers* 24, no. 3 (1996): 509–24.

Habermas, Jürgen, and Ciaran Cronin. 'The European Nation-State: On the Past and Future of Sovereignty and Citizenship'. *Public Culture* 10, no. 2 (1998): 397–416.

Habermas, Jürgen. 'Equal Treatment of Cultures and the Limits of Postmodern Liberalism', *Journal of Political Philosophy* 13, no. 1 (2005): 1–28.

Halklarin Demokratik Partisi Parti Programi (The HDP Party Program), www .hdp.org.tr/tr/parti/parti-programi/8.

Hargreaves, Alec G. 'Half-Measures: Antidiscrimination Policy in France'. *French Politics, Culture & Society* 18, no. 3 (2000): 83–101.

Harty, Siobhán. 'The Nation as a Communal Good: A Nationalist Response to the Liberal Conception of Community'. *Canadian Journal of Political Science* 32, no. 4 (1999): 665–89.

Hechter, Michael. *Containing Nationalism*. Oxford: Oxford University Press, 2000.

Heper, Metin. *The State and Kurds in Turkey: The Question of Assimilation*. Houndmills, UK: Palgrave Macmillan, 2007.

Hermine, G. L. 'French Regionals 2010: Second Round'. World Elections, https://welections.wordpress.com.

Heyes, Cressida J. 'Can There Be a Queer Politics of Recognition?' in Robin N. Fiore and Hilde Lindemann Nelson, eds. *Recognition, Responsibility, and Rights: Feminist Ethics and Social Theory*. Washington, DC: Rowman & Littlefield, 2003.

Higgins, Rosalyn. 'Conceptual Thinking About the Individual in International Law'. *British Journal of International Studies* 4, no. 1 (1978): 1–19.

Hirschler, Konrad. 'Defining the Nation: Kurdish Historiography in Turkey in the 1990s'. *Middle Eastern Studies* 37, no. 3 (2001): 145–66.

Hirschon, Renée. *Crossing the Aegean: An Appraisal of the 1923 Compulsory Population Exchange between Greece and Turkey*. New York, NY: Berghahn Books, 2003.

Hofmann, Tessa. *Armenians in Turkey Today: A Critical Assessment of the Situation of the Armenian Minority in the Turkish Republic*. Brussels: The EU Office of Armenian Associations of Europe, 2002.

Hogg, Peter W. *Canada Act 1982 Annotated*. Toronto, ON: Carswell, 1982.

Horowitz, Donald L. *Ethnic Groups in Conflict*. Berkeley, CA: University of California Press, 1985.

Hossay, Patrick. 'Recognizing Corsica: The Drama of Recognition in Nationalist Mobilization'. *Ethnic and Racial Studies* 27, no. 3 (2004): 403–30.

Hotham, David. *The Turks*. London: Taylor & Francis, 1972.

Houston, Christopher James. *Islam, Kurds and the Turkish Nation State*. Oxford: Berg, 2001.

Howe, Kenneth R. 'Liberal Democracy, Equal Educational Opportunity, and the Challenge of Multiculturalism'. *American Educational Research Journal* 29, no. 3 (1992): 455–70.

Howes, David and the Centaur Jurisprudence Project. 'A Clarification of Terms: Canadian Multiculturalism and Quebec Interculturalism'. Centre for Human Rights and Legal Pluralism, McGill University (2012):

1–14, http://canadianicon.org/wp-content/uploads/2014/03/TMODPart1-Clarification.pdf.

Hughes, James. 'The Chechnya Conflict: Freedom Fighters or Terrorists?'. *Demokratizatsiya* 15, no. 3 (2007): 293.

Human Rights Watch. 'Turkey "Still Critical"': Assessing the Scale of the Problem'. Human Rights Watch, www.hrw.org.

Human Rights Watch. *The Turks of Western Thrace.* New York, NY: Human Rights Watch, 1999.

Hurriyet Daily News '2011 Yili Genel Secim Sonuclari – the 2011 General Election Results'. *Hurriyet Daily*, www.hurriyetdailynews.com.

Hurriyet Daily News. 'Attacks on Pro-Kurdish Party's Election Offices Called "Political"'. *Hurriyet Daily News*, www.hurriyetdailynews.com.

Hutchinson, John. 'Nations and Culture', in Montserrat Guibernau and John Hutchinson, eds., *Understanding Nationalism.* Cambridge: Polity Press, 2001.

Ibrahim, Arwa. 'Inter-Kurdish Tensions Point toward HDP-PKK Divide'. Middle East Eye, http://middleeasteye.net.

Ibrahim, Arwa. 'Turkey's Regional Policy and the Kurdish Peace Process'. *Middle East Eye*, www.middleeasteye.net.

Icduygu, A., David Romano, and Ibrahim Sirkeci. 'The Ethnic Question in an Environment of Insecurity: The Kurds in Turkey'. *Ethnic and Racial Studies* 22, no. 6 (1999): 991–1010.

Ignatieff, Michael. *Blood and Belonging: Journeys into the New Nationalism.* New York, NY: Farrar, Straus and Giroux, 1993.

International Crisis Group. 'A Sisyphean Task? Resuming Turkey-PKK Peace Talks'. International Crisis Group, www.crisisgroup.org/en/regions/europe/turkeycyprus/turkey/b077-a-sisyphean-task-resuming-turkey-pkk-peace-talks.aspx.

International Crisis Group. 'Turkey: Ending the PKK Insurgency', in *Europe Report.* Brussels: International Crisis Group, 2011. www.crisisgroup .org/en/regions/europe/turkey-cyprus/turkey/213-turkeyending-the-pkk-insurgency.aspx.

Jacob, James E., and David C. Gordon. 'Language Policy in France', in W. R. Beer and J. E. Jacob, eds., *Language Policy and National Unity.* Totowa, NJ: Rowman & Allanheld, 1985.

Jayaratnam, R. 'Ruminations of a Sri Lankan Tamil'. *Sri Lanka Guardian*, February 17, 2010.

Jennings, Ivor. *The Approach to Self-Government.* Cambridge: Cambridge University Press, 2011.

Jones, Peter. 'Human Rights, Group Rights, and Peoples' Rights'. *Human Rights Quarterly* 21, no. 1 (1999): 80–107.

Jungius, Björn. 'Aziz Nesin Grundschule, Berlin: A Bilingual Turkish–German Public Elementary School'. *Migration Online Language and Integration* (2007*)*, http://migrationonline.cz/en/aziz-nesin-grundschule-berlin-a-bilingual-turkishgerman-public-elementary-school.

Kadioğlu, Ayşe. 'The Paradox of Turkish Nationalism and the Construction of Official Identity'. *Middle Eastern Studies* 32, no. 2 (1996): 177–93.

Kahraman, Hasan Bulent. 'From Culture of Politics to Politics of Culture: Reflections on Turkish Modernity', in F. Keyman, ed., *Remaking Turkey: Globalization*. Oxford: Lexington Books, 2007.

Kalyvas, Stathis, N. 'Ethnic Defection in Civil War'. *Comparative Political Studies* 41, no. 8 (2008): 1043–68.

Karasapan, Omer. 'Turkey and US Strategy in the Age of Glasnost'. *Middle East Report* 160 (1989): 4–10.

Karpat, Kemal. *Türk Demokrasi Tarihi Sosyal, Ekonomik, Kültürel Temeller (The History of Turkish Democracy: Social, Economic and Cultural Foundations)*. Istanbul: Istanbul Matbaasi, 1967.

Kasapoplu, Cagil. 'Murat Karayilan Announces PKK Withdrawal from Turkey'. *BBC World News*, www.bbc.co.uk.

Kaufmann, Eric. 'Liberal Ethnicity: Beyond Liberal Nationalism and Minority Rights'. *Ethnic and Racial Studies* 23, no. 6 (2000): 1086–119.

Keating, Michael. *Plurinational Democracy: Stateless Nations in a Post-Sovereignty Era*. Oxford: Oxford University Press, 2001.

Kidd, Andrew, and Barbara F. Walter. 'Sabotaging the Peace: The Politics of Extremist Violence'. *International Organizations* 56, no. 2 (2002): 263–96.

Killi, S. *Turkish Constitutional Developments and Assembly Debates on the Constitutions of 1924 and 1961*. Istanbul: Mentes Matbaasi, 1971.

Kirişci, Kemal, and Gareth M. Winrow. *The Kurdish Question and Turkey: An Example of a Trans-State Ethnic Conflict*. London: Frank Cass, 1997.

Kohn, H. 'Western and Eastern Nationalisms', in J. Hutchinson and A. Smith, eds., *Nationalism*. Oxford: Oxford University Press, 1994.

Kokce, H. K. 'Two Transformative Actors of Turkish Politics: Justice and Development Party and Kurds'. MA Thesis, *Middle East Technical University*, 2010.

Konda Research and Consultancy. *A Survey on Social Structure: Perceptions and Expectations in the Kurdish Question*. Istanbul: Iletisim, 2011.

Konda Research and Consultancy. *A Survey on Social Structure: Who Are We? Turkey*. Istanbul: KONDA, 2006.

Koulish, Robert. 'Hungarian Roma Attitudes on Minority Rights: The Symbolic Violence of Ethnic Identification'. *Europe–Asia Studies* 57, no. 2 (2005): 311–26.

Kozma, Troy. 'Liberalism and Civic Assimilation: A New Look at Minority Nations'. Paper presented at the annual meeting of the Midwest Political Science Association, Chicago, Illinois, April 20, 2006.

Kresl, Peter Karl. 'Quebec's Culture Policy: Will Increased Autonomy Matter?' *American Review of Canadian Studies* 26, no. 4 (1996): 499–521.

Kukathas, Chandran. 'Anarcho-Multiculturalism: The Pure Theory of Liberalism', in G. B. Levey, ed., *Political Theory and Australian Multiculturalism*. New York, NY: Berghahn Books, 2008.

Kukathas, Chandran. 'Are There Any Cultural Rights?' *Political Theory* 20, no. 1 (1992): 105–39.

Kukathas, Chandran. 'Liberalism and Multiculturalism: The Politics of Indifference'. *Political Theory* 26, no. 5 (1998): 686–99.

Kukathas, Chandran. 'The Life of Brian, or Now for Something Completely Difference Blind', in P. Kelly, ed., *Multiculturalism Reconsidered*. Cambridge: Polity Press, 2002.

Kurban, Dilek. 'Confronting Equality: The Need for Constitutional Protection of Minorities on Turkey's Path to the European Union'. *Columbia Human Rights Law Review* 35, no. 1 (2003): 151–214.

Kushner, David. *The Rise of Turkish Nationalism, 1876–1908*. London: Frank Cass, 1977.

Kutschera, Chris. *Le Mouvement National Kurde (The National Movement of Kurdish People)*. Paris: Flammarion, 1979.

Kuzio, T. 'The Myth of the Civic State. Hans Kohn Revisited: Civic and Ethnic States in Theory and Practice'. Paper presented at the Annual Convention of the Association for the Study of Nationalities, Columbia University, New York, April 13, 2000.

Kuzu, Durukan. 'A Self-Governing Group or Equal Citizens – Kurds, Turkey and the European Union'. *Journal on Ethno-politics and Minority Issues* 9 (2010): 32–65.

Kuzu, Durukan. 'Comparative Analysis of Political Systems and Ethnic Mobilization. Assimilation vs. Exclusion', *Comparative European Politics* 15, no. 4 (2017): 557–76.

Kuzu, Durukan. '"The Politics of Identity, Recognition and Multiculturalism. The Kurds in Turkey."' *Nations and Nationalism* 22, no. 1 (2016): 123–142.

Kymlicka, Will. 'Assessing the Politics of Diversity in Transition Countries', in F. Daftary and F. Grin, eds., *Nation-Building, Ethnicity and Language Politics in Transition Countries*. Budapest: Open Society Institute-ECMI/LGI Series, 2003.

Kymlicka, Will. *Finding Our Way: Rethinking Ethnocultural Relations in Canada*. Oxford: Oxford University Press, 1998.

Kymlicka, Will. *Liberalism, Community, and Culture*. Oxford: Oxford University Press, 1991.

Kymlicka, Will. 'Liberal Multiculturalism and Human Rights'. CEU E-Learning Site, https://ceulearning.ceu.edu.

Kymlicka, Will. *Multicultural Citizenship: A Liberal Theory of Minority Rights*. Oxford: Clarendon Press, 1995.

Kymlicka, Will. 'Multicultural Citizenship within Multination States'. *Ethnicities* 11, no. 3 (2011): 281–302.

Kymlicka, Will. 'Multiculturalism and Minority Rights: West and East'. *Journal on Ethnopolitics and Minority Issues in Europe* 4, no. 2 (2002): 1–26.

Kymlicka, Will. *Multicultural Odysseys: Navigating the New International Politics of Diversity*. Oxford: Oxford University Press, 2007.

Kymlicka. Will. 'National Minorities in Postcommunist Europe: The Role of International Norms and European Integration', in Zoltan Barany and Robert G. Moser, eds., *Ethnic Politics after Communism*. Ithaca, NY: Cornell University Press, 2005.

Kymlicka, Will. *Politics in the Vernacular: Nationalism, Multiculturalism, and Citizenship*. Oxford: Oxford University Press, 2001.

Kymlicka, Will. 'Testing the Liberal Multiculturalist Hypothesis: Normative Theories and Social Science Evidence'. *Canadian Journal of Political Science* 43, no. 2 (2010): 257–71.

Kymlicka, Will. 'The Rights of Minority Cultures: Reply to Kukathas'. *Political Theory* 20, no. 1 (1992): 140–46.

Kymlicka, Will, and Baogang He. *Multiculturalism in Asia*. Oxford: Oxford University Press, 2005.

Kymlicka, Will, Bruce Berman and Dickson Eyoh. *Ethnicity & Democracy in Africa*. London: J. Currey, 2004.

Kymlicka, Will, and Magda Opalski. *Can Liberal Pluralism Be Exported?: Western Political Theory and Ethnic Relations in Eastern Europe: Western Political Theory and Ethnic Relations in Eastern Europe*. Oxford: Oxford University Press, 2002.

Kymlicka, Will, and Alan Patten. *Language Rights and Political Theory*. Oxford: Oxford University Press, 2003.

Kymlicka, Will, and Eva Pföstl. *Multiculturalism and Minority Rights in the Arab World*. Oxford: Oxford University Press, 2014.

Lacy, Dean, and Niou Emerson. 'A Problem with Referendums'. *Journal of Theoretical Politics* 12, (1998): 5–31.

Larsen, Ronald J. *The Puerto Ricans in America*. Minneapolis, MN: Lerner Publishing Group, 1991.

Leopold, P. M. 'Autonomy and the British Constitution', in M. Suksi, ed., *Autonomy, Applications and Implications*. The Hague: Kluwer Law International, 1998.

Lerner, Melvin J. 'The Justice Motive: Some Hypotheses as to Its Origins and Forms'. *Journal of Personality* 45, no. 1 (1977): 1–52.

Levy, Jacob T. *The Multiculturalism of Fear*. Oxford: Oxford University Press, 2000.

Lichfield, John. 'Corsica: Installation of Nationalist Government Sparks Concern in Paris amid Renewed Calls for Independence'. *The Independent*, www .independent.co.uk.

Loughlin, John, and Francisco Letamendía. 'Lessons for Northern Ireland: Peace in the Basque Country and Corsica?' *Irish Studies in International Affairs* 11 (2000): 147–62.

MacCallum, Gerald C. 'Negative and Positive Freedom'. *The Philosophical Review* (1967): 312–34.

Mahoney, James. 'Qualitative Methodology and Comparative Politics'. *Comparative Political Studies* 40, no. 2 (2007): 122–44.

Mango, Andrew. *Turkey and the War on Terror: 'For Forty Years We Fought Alone'*. New York, NY: Routledge, 2005.

Mansfield, Edward D., and Jack Snyder. *Electing to Fight: Why Emerging Democracies Go to War*. Cambridge, MA: MIT Press, 2005.

Marcus, Aliza. *Blood and Belief: The PKK and the Kurdish Fight for Independence*. New York, NY: New York University Press, 2007.

Mardin, Şerif. *Türkiye'de Din Ve Siyaset (Religion and Politics in Turkey)*. Istanbul: Iletisim, 1992.

Margalit, Avishai, and Joseph Raz. 'National Self-Determination'. *The Journal of Philosophy* 87, no. 9 (1990): 439–61.

May, Stephen, Tariq Moodod and Judith Squires. *Ethnicity, Nationalism, and Minority Rights*. Cambridge: Cambridge University Press, 2004.

May, Stephen. 'The Politics of Homogeneity: A Critical Exploration of the Anti-Bilingual Education Movement', in James Cohen, Kara T. McAlister, Kellie Rolstad and Jeff MacSwan, eds., *Proceedings of the 4th International Symposium on Bilingualism*. Somerville, MA: Cascadilla Press, 2005.

Mazie, Steven V. 'Consenting Adults? Amish Rumspringa and the Quandary of Exit in Liberalism'. *Perspectives on Politics* 3, no. 4 (2005): 745–59.

McDowall, David. *A Modern History of the Kurds*. London: I. B. Tauris, 2000.

McGarry, John, and Brendan O'Leary. 'Consociational Theory, Northern Ireland's Conflict, and Its Agreement. 2. What Critics of Consociation Can Learn from Northern Ireland'. *Government and Opposition* 41, no. 2 (2006): 249–77.

McLaughlin, Theo, and Wendy Pearlman. "Out-group Conflict, In-group Unity? Exploring the Effect of Repression on Intra-movement Cooperation'. *Journal of Conflict Resolution* 56, no. 1 (2012): 41–66.

McQueen, Paddy. 'Social and Political Recognition'. Internet Encyclopedia of Philosophy, www.iep.utm.edu/recog_sp/.

McRoberts, Kenneth. *Misconceiving Canada: The Struggle for National Unity*. Oxford: Oxford University Press, 1997.

Metelits, Claire. *Inside Insurgency: Violence, Civilians, and Revolutionary Group Behavior*. New York, NY: New York University Press, 2009.

Michelucci, Alessandro. 'Rebel Island: Corsica's Long Quest for Autonomy', in Thomas Benedikter, ed., *Solving Ethnic Conflict through Self-Government: A Short Guide to Autonomy in Europe and South Asia*. Bolzano: EURAC, 2008.

Miller, David. *On Nationality*. Oxford: Oxford University Press, 1995.

Minority Rights Group International. *A Quest for Equality? Minorities in Turkey*. London: Minority Rights Group, 2007.

Minority Rights Group International. 'Hungary–Roma'. Minority Rights Group International, http://minorityrights.org.

Modood, T. *Multiculturalism*. Cambridge: Polity Press, 2007.

Morigiwa, Yasutomo, Fumihiko Ishiyama, and Tetsu Sakurai. *Universal Minority Rights?: A Transnational Approach: Proceedings of the Fifth Kobe Lectures, Tokyo and Kyoto, December 1998*. Stuttgart: Franz Steiner Verlag, 2004.

Müller, Jan-Werner. *Constitutional Patriotism*. Princeton, NJ: Princeton University Press, 2009.

Mumcu, U. *Kurt-Islam Ayaklanmasi 1919–1925 (Kurdish-Islamic Revolt 1919–1925)*. Ankara: Tekin Yayinevi, 1992.

Narli, Nilufer. 'The Rise of the Islamist Movement in Turkey'. *Middle East* 3, no. 3 (1999): 38–48.

Nations Online Project. *Turkey Map* (1998). Nations Online Project, www.nationsonline.org/oneworld/map/turkey-map.htm.

Necef, Mehmet Ümit. 'Who Started the War between the Turkish State and the PKK: Erdoğan or the PKK?' Researchgate, www.researchgate.net/publication/298722968_Who_Started_the_War_Betwen_the_Turkish_State_and_the_PKK_-_Erdogan_or_the_PKK.

New Policy Institute. *London Poverty Report: Ethnicity, Low Income and Work*. London: New Policy Institute, 2009.

Neyzi, Leyla. 'Zazaname: The Alevi Renaissance, Media and Music in the Nineties', in P. White and J. Jongerden, *Turkey's Alevi Enigma*. Leiden: Koninklikje Brill, 2003.

Nezan, Kendal. 'Kurdistan in Turkey', in G. Chaliand, ed., *People without a Country: The Kurds and Kurdistan*. London: Zed Press, 1980.

O'Driscoll, Dylan. 'Is Kurdish Endangered in Turkey? A Comparison between the Politics of Linguicide in Ireland and Turkey'. *Studies in Ethnicity and Nationalism* 14, no. 2 (2014): 270–288.

O'Neil, Mary Lou. 'Linguistic Human Rights and the Rights of Kurds', in Zehra Arat, ed., *Human Rights in Turkey*. Philadelphia, PA: University of Pennsylvania Press, 2007.

Okin, Susan. *Is Multiculturalism Bad for Women?* Princeton, NJ: Princeton University Press, 1999.

Olson, Robert. *The Sheikh Said Rebellion and the Emergence of Kurdish Nationalism: 1880–1925*. Austin, TX: University of Texas Press, 1989.

Ong, Paul M., Douglas Houston, Jennifer Wang, and Jordan Rickles. *Socioeconomic Status of American Indians in Los Angeles County*. Los Angeles, CA: University of California/United American Indian Involvement, 2002.

Oran, Baskin. 'Linguistic Minority Rights in Turkey, the Kurds and Globalization', in G. Gurbey and F. Ibrahim, eds., *The Kurdish Conflict in Turkey: Obstacles and Chances for Peace and Democracy*. New York, NY: St. Martin's Press, 2000.

Orhan, Mehmet. Political Violence and Kurds in Turkey: Fragmentations, Mobilizations, *Participations & Repertoires*, Vol. 77. New York, NY: Routledge, 2016.

OSCE. *National Minority Standards*. Strasbourg: Organization for Security and Cooperation in Europe: 2007.

Özbudun, Ergun. 'Democratization Reforms in Turkey, 1993–2004'. *Turkish Studies* 8, no. 2 (2007): 179–96.

Özbudun, Ergun, and Yazici Serap. *Democratic Reforms in Turkey (1993–2004)*. Istanbul: TESEV Publications, 2004.

Ozkirimli, Umut. 'Multiculturalism, Recognition and the "Kurdish Question" in Turkey: The Outline of a Normative Framework'. *Democratization* 21, no. 6 (2014): 1055–73.

Palmer, J., and C. Smith, *Modern Turkey*. London: George Routledge and Sons, 1942.

Parekh, Bhikhu C. *Rethinking Multiculturalism: Cultural Diversity and Political Theory*. Cambridge: Harvard University Press, 2002.

Patten, Alan. 'The Autonomy Argument for Liberal Nationalism'. *Nations and Nationalism* 5, no. 1 (1999): 1–17.

Pearlman, Wendy, and Kathleen Gallagher Cunningham. 'Non-state Actors, Fragmentation, and Conflict Processes'. *Journal of Conflict Resolution* 56, no. 1 (2012): 3–15.

Pentassuglia, G. *Minorities in International Law*. Strasbourg: Council of Europe Publishing, 2002.

Pfaff, William. *The Wrath of Nations. Civilizations and the Fury of Nationalism*. New York, NY: Simon & Schuster, 1993.

Phillips, A., and A. Rosas, eds. *Universal Minority Rights*. London: Institute for Human Rights Abo Akademi University and Minority Rights Group, 1995.

Phillips, Anne. *Multiculturalism without Culture*. Princeton, NJ: Princeton University Press, 2009.

PKK Terrorism Blog. 'PKK Terrorism Blog', http://pkkterrorismblog.net.

Pope, Huge. 'Turkey and the Democratic Opening for the Kurds', in F. Bilgin and A. Sarihan, eds., *Understanding Turkey's Kurdish Question*. Lanham, MD: Lexington Books, 2013.

Preece, Jennifer Jackson. *Minority Rights*. Cambridge: Polity Press, 2005.

Preece, Jennifer Jackson. *National Minorities and the European Nation-States System*. Oxford: Oxford University Press, 1998.

Przeworski, Adam. 'Minimalist Conception of Democracy: A Defense', in I. Shapiro and C. Hacker-Cordon, *Democracy's Values*. Cambridge: Cambridge University Press, 1999.

Quinn, David, and Ted Robert Gurr. 'Self-Determination Movements and Their Outcomes', in J. Hewitt, J. Wilkenfeld and T. Gurr, eds., *Peace and Conflict*. Boulder, CO: Paradigm, 2008.

Radikal Newspaper. 'Meclise Zaza, Laz ve Gürcü Dillerinde TV Kurulsun Dilekcesi' ('Petition to the Turkish Parliament to Demand TV Channels in Zaza, Laz and Georgian Languages'). *Radikal Newspaper*, www.radikal.com.tr.

Rawls, John. *Political Liberalism*. New York, NY: Columbia University Press, 2005.

Reinares, Fernando. 'Nationalist Separatism and Terrorism in Comparative Perspective', in T. Bjorgo, ed., *Root Causes of Terrorism: Myths, Reality and Ways Forward*. New York, NY: Routledge, 2005.

Reitz, Jeffrey G. 'Assessing Multiculturalism as a Behavioural Theory', in R. Breton and K. Dion, eds., *Multiculturalism and Social Cohesion: Potentials and Challenges of Diversity*. New York, NY: Springer, 2009.

Renan, Ernest. 'Qu'est-Ce Qu'une Nation? (What Is a Nation?)', in O. Dahbour, M. Ishay and R. Michelin, eds., *The Nationalism Reader*. New Jersey: Humanities Press International, 1995.

Rex, John. 'Equality of Opportunity and the Ethnic Minority Child in British Schools', in S. Modgil, G. Verma, K. Mallick and C. Modgil, eds., *Multicultural Education*. London: Falmer Press, 1988.

Rex, John. 'Multiculturalism in Europe and North America' in *Ethnic Minorities in the Modern Nation State*. New York, NY: Springer, 1996.

Roeder, Philip G. 'Clash of Civilizations and Escalation of Domestic Ethnopolitical Conflicts'. *Comparative Political Studies* 36, no. 5 (2003): 509–40.

Roeder, Philip G. 'Power dividing as an Alternative Ethnic Power Sharing' in Philip G.Roeder and Ronald Rothchild eds., *Sustainable Peace: Power and Democracy after Civil Wars* (Ithaca, NY: Cornell University Press, 2005), 51–83.

Romano, David. *The Kurdish Nationalist Movement: Opportunity, Mobilization and Identity*. Cambridge: Cambridge University Press, 2006.

Rumelili, Bahar. 'The European Union and Cultural Change in Greek-Turkish Relations'. *The European Union and Border Conflicts* 17 (2005): 1–31.

Saatci, Mustafa. 'Nation-States and Ethnic Boundaries: Modern Turkish Identity and Turkish-Kurdish Conflict'. *Nations and Nationalism* 8, no. 4 (2002): 549–64.

Safran, William. 'Pluralism and Multiculturalism in France: Post-Jacobin Transformations'. *Political Science Quarterly* 118, no. 3 (2003): 437–65.

Sanchez, W. Alejandro. 'Corsica: France's Petite Security Problem'. *Studies in Conflict & Terrorism* 31, no. 7 (2008): 655–64.

Sánchez-Cuenca, Ignacio, and Paloma Aguilar. 'Terrorist Violence and Popular Mobilization: The Case of the Spanish Transition to Democracy'. *Politics & Society* 37, no. 3 (2009): 428–53.

Sandel, Michael J. *Liberalism and the Limits of Justice*. Cambridge: Cambridge University Press, 1998.

Saracoglu, Cengiz. 'Exclusive Recognition: The New Dimensions of the Question of Ethnicity and Nationalism in Turkey'. *Ethnicity and Racial Studies* 32, no. 4 (2009): 640–58.

Sarigil, Zeki, and Ekrem Karakoc. 'Who Supports Secession? The Determinants of Secessionist Attitudes among Turkey's Kurds'. *Nations and Nationalism* 22, no. 2 (2016): 325–46.

Schertzer, Robert, and Eric Taylor Woods. 'Beyond Multinational Canada'. *Commonwealth & Comparative Politics* 49, no. 2 (2011): 196–222.

Schleifer, Yigal. 'Religious Kurds Become Key Vote in Turkey'. *Christian Science Monitor* 101, no. 7 (2009), www.aina.org/news/20090104162455.pdf.

Selek, S. *Ismet Inonu Hatiralar (Memoirs of Ismet Inonu)*. Ankara: Bilgi Yayinevi 2006.

Serrano, I. 'France: The End of the Corsican Question', in *Annual ASEN Conference 2007*. London: LSE (2007).

Shachar, Ayelet. 'On Citizenship and Multicultural Vulnerability'. *Political Theory* 28, no. 1 (2000): 64–89.

Shankland, David. *Islam and Society in Turkey*. Hemingford Grey, UK: Eothen Press, 1999.

Sherman, A. V. 'Turkey – A Case in Constructive Nationalism'. *Commentary* 30, no. 2 (1960): 93–101.

Shils, Edward. 'Primordial, Personal, Sacred and Civil Ties: Some Particular Observations on the Relationships of Sociological Research and Theory'. *British Journal of Sociology* 8, no. 1 (1957): 130–45.

Show News. 'DTP de Kürtçe Bilmeyen Kaç Milletvekili Var?' ('How Many MPs in the DTP Do Not Know Kurdish?'). Showhaber.com, www.showhaber .com.

Siddique, Abubakar. 'Turkey's New Kurdish TV Hopes to Win Hearts and Minds'. Radio Free Europe Radio Liberty, www.rferl.org/.

Silian, Alina. *Liberal Nationalism and Deliberative Democracy*. Unpublished master's thesis submitted to Central European University Nationalism Studies Program, Budapest, Hungary, 2002.

Simsir, B. *Kurtculuk 1924–1999 (Kurdism 1924–1999)*, Vol. II. Ankara: Bilgi Yayinevi, 2009.

Siyasi Haber. 'Kütahya'da Kürt İşçilere Linç Girişimi: Kaldıkları Barakalar Ateşe Verildi' ('A Mob Looted and Set Fire to Kurdish Workers' Dwellings in Kutahya'). *Siyasi Haber*, http://siyasihaber3.org.

Smith, A. D. *Ethnic Origins of Nations*. Oxford: Basil Blackwell, 1986.

Smith, A. D. *National Identity: Ethno-Nationalism in Comparative Perspective* (Reno, NV: University of Nevada Press, 1993).

Smith, A. D. *Nationalism and Modernism*. London: Routledge, 1998.

Smith, Thomas W. 'Civic Nationalism and Ethnocultural Justice in Turkey', *Human Rights Quarterly* 27, no. 2 (2005): 436–70.

Somer, Murat. 'Defensive and Liberal Nationalisms: The Kurdish Question and Modernization and Democratization', in E. F. Keyman, ed., *Remaking Turkey: Globalization* (Oxford: Lexington Books, 2007), 103–35.

Sonn, Christopher C., and Adrian T. Fisher. 'Identity and Oppression: Differential Responses to an In-Between Status'. *American Journal of Community Psychology* 31, no. 1–2 (2003): 117–28.

Soysu, Hâle. *Kavimler Kapısı (The Gate of Ethnicities)*. Istanbul: Kaynak Yayınları, 1992.

Staniland, Paul. 'Between a Rock and a Hard Place: Insurgent Fratricide and Ethnic Defection in Kashmir and Sri Lanka'. *Journal of Conflict Resolution* 56, no. 1 (2012): 16–40.

Stilz, Anna. *Liberal Loyalty: Freedom, Obligation, and the State*. Princeton, NJ: Princeton University Press, 2009.

Stirling, Paul. 'Religious Change in Republican Turkey'. *The Middle East Journal* 2, no. 4 (1958): 395–408.

Sullivan, John. *ETA and Basque Nationalism (RLE: Terrorism & Insurgency): The Fight for Euskadi 1890–1986*. New York, NY: Routledge, 2015.

Tamir, Yael. *Liberal Nationalism*. Princeton, NJ: Princeton University Press, 1995.

Taspinar, Omer. *Kurdish Nationalism and Political Islam in Turkey: Kemalist Identity in Transition*. London: Routledge, 2005.

Taylor, Donald M., and Fathali M. Moghaddam. *Theories of Intergroup Relations: International Social Psychological Perspectives*. Westport, CT: Greenwood, 1994.

Tekeli, I. 'Osmanli Imparatorlugundan Gunumuze Nufusun Zorunlu Yer Degistirmesi Sorunu (The Problem of the Forced Resettlement of the Population since the Ottoman Empire)'. *Toplum ve Bilim* no. 50 (1990): 49–71.

Teske, Raymond H. C., and Bardin H. Nelson. 'Acculturation and Assimilation: A Clarification'. *American Ethnologist* 1, no. 2 (1974): 351–67.

Tezcür, Güneş Murat. 'Kurdish Nationalism and Identity in Turkey: A Conceptual Reinterpretation'. *European Journal of Turkish Studies*, no. 10 (2009): 1–18.

Tezcür, Güneş Murat. 'Violence and Nationalist Mobilization: The Onset of the Kurdish Insurgency in Turkey'. *Nationalities Papers* 43, no. 2 (2015): 248–66.

Tezcür, Güneş Murat. 'When Democratization Radicalizes: The Kurdish Nationalist Movement in Turkey'. *Journal of Peace Research* 47, no. 6 (2010): 775–89.

The Commission to the European Parliament and the Council. 'Turkey 2013 Progress Report'. European Commission, http://ec.europa.eu.

The Council of Europe. 'Draft European Charter of Self-Government', June 5, 1997, Art. 2(1). Centre Virtuel de la Connaissance sur l'Europe, www.cvce .eu/.

The Council of Europe. 'European Charter for Regional or Minority Languages'. Council of Europe, www.coe.int.

The Council of Europe. 'Framework Convention for the Protection of National Minorities, Article 14'. Council of Europe, https://rm.coe.int.

Toprak, Binnaz. *Islam and Political Development in Turkey*. Leiden: Brill, 1981.

Trickett, Edison J., Roderick J. Watts, and Dina E. Birman. *Human Diversity: Perspectives on People in Context*. San Francisco: Jossey-Bass, 1994.

Turner, Terence. 'Anthropology and Multiculturalism: What Is Anthropology that Multiculturalists Should Be Mindful of It?' *Cultural Anthropology* 8, no. 4 (1993): 411–29.

Tuzun, Baycan-Levent. 'The Demographic Transition and Urban Development in Turkey', in H. S. Geyer, ed., *International Handbook of Urban Systems: Studies of Urbanization and Migration in Advanced and Developing Countries*. Cheltenham, UK: Edward Elgar, 2002.

Uppsala Conflict Data Program. 'Turkey: Kurdistan – Entire Conflict'. Uppsala Conflict Data Program, http://ucdp.uu.se.

US Department of State. '2013 Human Rights Reports: Turkey'. US Department of State, www.state.gov.

Vaghefi, Sanem. 'Turkey's Kurdish Movement: In Search of 'Real Islam'. *Open Democracy* (6 June 2015) www.opendemocracy.net/sanem-vaghefi/turkey %E2%80%99s-kurdish-movement-in-search-of-%E2%80%9Creal-islam %E2%80%9D.

Van Bruinessen, Martin. *Agha, Shaikh, and State: The Social and Political Structures of Kurdistan*. Utrecht: University of Utrecht, 1978.

Van Bruinessen, Martin. 'Genocide in Kurdistan? The Suppression of the Dersim Rebellion in Turkey (1937–38) and the Chemical War against the Iraqi Kurds (1988)', in G. J. Andreopoulos, ed., *Conceptual and Historical Dimensions of Genocide*. Philadelphia, PA: University of Pennsylvania Press, 1994.

Van Bruinessen, Martin. 'Kurds, Turks and the Alevi Revival in Turkey', *Middle East Report*, no. 200 (1996): 7–10.

Varin, Caroline. 'Education in a Federal System: A Case-Study of Belgium'. *CUREJ: College Undergraduate Research Electronic Journal*, June 28, 2006, Philadelphia, PA: University of Pennsylvania Press, http://repository.upenn .edu.

Waldron, Jeremy. 'Minority Cultures and the Cosmopolitan Alternative'. *University of Michigan Journal of Law Reform* 25, no. 3 (1991): 751–93.

Walker, Jack L. 'The Origins and Maintenance of Interest Groups in America'. *American Political Science Review* 77, no. 2 (1983): 390–406.

Walker, Kate. 'Success with Separatism? Brittany, Corsica, and the Indivisible French Republic'. Paper presented at the 40th Annual Meeting of the Alabama Political Science Association Conference Tuscaloosa, May 2, 2013, 25.

Watts, Nicole F. 'Activists in Office: Pro-Kurdish Contentious Politics in Turkey'. *Ethnopolitics* 5, no. 2 (2006): 125–44.

Weller, M., ed. *Universal Minority Rights: A Commentary on the Jurisprudence of International Courts and Treaty Bodies*. Oxford: Oxford University Press, 2007.

White, Paul. 'Ethnic Differentiation among the Kurds: Kurmancî, Kizilbash and Zaza'. *Journal of Arabic, Islamic, and Middle Eastern Studies* 2, no. 2 (1995): 67–90.

Wimmer, Andreas. 'The Making and Unmaking of Ethnic Boundaries: A Multilevel Process Theory'. *American Journal of Sociology* 113, no. 4 (2008): 970–1022.

Wolfgang Deutsch, Karl. *Nationalism and Social Communication: An Inquiry into the Foundations of Nationality*. Cambridge, MA: MIT Press, 1953.

World Bulletin. 'Kurdish Militants Threaten to Attack Turkish Dam Sites'. World Bulletin, www.worldbulletin.net.

Wright, Jane. 'The Protection of Minority Rights in Europe: From Conference to Implementation'. *The International Journal of Human Rights* 2, no. 1 (1998): 1–31.

Wynne, Eimear. 'Reflections on Recognition: A Matter of Self-Realization or a Matter of Justice?' Paper presented at the Thinking Fundamentals. IWM Junior Visiting Fellows Conferences, Vienna, 2000. www.iwm.at/wp-content/uploads/jc09–06.pdf.

Yack, Bernard. 'The Myth of the Civic Nation: A Critical Review', *Journal Politics and Sociology* 10, no. 2 (1996): 193–211.

Yanmis, Mehmet. *The Resurgence of the Kurdish Conflict in Turkey: How Kurds View It*. Washington, DC: Rethink Institute, 2016.

Yavuz, M. Hakan. 'Five Stages of the Construction of Kurdish Nationalism in Turkey'. *Nationalism and Ethnic Politics* 7, no. 3 (2001): 1–24.

Yeğen, Mesut. 'Citizenship and Ethnicity in Turkey'. *Middle Eastern Studies* 40, no. 6 (2004): 51–66.

Yeğen, Mesut. '"Prospective-Turks" or "Pseudo-Citizens": Kurds in Turkey'. *The Middle East Journal* 63, no. 4 (2009): 597–615.

Yeğen, Mesut. 'The Kurdish Question in Turkey: Denial to Recognition', in M. Caiser and J. Jongerden, eds., *Nationalism and Politics in Turkey*. New York, NY: Routledge 2011.

Yeğen, Mesut. 'Turkish Nationalism and the Kurdish Question'. *Ethnic and Racial Studies* 30, no. 1 (2007): 119–51.

Yildiz, A. *Ne Mutlu Turkum Diyebilene: Turk Ulusal Kimliginin Etno-Sekuler Sinir-lari (1919–1938) (How Happy Is the One Who Can Say 'I Am Turkish': The Ethno Secular Borders of Turkish National Identity (1919–1938)*. Istanbul: Iletisim, 2001.

Yildiz, K. *The Kurds in Turkey: EU Accession and Human Rights*. London: Pluto Press, 2000.

Yildiz, Kerím. 'Turkey's Kurdish Conflict: Pathways to Progress'. *Insight Turkey* 14, no. 4 (2012): 151.

Young, Iris Marion. 'A Multicultural Continuum: A Critique of Will Kymlicka's Ethnic Nation Dichotomy'. *Constellations* 4, no. 1 (1997): 48–53.

Young, Iris Marion. *Justice and the Politics of Difference*. Princeton, NJ: Princeton University Press, 1990.

Young, Iris Marion. 'Polity and Group Difference: A Critique of the Ideal of Universal Citizenship', in Ronald Beiner, ed., *Theorizing Citizenship*. Albany, NY: New York University Press, 1995.

Zaman. '1/3 of MPs from the DTP Did Not Understand Speech in Kurdish'. Haber7.com, www.haber7.com.

Zeldin, Wendy. 'Turkey: Adoption of New Law Aimed at Ending Terrorism and Achieving Social Integration'. Global Legal Monitor, www.loc.gov.

Zeydanlıoğlu, Welat. 'The White Turkish Man's Burden: Orientalism, Kemalism and the Kurds in Turkey', in G. Rings and A. Ife, eds., *Neo-Colonial Mentalities in Contemporary Europe: Language and Discourse in the Construction of Identities*. Newcastle upon Tyne, UK: Cambridge Scholars Publishing, 2008.

Zeyneloglu, Sinan, Yaprak Civelek, and Ibrahim Sirkeci. 'Inter-regional Migration and Intermarriage among Kurds in Turkey'. *Economics & Sociology* 9, no. 1 (2016): 143.

Zhou, Min. 'Segmented Assimilation: Issues, Controversies, and Recent Research on the New Second Generation'. *International Migration Review* 31, no. 4 (1997): 975–1008.

Zimmer, Oliver. 'Boundary Mechanisms and Symbolic Resources: Towards a Process Oriented Approach to National Identity'. *Nations and Nationalism* 9, no. 2 (2003): 173–93.

Zolberg, Aristide. 'Modes of Incorporation: Towards a Comparative Framework', in V. Bader, ed., *Citizenship and Exclusion*. New York, NY: St. Martin's Press, 1997.

Index